SONNY GIRARD'S
MOB READER:

An Organized Crime Primer

by

Sonny Girard

THIS WORK IS DEDICATED TO MY THREE
KIDS AND SEVEN GRANDKIDS, WHO MAKE
WAKING UP WORTHWHILE.

Table of Contents

MOB SNAPSHOTS:

ACKNOWLEDGMENTS

Cover Photos Google Public Domain. Individual details upon request.

MOB BLOG #1:

Amnesty

Fooled you, huh? Thought I was talking about illegals crossing the Mexican border? No, I'm talking about legal citizens who do illegal things, specifically members and associates of traditional organized crime whose roots begin hundreds of years ago in Sicily and Southern Italy (*both were part of what was known as "The Kingdom of the Two Sicilies*). Why that group? Because it was the most powerful organized criminal group in the history of the United States, and now it's old and tired at a time when we can better use resources to combat more brutal new gangs and the thing that threatens us all: terrorism.

How and why Sicilian-rooted organized crime peaked for such a long time is based in its history. Every immigrant group that arrived on our shores was forced into ghetto areas and had criminal gangs. Read Herbert Asbury's classic study, "The Gangs of New York," or watch Martin Scorsese's film of the same name, and you will understand how powerful and pervasive Irish gangs with names like the Plug Uglies, Dead Rabbits, and Five Pointers were in Lower Manhattan in the last half of the Nineteenth Century. As a matter of fact, by the beginning of the Twentieth Century, when immigrants from Southern Italy were replacing the Irish in their former ghettos as the latter moved up in society, the transitional leader of the Five Points Gang, Paul Kelly, was actually named Paolo Vacarelli. He was the bridge between remaining Irish criminals and new Italian gang members. The Five Points Gang, operating out of Lower Manhattan, turned out major mob names, including that of Lucky Luciano.

There were plenty of Jewish gangsters also that came out of inner city ghettos in the early to mid-part of the Twentieth Century. Monk Eastman, Lepke Buchalter, Gurrah Shapiro, Meyer Lansky, Bugsy Siegel, and most members of Murder Incorporated, were all of Jewish descent. They were not all one group. Siegel and Lansky had their own Manhattan based Bug & Meyer Mob aligned with Lucky Luciano and Frank Costello (*later called the Genovese Family*), while Murder Incorporated under the banner of Albert Anastasia (*later known as the Gambino Family*) was primarily from Brownsville and East New York areas of Brooklyn.

Why then, did all these Irish and Jewish mobsters fade from the public consciousness while Italians/Sicilians did not? History and perception. Irish and Eastern European Jews always had problems with oppression, but it had not been consistent centuries-long foreign oppression. Russian Jews had been brutalized for centuries by Russians. It was the Jews who were as much as foreigners in their Mother Russia. Irish Catholics and Protestants had battled in the old country, with foreign Brits allied with many of their own countrymen. Sicilians and Southern Italians, on the other hand, had always been at the mercy of foreigners who ruled their land. French, Spanish, Arab, and Greek military forces had dominated their island for nearly a thousand years. Sicily's architectural diversity attests to the various invaders who left their mark. Where were Sicilian natives supposed to get justice? They didn't even speak the languages of the various troops or, more importantly, courts. The answer: a sub-rosa government (*Mafia*), with the ability to tax (*extortion, kidnapping, etc.*), and the means to enforce the law (*violence or death*).

When Sicilian and other Southern Italian immigrants landed in the United States, they found a familiar situation. They were considered the lowest element in society (*many Americans wanted them deported back home*), didn't speak the language, and couldn't get justice. They also found a familiar sub-rosa government in their areas to get that justice from; to go to when a daughter had been violated, as portrayed in Francis Ford Coppola's operatic film, "Godfather."

What that did was continue history for them, and, in turn, give them a different perception of crime from the other groups. Irish and Jewish mobsters, in large part viewed their criminal activities as a vehicle to get them from poverty to affluence, with the idea that their children and grandchildren would not have to follow that path. I know descendents of Lansky, Shapiro, and others. Sam Jacobson was a major star in Lansky's organization. Sam's son went to college and was, when I saw him last, a distributor of packaged bakery products to supermarkets. Henry Shapiro, Gurrah's son, owned a trendy men's clothing store when I first met him. Max "The Jew" Schrager was part of the same Lansky group and ran a Williamsburg, Brooklyn numbers bank. His son went to law school, became a partner in the legendary Studio 54, and now is a world class hotel entrepreneur, with names like the Delano in Miami and Mondrian in L.A. as part of his chain.

On the other hand, Sicilians/Italians saw crime as a way of life; something to be handed down to their sons and their sons' sons. Joe Colombo Sr.'s father was a mobster who was murdered, Joe himself became the namesake of the former Profaci Family, and every one of Joe's sons has done prison time. Same with the Persicos; three generations either in prison or released from it; not to mention John Gotti's dragging his son into the family business. Unfortunately, those three families are by no means anomalies. You can go from biological family to biological family, across all mob family lines and find an enormous number of father and son or grandson mob affiliations.

All of the above brings us to the present time. From my inside view of organized crime, I know it's done for...*finito*. Some bodies still standing are just waiting to die in bed. The younger generation, with hopes of mob glory? *Fuggetaboutit*. There's no mob worth getting involved with today, and for you wannabes reading this, you aren't up to snuff if there was. Why? Because conditions create toughguys, not dreams or bloodline. None of today's wannabes grew up in conditions where, when that prison gate clangs behind them, they can honestly say to themselves, "This isn't as bad as where I grew up." Historically, if one looks at the heyday of the mob with big names like Lucky Luciano, Albert Anastasia, and Al Capone, he or she also see a bunch of big name fighters coming out of the same ghetto areas, like Rocky Graziano, Jake LaMotta, and Joey Giardello. Mob guys were saying, "Shoot me, lock me in jail, I don't care, but I ain't going back there." Fighters coming out of the same areas, through actions said, "Hit me, bang my face up, do what you want, but I ain't going back there." See any consequential number of Italian-American prizefighters today? What does that say about mobsters? There is no more "back there" to turn out effective participants in either life in any significant number. Those with hopes of becoming mobsters take heed. Old timers who even consider dealing with young new members and associates take even more heed. Your lives depend on it.

Getting back to the point of amnesty, the mob today can be compared to gunslingers of the old Wild West. Gunslingers had their moment in time; traditional organized crime mobsters had theirs. One day the gunslingers were shooting it out on the streets of Dodge City; a short time later Dodge had high-rise buildings and automobiles. Same with the mob. Conditions when they immigrated to America and especially Prohibition vaulted them into decades of power and wealth. Had it not been for Prohibition, those Sicilian/Italian gangs would have been just that: gangs. Prohibition gave them national exposure and enough money and influence to continue on for decades, without considering the fact that the United States was not Sicily; that their children would speak the language and meld with American society; that there would be no further need of a sub-rosa government. At one time, given conditions at the time, there was minimum exposure to punishment and maximum profit. Today, it's the complete reverse.

There was one big difference at the end of the Wild West from today. Authorities at that time were forgiving. They periodically issued amnesties to the gunslingers if they would hang up their weapons. It worked. There was no overcrowding of western prisons. Old gunslingers just faded into the sunset with no fuss. Today, with organized crime on its last legs, the time has come to offer a conditional amnesty to mob members and associates if they come forward and agree to retire. There would be immunity for past crimes outside of murder, a financial declaration, and a suspended amnesty sentence that would automatically be enforced if another crime was committed. If the conditions were right, plenty of real mob figures would flock to the U.S. Attorneys' offices around the country to sign up. The wannabes would have no place to be. They'd just be called wannas. Traditional organized crime, as we knew it, would be completely dead. R.I.P.

The problem is that organized crime is a cash cow, not for the criminals any more, but for the authorities. There remains a dangerous aura about the mob that government officials can exploit for various reasons. A while ago a totally bogus story was given to the media about government fears of organized crime figures hooking up with terrorists. Wow, headlines, a call for more funding, a little intrigue (*the truth is that traditional organized crime figures are generally very patriotic*). An even shorter time ago, Jeffrey Holder staged a dog and pony show where he arrested 167 alleged mobsters from sixteen different indictments on one day. Many, if not most of those guys will get little or no time. One, Andy Russo, of the Colombo faction, is indicted for sitting down with members of the Gambino crew to work out a settlement whereby one of the Gambino pals who shot one of his pals would pay the medical expenses of the victim. The charge: extorting money from the Gambino Family. What??? How blind or stupid is the public to buy this crap from its Attorney General and his gang?

Just ask yourself how many FBI Agents and U.S. Attorneys around the country are working on catching bookmakers, shylocks, and mob swindlers? Wouldn't their expense and effort be better utilized in protecting Americans from terrorists? Not as cushy an assignment as a mob that's got one leg in the coffin. Traditional organized crime figures as a rule do not harm federal agents, while terrorists might target them. Terror-chasing is not as glamorous either. One organized crime figure, for example, was offered a plea deal of twelve years on a fraud case, while an attorney who carried terrorist messages from the sheik who participated in the first World Trade Center bombing received a mere twenty-eight month sentence when convicted. One bunch of mobsters was so old when arrested that the newspapers dubbed them the "Mob-fogies." Give me a break.

Common sense would dictate that the time has come to move federal authorities out of the organized crime business and into the more difficult and dangerous task of protecting us from terrorism. Forget amnesty for illegal immigrants, the real benefit to the public of an amnesty is one for last century's organized crime figures.

MOB BLOG #2:

Good Friends Who Did Dumb Things

In the course of my life in the streets, I have had some friends, who, while they did some bad things...okay, a lot of bad things (*after all, they were mobsters*), did some really dumb things that resulted in their deaths. You probably won't recognize their names, but they were here...and, as I look back on memories, I remember them to you.

1) Tony "Gawk" Augello: "The Gawk," as he was known to friends and law enforcement, was a giant of a man, whose handshake reached halfway to my elbow, in a subculture where most participants ranged from average to height-challenged. Personally, I had trouble trusting anyone over 5' 9" or so, as they met the height requirements for police or FBI work. Gawk was an exception. He was a proven guy who law enforcement claimed "pissed ice water." He caused so much trouble in state prison that they used to have him strip naked and hose him down in his cell as punishment. One time, when he was incarcerated, he set up a meeting with the FBI to discuss rolling over and changing sides, which, for wiseguys at that pre-Sammy the Bull time, was the exception rather than the rule, as it is today. Tony's lawyer, Ira Cooper, who was also one of mine, was in shock. Couldn't be that one of the toughest guys he knew would become a rat? Gawk got everyone together in a big courthouse conference room: the two Assistant U.S. Attorneys for the Eastern District of New York who were handling his case, FBI Agents, our aforementioned attorney, and last but not least the court stenographer he insisted on. He then went about telling prosecutors and agents how he'd had sex with their mothers and sisters at various times over the last year. They dragged him out and practically had to carry the shocked attorney out on a stretcher.

But Gawkie had two major problems. First, he was terrible at sitdowns with other mob guys. To me, he had an uncanny ability to snatch defeat from the jaws of victory. He also knew it, and sometimes begged off meetings with a feigned illness, so someone else could represent his side. Gawk was usually surprised if whoever had taken his place won. More important, and ultimately deadly, he was scared to death of his bosses. He'd actually get physically sick...no faking...if he got called downtown by higher ups. Then he screwed up and got in trouble...the kind of trouble...drug selling trouble...that mandated a death sentence for anyone in the crew. He had befriended a black drug dealer in prison, who offered him a deal when they both hit the streets. No one outside of the guys he was dealing with, including a couple of mob guys willing to play that game, knew what he was up to. When the arrest came, no one could be more shocked than I was that he would take a chance like that. Once the arrest came, he knew his fate. Was he worried about dying? No. What worried him was that if he was killed and his body was made to disappear, his family's properties and cash that they put up for his bail would be forfeited.

Now he had real pressure from the Feds too, since he already owed parole time. Couldn't rat; couldn't hide. What to do, what to do? Gawk decided that the best thing was to go to a McDonald's parking lot pay phone, call some friends to say goodbye, then blow his brains out on the spot. Dumb. Discretion dictates that I can't tell you what he should have done, but that wasn't it. He even left a note that blamed FBI pressure for his suicide. Tony Gawk was honorable in a way that went far beyond the call of mob duty. Just a dumb thing. R.I.P. Gawk.

> 2) Richie "The Wig": Richard Pagliarulo was a person at war with himself; at war with who he believed he was and how he was accepted or not by others important to him. The root of his problem began before he was born, when his future father's sister married a soon to be well known mobster. As he grew up, he also grew to love and idolize his legendary uncle, and ultimately prove himself worthy of being a member of his crew.

16

Richie was not "The Wig" then, just "Little Richie"; he still had hair, much of which he lost as a result of a nasty head wound sustained when he was a passenger in a car being chased by police (unfortunately, I was driving). If Richie hadn't had much too much to drink and was not too limp to be tossed around like a rag doll, he would have probably lost his life along with his hair.

In an effort to prove himself, he often did bizarre things. For example, he would leave his girlfriend sitting alone at the bar in a club where his uncle's crew hung out. If a guy approached the girl, whose legs were long and skirt was short, Little Richie would rush over and, without a word, knock the guy cold. For a little man, no more than 5'5", he packed a giant's punch. He wasn't known for a having a great mind, but certainly had balls, and proved it on a number of occasions.

His world began to unravel when his uncle died of natural causes at only forty-one years old. Instead of being embraced, Richie found himself on the outs with those members of the crew that hadn't transferred over to other groups within the Colombo Family. He wasn't accepted the same way as he was when "Unc" was alive. The King was dead; long live the King. All the promises his uncle had made for his future were gone.

After a few years of ups and downs and a couple of murders surrounding him; deaths of close associates, he landed with Anthony "Tony Gawk" Augello. For political and some financial considerations, Gawk kept Richie off the record; never officially listing him as an underling of his with the family bosses. That worked for Richie for awhile. He was a good earner who wasn't a big spender. He was not an extravagant dresser or someone who lived in luxurious digs. Because he wasn't on record with the Gawk and didn't have the flash that drew attention, he was able to exist in his mob nether world and also hang on to a lot of his money that higher ups would have taken in taxes.

However, once again, Richie lost a "rabbi." Tony Gawk, pressured by the FBI and his bosses after a drug arrest, blew his brains out at the payphone in a McDonald's parking lot. When family higher ups wanted to know what was going on and wanted to assign some of his men to Benny "The Sidge" LoCicero, Patty "Fat Patty" Catalano asked others that knew of Richie's non-person status not to mention him. He said that he could move Richie quietly to the Lucchese crew, where he would be treated better and have a real chance to be "made." Little did Patty know that his good intentions were actually signing a death warrant for Richie Pagliarulo.

As intended, Richie wound up with the Lucchese crew, and eventually became a right hand shooter for his boss, Anthony "Gaspipe" Casso. When Gaspipe began murdering everyone he dreamed might betray him, and it was in madman numbers, Richie started dropping bodies for him all over the place. It never dawned on Richie that the numbers were becoming bizarre, and that getting rid of Casso would have ended the fratricide. He just kept shooting; piling up bodies for a pat on the head from a guy who would soon become a government witness. When, after being arrested for carrying out a good part of Gaspipe's bloody rampage, Richie was offered a plea where he would have a chance to see daylight sometime in his life, he refused and insisted on going to trial. He was convicted in a matter of a few hours. According to "Gangbusters," by Ernest Volkman, when Judge Nickerson sentenced Richie, he prefaced the sentencing by mentioning that the defendant been convicted of forty-eight murders, Richie interrupted the judge by correcting the number as forty-nine. He got life. Again, he proved he had more balls than brains.

Once in prison, it dawned on the forty-something year old that he would never see the street again. He started coming apart at the seams, writing letters that seemed unrealistic and unfocused. Richie didn't fully bust a seam, but his heart did. If there were an organization for dumb, just those last acts for Gaspipe and the correction in front of the judge would have made him its poster boy. R.I.P.

3) "Hickey": I met Hickey when we were in prison together. We became good friends. He was a bug, but a bright bug, and was great company. As with many extremely bright people, he was also a little off kilter mentally. His crazy acts delighted those inmates who were friends through mob relationships, and scared the hell out of others. Hickey was once released from MCC (*the Manhattan Federal House of Detention*) on a furlough to go to his dentist, which was common practice at that time. Unfortunately for anyone who wanted a furlough from that point, he came back to the jail five years later, by way of Argentina. Sometime after being released when he completed the sentence he got upon his return, he had some problems within his crew. Instead of being able to squash the problem, it became more serious. When he saw a couple of guys lurking outside his house in New Jersey, he thought he was under attack and shot at them. Surprised when they identified themselves as FBI Agents, Hickey did what any lunatic in that situation would do. He stripped naked and ran out into the arms of the agents, while screaming about the aliens that had come down from outer space to take him back. He got a parole violation, which saved him at least for that time. When he was released, his problem was a serious as it had been before his sentence, so he took off for another state, far away from New York.

As I said, Hickey was a smart guy. He had been involved in the case where Vatican banker Maurice Sindona got fleeced of millions of the Roman Church's money. After being released from jail and still under fire from his mob bosses, he chose to take off for the West Coast, where he could enjoy life while those back East were making excuses why they couldn't go to a strange place and dispose of him without getting caught.

Then Hickey got dumb. The same homesickness that brought him back from Argentina after five years afflicted him. When he got a message that all was forgiven (*the oldest trick in the book*), he came back to N.Y. Dumb. R.I.P. Hickey.

These guys are all fairly unknown criminals. They were bad guys in a time when it was made easy to be a bad guy by bribe-taking police and judges, and neighborhoods that spawned mobsters as well as boxers. As Michael Corleone reminded a Senator in Godfather II, "We're all part of the same hypocrisy." Don't misunderstand, I cannot and will not defend the bad things they did, and, believe me, they did a lot, but, in their own way each had a human side to the people who knew them intimately, including me. To us, they were also funny guys, tough guys, standup guys, sometimes sad or tormented guys, and good friends. Each died because they did something dumb. R.I.P. guys.

MOB BLOG #3:

Eric Holder's Sleight of Hand

On Thursday, January 20, 2011, U.S. Attorney General Eric Holder flipped a damaging card off the table as he played a shell game with America. On that day, he had more than 800 FBI personnel arrest 127 alleged mobsters. It looked really impressive, and immediately took the heat he'd been taking over holding terrorist trials in GITMO. All he needed was a couple of days till Obama's State of the Union speech would dominate print and airways. Due to the complicity of the media, he got it. No one I saw on TV really understood what was going on, and if they did they weren't saying. Instead, they ballyhooed the arrest as if they had captured the entire upper echelon of Al Qaeda. In fact, I was contacted that day by one national TV news organization, asking if I would be willing to appear on air to discuss the arrests. In all fairness, they were having a little trouble coordinating a crew to interview me, but, I believe they decided against it after they asked what my thoughts were on the subject, and I told them.

First, numbers don't lie. The 127 men were arrested under sixteen separate indictments. Does anyone believe they were all handed down on or even around the same day? There were so many arrested that they couldn't even book them in proper surroundings, but had to set up an ad hoc processing center at Brooklyn's Ft. Hamilton army base. Was that necessary? Add to that more than 800 FBI personnel took part in the arrests. 800! Who was overseeing potential terrorist activities in New York? Imagine, God forbid (Yes, libs, God!), that an explosive device went off in Manhattan that Thursday? Eric Holder would be hiding in an Afghan cave and ducking drone missiles right now.

How about the number of alleged "mobsters" arrested: 127. How many of those 127 are real? How many are wannabes, stumblebums, pretenders, or gofers? My guess is that more than three quarters fit into the latter category. If you read the indictments you find a minor gambler, someone who cashed a check, someone involved in bringing coffee to construction workers, and the killer of Cock Robin. One of the most laughable of all charges is against Andy Russo, who is alleged to be the acting boss of the Colombo crew. It seems one man allegedly affiliated with the Gambinos stabbed someone allegedly affiliated with the Colombos. A meeting was held to keep the situation from escalating into a deadly one when the victim recovered. At the meeting, Andrew suggested that the assaulter pay the hospital bills of the guy who had been sliced and diced. That launched an indictment against Andy Russo for "extorting the Gambino Family." WHAT??? Are crime families now under the protection of Eric Holder and his gang? Will executives of the Obama-Holder Family now conduct sitdowns to settle mob disputes? Will they get a piece of the action? Are they jockeying for a seat on the Commission? It is so ridiculous that if a man's freedom was not at stake, it would be a real rib tickler.

When a Muslim officer screamed "Allah Akbar" and shot fellow military people at Fort Hood, the President and his Attorney General cautioned us "not to jump to any conclusions," yet when it comes to parading out "alleged" mobsters there isn't any presumption of innocence.

This Ringling Brothers spectacle brings out another factor that is generally whispered but not said in mixed company and certainly not even mentioned by the mainstream media: there is a racist element to this President and his administration. When Harvard Professor Gates, a black man, became an issue after his arrest, Obama, after stating that he didn't know all the facts, claimed, "The police acted stupidly." There has been no similar misgiving about the FBI arresting 127 men on one day based on sixteen separate indictments. AFTER New Black Panther thugs were found guilty of voter intimidation, Eric Holder dropped the charges. Don't hold your breath for similar treatment of those arrested on the mob case in question.

Joe Colombo was ahead of his time in fighting the Government for their persecution of Italians. He also understood the changing society and wanted to have his people adapt. He recognized that organized crime, both here and in Italy/Sicily had two intertwining threads, crime and honor...it was a near thousand year old way of life...and for the latter to survive, the former had to be discarded and the latter strengthened and preserved. The organization could be modeled after the Masons, he'd said, with money being circulated between businesses owned by members. It could even have an initiation ceremony modeled after the classic one, including burning a picture of a saint during the process. The problem Joe had then, which will remain the same in the future, is that the enlightened members, if they do not number one-hundred-percent, will always be dragged down by those who refuse to advance. What to do when the nitwit who wants to shake down those former mobsters making money? Clip him? Back where you started. Stupid sucks.

A check of results one year from the date of the Holder extravaganza, on January 20, 2012, will show that the majority of the 127 arrested got little or no prison time, that most of those heavy hitters rolled over and made deals for a slap on the hand, and that a relatively few old timers, like Andy Russo, will wind up in prison for a more substantial amount of time. The money wasted will never be accounted for, the whole hoopla surrounding the events will be forgotten, and for Eric Holder the joke will be on the rest of us.

Sonny Girard

Mob Blog #4:

License to Bash Italians &

The Assault on San Gennaro

It seems I get more infuriated each day by the official hypocrisy of the media and government in this country, and the general sheep-like acceptance of any crap by citizens who are either too distracted, too self-absorbed, or just too damn stupid to realize what's going on around them.

Going back over a century or more, Italians have been a silent minority group that could be officially abused without any recourse. To say that they didn't bring any of it on themselves would be a lie. However, history should be truth. Lately, it has become skewed toward political correctness. In going over history homework with my school age grandchildren, I have found entire paragraphs focused on minority players with good but relatively minor accomplishments while famous white inventors have been minimized to one line. That minimization of Italian/white discrimination was no more apparent than after FDR locked up people he deemed a threat to security after WWII began. Over the years, a lot has been made of how unfair it was to Japanese immigrants, including books and movies, while I would be willing to bet that a majority of those reading this now do not realize that a large number of Italians were interned too...and their countrymen didn't bomb Pearl Harbor! In fact, the latter internment is known to Italians as *"La Storia Segreto,"* or "The Secret Story." Rather than bitch and moan about the situation, Italians felt ashamed that they would be considered anything less than lovers of America, and buried the whole affair. Google it to learn more.

Now to the related story that ticked me off today:

NEW YORK POST Updated: Sun., Feb. 20, 2011, 6:46 AM

Nolita boutiques fighting 'greasy' Feast of San Gennaro

By SUSAN EDELMAN

Last Updated: 6:46 AM, February 20, 2011

Posted: 12:06 AM, February 20, 2011

It's a clash of cannoli vs. couture.

Supporters of Little Italy's famed Feast of San Gennaro -- set to celebrate its 85th year in September -- are fighting a newly passed Community Board 2 resolution urging the city to consider shrinking the boisterous, sausage-filled festival by three blocks -- including one that includes beloved St. Patrick's basilica.

The recommended cutback -- blasphemous to Italian-Americans who revere the celebration -- stems from gripes by owners of snooty Nolita boutiques about the noise, crowds, cooking smoke -- and even customers attracted to the 11-day event.

"They come in with greasy hands" and stain the leather handbags and $300 dresses, said Ying Ying Chong, owner of White Saffron, one of the hip shops that have popped up on Mulberry Street between Kenmare and Houston streets -- the blocks where the festival would be banned.

"I have cannolis frying in front of my store!" she said.

Heewon Kim, a co-owner of Coqueta, a lingerie shop across the street, said she sprays Febreze on the lacy undies to kill the smoky odor.

The street fair, scheduled for Sept. 15-25, normally stretches seven blocks on Mulberry, from Canal to Houston Streets, and fills four more blocks on side streets.

The Nolita opponents say the food and game booths hinder access to their clothing, jewelry and bag boutiques. Despite foot traffic of 100,000 people a day, "it's not our target clientele," Ying sniffed.

San Gennaro organizers are hotter than freshly fried zeppole.

"You can't understand the emotion we have -- the anger -- when we feel we're being attacked," said John Fratta, president of the Little Italy Restoration Association, who was raised in the neighborhood and whose grandfather co-founded the feast in 1926.

"This is our culture and our heritage."

More than 100 Little Italy residents and boosters jammed the community-board meeting Thursday to voice opposition to stopping the revelry at Kenmare Street.

That explosive recommendation was tucked into a larger resolution, quietly passed on Jan. 26, that approved other permit logistics. Vowing a "full-court press," supporters distributed fliers urging community members to bombard Mayor Bloomberg and other elected officials with calls and e-mails to keep the feast intact.

Fratta and others say Nolita boutiques are always empty anyway -- and can't blame the feast if their pricey apparel doesn't sell.

As an olive branch to Nolita, the feast organizers agreed to give the shops a discount on booths to hawk their stylish wares -- and even the chance to stage a fashion show on Mulberry Street. Both offers were refused.

To prove that funnel cake and fashion can co-exist, the San Gennaro group wants to ask Giorgio Armani or another top designer, preferably Italian, to create a catwalk for the festival.

The only taboo attire will be T-shirts with words like "Mafia," "Sopranos" and "Cosa Nostra." For the first time in its history, the feast will ban the sale of garb that glorifies organized crime.

Figli di San Gennaro, a nonprofit that has run the feast since 1996, has donated $1.6 million to charities and schools from fees charged to vendors. The city collects 20 percent of the fees.

"They come in with greasy hands." The "Nolita" (*North Little Italy*) merchants bitch about the smell of cooking that bothers them. First, these complaining Asian shop girls, like *Ying Ying Chong* and *Heewon Kim,* should walk through the "Solita," or Chinatown side of the area south of Little Italy, on any summer day or night, where rotting entrails and other discards from restaurants permeate the air, before they talk about offensive smells. This is where the politically correct reverse racism I mentioned earlier comes into play. Imagine the same kind of statements being made about the smell of the Caribbean Day Parade and celebration? Or about the greasy hands of those eating in Bed-Sty fast food stores leaving fingerprints on store merchandise? Or rumors of cats being served in Chinatown? It would be a national media outrage. Reverand Al might even be leading pickets to get the stores of those who made the remarks shut down. But for a religious Italian feast and celebration, no big deal. And how many pickets and cameras would be outside Community Board 2, the creeps trying to cut down the area of the Feast, which has been in that area for a time closing in on a century if they were trying to limit the growth of Chinatown, which has spread over the area like the BP oil spill?

Now a word for the *Figli di San Gennaro* wimps running the Feast: You guys should be ashamed of yourselves. Instead of bending over for SoHo wannabe snobs, and offering them to have a fashion show, you should be fighting to preserve the tradition of probably the most famous Italian feast in America. You should also go read the First Amendment of the Constitution of the United States before joining Giuliani and Bloomberg in Feast bashing by banning free speech in the form of tee shirts with sayings about Sopranos, or Mafia, or any reference to the mob. If you're so self-loathing or wimpy, get out and let somebody else run the Feast. Like it or not, guys, organized crime is part of America's history, and Italians have played a major role. You should be more ashamed of the rats that testify against their own brothers and fathers (*are you going to allow Sammy The Bull, or Henry Hill, or John Franzese Jr. tee shirts?*). Your actions would never be tolerated in an area where tee shirts carry messages about killing snitches, or spew anti-American rhetoric about Mexico taking over the West, or support Hamas or Hezbollah. The ACLU would be in court immediately in those cases. In fact, I hope the ACLU takes you guys to court and forces you to pay for Soprano tee shirts out of your own pockets for anyone who shows up...and to wear them for photos. I'll reserve a Paulie Walnuts shirt now: extra large.

Unfortunately, this deterioration of a neighborhood that many love and owe a lot to is something I wrote about two years ago, in my article, MOB BLOG #12: "*Arrivederci, Little Italy.*" It is also unfortunate that my anger may have turned out an article today that is less than fully coherent and less than what I really want to say. That anger would be just as vehement if a group were looking to decimate Chinatown or any other historic ethnic area. New York is loved because it, in spite of its faults, is a city made up of diverse areas with different and unique textures. Kill one and you can kill them all. Too bad.

P.S. I suggest all of you who are as incensed as I am, and are anywhere near Little Italy, stop in and tell Heewon Kim (*photo below—too cute to be so miserable*) and Ying Ying Chon how much you appreciate their interest in the area. Bring Ying Ying some cannolis.

You can also write to the Post's author, Susan Edelman at

susan.edelman@nypost.com

She has no part in the issue, but is just reporting it. Let her know how you feel about what's going on. Let me know too.

Sonny

MOB BLOG #5:

Unions

I read a post on Twitter that asked, "When did unions become gangsters and thugs?" I tweeted back, "Gangsters ran unions from the earliest days." Of course, that was a simplification, but tweets are tweets.

The union movement as we know it today was basically born after the massive immigration of mostly poor Southern Italians and Eastern European Jews in the early days of the Twentieth Century. It was also fueled by the success of the Bolshevik Revolution. Of course, unions in the U.S. had begun during the 19th Century, but they faltered and sometimes failed until the first two decades of the 20th, when the movement blossomed. To counter the strength of the numbers of workers who would picket a clothing plant or food distributor, the owners, often immigrants themselves, would hire local thugs to disperse the crowd. Though they had overwhelming numbers, workers were still no match for the hoodlums who set upon them with bats, two-by-fours, or iron pipes. To respond, they also hired mobsters to fight on their behalf. Once mobsters were the muscle on both sides, they became the controllers; they made deals that kept peace and lined their pockets as well. One of the early mob leaders to take advantage of the worker-management situation was Louis "Lepke" Buchalter, the de-facto boss of Murder Incorporated.

Lepke was far ahead of many other racketeers during the waning years of Prohibition. Some were preparing by putting a large fund together to finance legitimate operations...remember, at a time when men's leather shoes cost $3.45 and a meal could be bought for a dime, a $25 case of illegal whiskey brought back a total of one thousand dollars. Others, like Dutch Schultz, ventured heavily into gambling, taking over the numbers business in black Harlem. For Lepke, who had his finger in all of the above and more, union control presented a lucrative and long lasting future. He saw that when speakeasies became restaurants and supper clubs he could unionize bartenders, and those who delivered linens, and those who trucked in food and booze. However, what interested him most was the clothing business.

New York's garment center hired many from the immigrant community to work long hours under terrible conditions. What's more, there were a variety of steps that had to be taken to get a garment from factory to store: design, cutting, sewing, finishing, trucking, etc. Lepke realized that by controlling a union of those necessary to any of the steps along the way, he could control the whole industry; shut it down whenever he chose. He started by organizing the cutters. Other mobsters followed him and either partnered with him or unionized under their own banners for the next decades: Carlo Gambino, Tommy Lucchese, Joe Bonnano, Johnny Dio, and on and on. Some, like Jersey's Tony Provenzano, focused on trucking, while others, like Albert and Tough Tony Anastasia tied up longshoremen. I use a fictitious incident involving Lepke in my forthcoming novel, "Night of the Vespers," a three generation saga that begins in 1931, to illustrate the incestuous relationship the mob had in the early days of unionization

That fictional situation closely resembles a real one that I was part of while working with a catch-all union (*a union chartered for non-specific membership, unlike those whose membership is exclusive to one trade*) while in my twenties; a time when I learned first-hand what unions were about and how much mob power fellow mobsters exerted within them. "Spike" Bernstein, who ran the union, and I would stop into a chosen business and threaten the owner with pickets outside his place. Most were restaurants and nightspots we believed were "connected." At least we hoped they were. If all went well, the owner would run to whatever crew he was attached to and a meeting would be set up with Spike's boss in the Genovese Family. The deal invariably worked out was that the owner would join the catch-all to avoid being unionized by a so-called "communist union," which would, in reality, sooner close down a business than modify its demands. He would get minimal benefits for his employees, but would bring a "Christmas gift" that would be split between the union and the business owner's mob connection. If businessmen did not know any mobsters, they would sign for a sweetheart deal bonus under the table for the union, or pay for bigger benefit packages for their employees once the union got them to join and was not as hospitable.

One example of the former, connected situation, was that of the Steak Loft chain, owned by Steve Rubell, who went on to own the celebrity-infested discotheque, Studio 54. Spike was tipped off to put the squeeze on Rubell by the made guy the chain was connected to, who happened also to be in the same crew. Spike and I met with Rubell and his attorney, Ian Schrager, son of Lansky numbers banker, Max "The Jew" Schrager. Ian went on to become a partner in 54, testify for the government, and now own chiq hotels like the Delano in Miami Beach and the Mondrian in Los Angeles. Rubell said he didn't need a union; that he kept his employees happy with constant partying and an ample supply of drugs. He and Schrager were pains in the ass, but a payoff deal was reached behind the scenes that they had to go along with.

Mob involvement was not always a bad thing. For one, they often did save businesses from the excessive demands of communist locals that would bankrupt them. Another example is the widely known connection of the Teamsters to the mob. Members of the Teamsters will all tell you how much they have benefitted from their union's support; their pay and benefit packages are above the national average. Teamster loans to build Las Vegas hotels and casinos have been much maligned by authorities, the press, and filmmakers. However, just stop and think what Vegas would be like without those loans and the influence of organized crime figures? Harry Reid might be the biggest personality in the desert (*Good grief, Charlie Brown*). Anyone who passes through Vegas should stop at the Tropicana Hotel's Mob Museum that brings the contributions of the mob to that city to life.

Another example of good works by a mob-union connection is that of Anthony "Tony Gawk" Augello and the New York Coliseum. Gawk was no angel, but he used his authority with the union of those installing and removing displays at the Manhattan convention center to settle disputes and, above all, have a place to put guys coming out of prison a job. Granted, sometimes, in the case of mob higher ups, the jobs were "no show," just to get them into halfway houses or satisfy their parole requirements. However, many of those connected guys came out of prison broke and needed the work, which was not a steady nine to five, but required men when a show was about to open and when it was closing. The pay was good and it left plenty of free time to readjust to life on the streets; sometimes to get back into criminal activities and sometimes not. Oddly enough, Gawk wasn't interested in personally earning from his influence as he was being able to provide the jobs as favors to mob brothers. That influence died when he did, as his captain, only interested in money, backed away from the union when he learned there was responsibility without pay. His words, when told that it should be kept to provide for guys in jail who need a job when they come home was, "F-ck the guys in jail! If there's no money, get rid of it." That overt greed marks the changing face of the mob and is a major contributor to its demise. Mob guys also no longer contribute to the well being of the neighborhoods they inhabit, and thereby have no citizen support.

The tweet that asked since when unions became gangsters referred to an incident recently in Wisconsin, where a non-union business owner, John King, was apparently shot by a union thug. The case is currently under investigation. My answer to the tweet was correct, that unions have always been aligned with gangsters. The difference in the beginning was that employees worked in sweatshops and under deplorable conditions that demanded someone help them lift their heads, and today the battle is just about greed.

Hey, Gordon Gekko, greed is not always what it's cracked up to be.

MOB BLOG #6:

Prison vs the Mob

Reputed mob boss Andy Russo was shot in the back eight times. Mob war? No, he was shot by Metropolitan Detention Center guards while on the phone during last week's New York earthquake. Since he was the only one who got hit with those eight non-lethal bullets, it begs the question, "Was it a hit by the prison guard mob against a well known street guy?" Seems absurd, but eight? Andrew is in for a very serious crime too. When a friend of his got stabbed by a guy linked to the Gambino's, he met with the Gambino rep to work out a deal so that their friend paid for the victim's medical expenses. The charge by Eric Holder (yes, the same AG who dropped voter intimidation charges on the New Black Panthers AFTER they'd been judged guilty), is that Russo "extorted" the Gambinos. Sound stupid? Yes, it is.

With any luck, the 77 year old Andrew will receive a "Get Out of Jail Free" card for not bringing a lawsuit against the Bureau of Prisons. That is not uncommon. "Little Dom" Cataldo earned one by having boiling water accidentally spill on him while working in a prison kitchen. He filed suit, but got an offer he couldn't refuse: "Drop the suit and go home." Dom did exactly that...that time. He wound up back on another case and died in prison of natural causes. The Russo incident also brings up the issues of other mobsters harmed or killed in prison by staff.

Nino Gaggi was a well known Gambino captain. He became famous or infamous, depending on whether or not you lived that life, off the media exposure of his underling, "Fat Roy" DeMeo, in the book "Murder Machine." DeMeo, who was himself murdered, was supposedly a bloodthirsty fiend who killed on orders given him by Gaggi, who, in turn, got them from Paul Castellano. In the interest of full disclosure, Fat Roy was a long time friend of mine, and was no bloodthirsty fiend. Fat Roy woke up in the morning focused only on getting a pat on the head from those higher up in his crew. Back to Gaggi. Nino was in Metropolitan Correctional Center, on Park Row, Manhattan, awaiting trial on multiple murders with Paul Castellano et al, when he was struck by chest pains that signaled more than just indigestion. He complained to the guard on duty several times, and insisted that he see some medical practitioner (*most times there are no doctors on premises, but physician's assistants*). The sicker Nino felt, the more insistent he became that he get medical attention, the more irritated the hack became. Finally, the guard had a solution. He handcuffed Nino to a chair so he wouldn't bother him until such time as he was good and ready to take care of the situation. Nino Gaggi had a massive heart attack in that chair, and died in the prison hospital.

Case three: Allie Romano was a relative of mine through marriage. Allie was one of the longest running drug kingpins until drugs were outlawed for most families in 1957, and also a captain in the Gambino Family. He was a connection to the French Connection, and had brought narcotics in from France and Corsica since the 1920s. According to the paperwork in the thirteen year old indictment Allie was arrested on (*yes, five year statute of limitations, but was renewed after the first five years then again after ten*), a single load broad in by ship consisted of more than three hundred kilos of pure heroin. Okay, so Allie made a shitload of dirty money and eventually was sentenced to thirty years in prison in his later years for it. An older, sicker man when he entered the penitentiary in Atlanta, Georgia, Allie had already had a major operation on his lungs. One night, his chest felt like it would explode. His younger brother, Dominick, who was his innocent co-defendant (*that's another story for another day*) and cellmate, screamed for help. It wasn't long before Allie, in the throes of an attack, was wheeled into the infirmary, where a physician's assistant (*remember, no doctors*), rushed to take care of him. Had he thoroughly gone over Allie's medical history, he might have guessed that it could be a collapsed lung that merely had to be blown up. Instead, he assumed it was a heart attack and pounded on Allie's chest. Allie Romano died on that table.

Sure, the BOP has saved many more wiseguys than they have killed...especially in the prison hospitals, like at Springfield, Missouri. On the other hand, they are no different than any massive institutional or medical complexes; there are errors made all the time that we read about or see on the television news. It just happens that the incident with Andy Russo at MDC, while serious, tickled something dark and humorous in me at the same time. In my mind, it could have been a scene from a Naked Gun-type movie.

However, there is a truly dark side that is always an underlying thought to inmates of prisons, but never spoken about in public. That is the rumor that in case of an invasion of or nuclear attack on the U.S., prisoners in penitentiaries would be immediately killed; probably gassed. True? I have no idea. But it is a plausible rumor and has never been addressed in any open forum. Does anyone care if convicted thieves and murderers incarcerated in New York State's Dannemora or Attica will be eliminated to avoid them roaming the streets? Or terrorists in the Feds' Super-Max prison in Colorado that also housed John Gotti and is the current home to Vinny "Gorgeous" Bascione? But what if anyone in those facilities is a relative? Shouldn't we know for sure?

Sonny Girard

MOB BLOG #7:

Hollywood Molls

It's no secret that females have always been attracted to mobsters. Anyone who visits a nightclub or restaurant where mob guys hang out will see the hens flock around those criminal roosters. And why not? Mobsters usually have great cars and clothing, have disposable cash, have plenty of spare time to entertain in and out of the bedroom, and, most of all bring an aura of daring and violence that women find vicariously thrilling. For those who haven't been around the mob, take my word for it. As a young man, I once had a fling with an Irish beauty who had mistakenly been told that I was my infamous boss (*we were dressed similarly and standing next to each other when she had inquired with the bartender*). I also had the wives of men who wanted to hang around with mob guys like me make offers of affairs and one girl who wouldn't give me the time of day till she saw me beat a drunk in a barroom incident (*I almost got pinched by two undercover detectives who were also watching the incident*). What proves that the money and flashy possessions take second place to the aura of violence? Just look at the Hollywood harem that jumped into bed, and were rumored to have jumped into bed with wiseguys, as those females wondered how much blood was on the hands that sizzled on their naked flesh.

Not all relationships wound up well. Thelma Todd was a former Miss Massachusetts (1925) who made her way to Hollywood and worked in more than forty mostly comedy films of the late 1920s and early 1930s with names like the Marx Brothers, Laurel and Hardy, Buster Keaton, and Jimmy Durante. In the early 1930s, she opened a cafe at Pacific Palisades, called Thelma Todd's Sidewalk Café. The eatery became a hit and became a place where Hollywood celebrities could be seen, which attracted tourists as patrons. With beauty and business success, came a series of relationships, including one with her jealous partner, Roland West, and another with a mob connected ex-husband involved in bootlegging and prostitution, Pat DeCicco. That ex-hubby also had a record of violence against women. On the night of December 15, 1935, Thelma had a nasty exchange with Pat at a party at the Trocadero, one of the most popular nightspots in L.A., run by actress Ida Lupino's father, Stanley Lupino. She dismissed DeCicco, and went on to become the life of the party. The next morning she was dead; found in a car in her garage with the motor running. The police ruled it a suicide (*Why the hell would a successful, beautiful, party girl commit suicide?*), but rumors and alternate theories have continued to this day, one of the most popular being that she refused to allow DeCicco and others in Lucky Luciano's family to use her club as a front for a gambling operation, and for her to participate in orgies that Lucky seemed to be fond of (*and who isn't?*). More likely, DeCicco would have been angered because of jealousy or a refusal by his ex- to put him on her payroll.

Gypsy Rose Lee, real name Rose Louise Hovick, was a living burlesque legend of the day at the same time Thelma Todd was having her best days. Raised under poor conditions by a whacky mother, Gypsy was drawn to vaudeville at an early age. By the age of thirteen she married. Mama Hovick had her young son-in-law arrested, but blew the case when she met him at the police station with a gun. She tried to shoot him, but the safety was on. The cops were happy to get rid of everyone in that crew, and filed no charges against anyone. Mama Hovick eventually shot a man to death, which, with the influence of her daughter's fame and money, was ruled as a suicide by the victim. Gypsy was a world renowned stripper who needed constant stimulation, mentally and sexually. Her string of lovers and husbands included the famous, like film icon Otto Preminger and international promoter Mike Todd, a number of unknowns, some women, and a gangster: Waxey Gordon. Waxey was a bootlegger and high level associate of the most infamous names of the day: Lansky, Luciano, Costello, etc. He was tough as nails and ran his own gang. That excited Gypsy, whose appetite for excitement was insatiable. The fact that she could tame the thuggish Gordon was orgasmic. He was also tough enough to make sure no one gave her a hard time, and was so enthralled with her that he gladly put up with her quirks, like having monkeys perform sex acts at her parties and orgies, and was there to intimidate anyone who had a beef with her. But Waxey seemed to have picked up some of the craziness that Gypsy had inherited from her mother, and, egged on by Gypsy, got into a pissing match with Meyer Lansky that went to the brink of all out war. Luciano and Lansky believed that a "War of the Jews" would be bad for business, and sent Meyer's brother Jake to the IRS with Gordon's second set of records. Waxey was convicted and went to Federal Prison. Gypsy had no control now on her behavior, and as her public career faded she remarried and divorced again, but had financial success as a film writer, art collector, and entrepreneur...and never forgot Waxey, who eventually was released, later rearrested for heroin trafficking, and sent to prison, where he died. Did she need Waxey's money? No. Was it his good looks or stunning personality? Certainly not. Once again, it was the aura of danger that surrounded him and excited a successful Hollywood star.

Janice Drake was another celebrity whose fascination with the mob led to tragedy. Janice, the wife of comedian Alan Drake, liked to move around as eye candy in mob circles...not that she brought them any good luck. She was with Albert Anastasia the night before he was shot to death in the Park Sheraton Hotel, presumably by Joey Gallo as a favor to Vito Genovese. She also dined with a garment center mover named Nat Nelson the night he was killed. That alone should have made mobsters...hell, men in general... treat her like a leper. But the ever imprudent Li'l Augie Pisano, whose real name was Anthony Carfano, never met a...how do we say this delicately?... female body part he didn't want, decided to take a chance with destiny and have a fling with Janice, who was later believed to have provided some service to the mob on the occasions of the murders and as a courier at other times. Bad luck caught up with her when she didn't get out of the way of Li'l Augie's body being aerated in his car. Or, was it Janice they were after? Or both, taking care of two birds with one stone? In either case, it was

Mrs. Drake's fascination with the mob that made her famous...and dead...slumped in a car; a bullet hole clean through her forehead.

Famed Schwab's soda counter discovery turned international pinup girl and top actress, Lana Turner, also had a tragic turn with a minor mob character, Johnny Stompanato, who was particularly associated with Mickey Cohen. Lana loved being around mobsters and being known as the tough girl who walked the walk, and a sexually active female who had had a stable of lovers. One old time mob guy told me a story about how Sinatra, who was rumored to have been "made" by Sam Giancana, finally broke up with red-hot beauty, Ava Gardner, that involved Lana Turner as well. He claimed to have been in a Luciano crew wiseguy's after hours club in Harlem when the two beauties stopped in after bouncing around the city's top night spots. Half lit, they proceeded to drink it up and entertain the crowd of wiseguys and their associates with racy jokes and sexy body language. According to the old mobster, a few more drinks and the two actresses were bare-assed on the bar, with each one's legs wrapped around the other's head and tongues flicking away at high speed.

When word hit Giancana's ears, he immediately gave Ol' Blue Eyes a choice: her or us. Sinatra was heartbroken, but chose the latter. Johnny Stompanato had no such scruples. He was also known as a male gold digger to mobsters, and they ignored him. The relationship didn't end well when supposedly her fourteen-year-old daughter, Cheryl, stabbed Johnny to death when he was having another of his violent fights with her mother. At fourteen, Cheryl was a sympathetic character, and never really at risk of going to prison. The case was ruled justifiable homicide. However, popular underworld theory, which is usually more accurate in matters of murder, was that Lana was actually the one who killed him when she caught him having sex with her daughter. A film is in the works about that affair.

One of the most famous celebrity-mobster romances was that of singer Phyllis McGuire, youngest of the popular McGuire Sisters, and Chicago crime boss, Sam "Momo" Giancana. That romance was immortalized in a Showtime movie "Sugartime," with John Turturro playing the smitten Giancana. That romance was at the center of Frank Sinatra losing his license to own part of the Cal-Nev Casino, in Lake Tahoe, Nevada, on the California border. In July of 1963, Giancana, who was staying in the hotel, had a battle with Phyllis' road manager, Victor Collins. Before long it turned into a physical battle, which drew the attention of the Nevada Gaming Commission, which, after interviewing Sinatra about Giancana's presence (*he was banned as an undesirable character*) at his hotel, the singer's license was pulled and he had to sell his ownership position. Giancana, who would never be considered handsome, went on to another famous affair when he shared Judith Campbell Exner with President Kennedy. The old mob boss also went on to become enmeshed with the CIA in a plot to kill Fidel Castro and possibly one to assassinate the President. He wound up with fatal lead poisoning...from a bullet...under conditions that smacked of a government hit (*he was under FBI surveillance at his home when a seemingly invisible assassin slipped into the house, killed him, and left, again unseen*).

Many other female celebrities have been rumored, and not always confirmed, to be associated with mobsters: Redheaded actress Rhonda Fleming with "Crazy Joe" Gallo; Marilyn Monroe with Sinatra and his pals; Virginia Hill with Bugsy Siegel; Singer Janice Harper with Joe Carlo; a still living former *very famous* TV sitcom star with my deceased pal, Benny, when she met him at a crap game he was running; a famous comedienne who, upon meeting another friend at a house party, was so impressed by his mob position that she gave him oral sex in the kitchen. Yes, it is common knowledge that the money, power, and violence of mob guys are an aphrodisiac for many women who find their own lives dull by comparison. But celebrity life is far from mundane, yet the attraction seems to be just as strong. Go figure.

Sonny Girard

MOB BLOG #8:

America and the Mob: 1932-1946

In 1932, representatives of New York's newly re-organized crime attended the Democrats' Presidential Convention in the city most infamous for corruption, Chicago, Illinois. They had made untold millions as a result of Prohibition that they'd used to put law enforcers, judges, and politicians in their pocket. Now, they were going for the biggest prize of all. They would own the next President of the United States.

The three main contenders for the office were Governor of New York, Franklin Delano Roosevelt, Speaker of the House of Representatives, Texan John Nance Garner, and Al Smith, a former Governor of New York and failed Presidential candidate four years earlier, in 1928. It was supposed to be an easy win for FDR, but it didn't work out that way. He wasn't able to muster the two-thirds he needed on the first and second votes, and back room deals went full force. One of those deals was with the mob.

A number of years ago, I got a message from Vincent "Jimmy Blue Eyes" Alo. As a lifelong mobster myself, Jimmy Blue Eyes was one of my early heroes. What he wanted to possibly do was write a book strictly about the 1920s and 1930s, when he, Frank Costello, Lucky Luciano, and Meyer Lansky controlled the Democrat machine in New York, known as "Tammany Hall." They were able to make mayors, judges, and councilmen, and had their way with any legal question, from criminal charges to licenses. One of those was the Presidency, in 1932. We never did the book because Jimmy, ever the loyal soldier, asked the boss of his family, the Genovese Family, for permission...and was denied. That denial came directly from Vincent "Chin" Gigante. Though

I was disappointed (*I would have given anything just to hear the details, even if I couldn't write about it*), I was impressed that Chin had stuck to the letter of the law...mob law...without exceptions or excuses. That being said, it didn't change the fact that those who controlled Tammany were at the Convention, and that they had a hand in electing the President.

In true Machiavellian fashion, the New York contingent of organized crime split up and infiltrated the camps of both FDR and Al Smith. They never really had any confidence that Garner would be anything more than a spoiler, and, in true Texas Congressional manner, would cut a deal with one of the other two *(he wound up as FDR's Vice President)*. The mob had an earth shaking decision to make, and they wanted to make it right.

Luciano assigned himself to Al Smith, while Costello, a big fan of FDR's, kept close to the candidate and actually got a brief audience with him to discuss support. Both offered the candidates not only money, but votes in key areas around the country. All Lucky and his guys had to do was send a message to Santo Trafficante in Tampa, Nig Rosen in Philadelphia, Waxey Gordon in Jersey, Nick Civella in Kansas City, or any of the bosses of major cities from coast to coast to get their troops out to pile up votes for their candidate, legally or illegally. They negotiated directly with the candidates and finally decided, with no doubt swayed by Costello's admiration, to throw their full and unified weight behind Franklin Delano Roosevelt.

The news shattered Al Smith. He practically cried when he was told of their decision. He also told them that they'd made a huge mistake; that he came from the same kind of background they did, including being part of the Tammany machine, and could be trusted to keep any word he gave them, while the patrician Roosevelt would promise them anything but betray them in the end. The decision had been made. FDR won, and immediately empowered Samuel Seabury to investigate organized crime and its political connections, especially Tammany Hall, which had spawned his former rival, Al Smith. For all their dreams, efforts, and thoughtfulness, Lucky Luciano, Meyer Lansky, and Frank Costello had made a mistake; they'd picked the wrong horse and would be trampled by their choice. Oddly enough, mobsters repeated their error in 1960, when their support helped their fellow bootlegger's son, John F. Kennedy, attain the Presidency. He also turned on them once in office, and had his brother, Robert, as Attorney General, go after organized crime with a vengeance. In fact, the R.I.C.O. Act, so effective in mob prosecutions, was written during RFK's reign as AG.

It was only ten years after Roosevelt's election, in February of 1942, with the United States embroiled in World War II for only two months that the superliner Normandie burned and capsized at its dock in New York Harbor. It wasn't just that it was one of the fastest luxury liners ever built, but it was to be refitted to carry Allied troops. There was not a U-boat of the Fuhrer's that could keep up with the Normandie. It wasn't just a fire. The Government saw it as an act of wartime sabotage.

At that time, many of those who worked the New York piers were of Italian descent, and the U.S. was at war with Mussolini's Italy. Control of the piers was also commonly known to be in the hands of organized crime. After intense discussions, it was decided by the Office of Naval Intelligence officials that they would approach the alleged Luciano boss of the piers, Joseph "Socks" Lanza, and appeal to his patriotism to help protect the docks from further sabotage. (*Albert Anastastia and his brother, Anthony "Tough Tony" Anastasia, controlled waterfront interests for what would eventually become the Gambino Family*)

Ever the loyal soldier, Lanza, through Meyer Lansky, contacted his boss, Lucky Luciano, who was serving a multi-decade sentence on a trumped up prostitution charge in Dannamora maximum security state prison in Clinton, New York. Lansky met with Lucky in the comfort of his decked out cell and worked a deal to have stevedores guard the piers against further sabotage. For his part, Luciano might get some kind of consideration once the war was over, but would also immediately be moved from close to the Canadian border to Sing Sing prison, just outside New York City, in Ossining, where he could have an enhanced visitation life. Later, before his death, Lucky claimed that he had ordered the Normandie burned in order to get the Navy to come to him for help. Since there had never been an instance that would lead him to believe that at the time, the statement should be taken with a grain of salt as an old mobster trying to sell a book. In fact, mobsters happen to be extremely patriotic. Meyer Lansky and Bugsy Siegel led their thugs to disrupt Nazi Bund meetings in Yorkville, Manhattan, not for any consideration, but just to break the asses of Jew haters. In fact, patriotism ran through the Lanskys' blood, with one of Meyer's nephews later becoming an Army Intelligence Officer.

Luciano's reputation among the United States war machine brass was golden. Years later, when the Allies were preparing to invade Sicily in the final push to defeat Hitler, Lucky was again approached; this time by the United States Army Military Intelligence. They were unsure how they would be greeted when they hit the shores of Sicily. Would they be given up to German troops? Would diehard believers in the now dead Il Duce engage them in battle? They knew he was well connected with Sicilian Mafia bosses, and assumed he could pave the way for an invasion unimpeded by Sicilian paisani. A firm promise was given that when the war ended, he would be released from prison and deported to Italy. Luciano, loyal to both Sicily and the United States, and very pleased with the promise, assured them that it was a done deal.

As the invasion was launched, Luciano had a yellow handkerchief with his crest dropped from a U.S. plane over Sicily. That signaled underground Sicilian partisans to come forward and join the Americans to expel Hitler's troops from their soil. For Mafiosi, who had been brutalized by Mussolini, which included the imprisonment of the most revered don in the history of the country, Don Vito Cascio Ferro, it meant a return of influence and power once Luciano's Americans cleared the island of Nazis. Mussolini was already dead and the Mafia was thoroughly ingrained in Sicilian society. In fact, once the Germans had been routed with Sicilian support, at Luciano's recommendation,

American officials in charge installed many Mafiosi as mayors of various towns and in other top political positions.

In this case, Army Intelligence kept its word, and Luciano, who had been railroaded by future Presidential candidate Thomas Dewey (*it is inconceivable that Luciano, the most powerful mobster in America at the time, confided his interests in a prostitution business to a druggie hooker named "Cokie Flo," whose testimony convicted him*), was released from prison in January, 1946, and deported to Italy. Since Sicily didn't want him, Lucky was exiled to Naples, where he resided, with intermittent trips for mob meetings in Sicily and Cuba, until his death in January, 1962.

Those twelve years, from 1932, when mobsters participated in a Presidential convention, and 1946, when Luciano was released from prison and deported, were unique in that they covered two major upheavals in American history: the Great Depression and World War II. However, the U.S. Government using mob figures when they weren't trying to lock them away, continued during America's crises in the following decades, although usually with the mobsters getting the short end of the stick. Chicago mobsters Johnny Roselli and Sam "Momo" Giancana were both enlisted to work with the CIA during the Kennedy years to try to assassinate Fidel Castro. Both Roselli and Giancana were murdered. Roselli washed ashore in an oil drum on the California coast; Momo was mysteriously shot to death in his basement apartment while under twenty-four hour FBI surveillance. Vito Genovese's godson recounted to me going to a hidden Florida beach with his godfather just before the Bay of Pigs fiasco, where they picked up a suitcase of money for weapons from para-military men. Vito's quiet role helped him survive.

More successful in his dealing with the Government was Colombo mobster turned rat, Greg Scarpa, who was conscripted by the FBI to find the bodies of three freedom marchers who had disappeared in Mississippi. Scarpa grabbed a general store owner who the FBI was sure knew where the three men had been buried. He tied the storeowner up and tortured him until he revealed where the graves were. Scarpa earned himself an FBI "license to kill" until his death from AIDs.

The Government and the mob have been more interrelated than most people realize. The Government has always found organized crime an easy target when it needs more funding or a diversion from other problems. In between, they have no compunction about using mobster crackdowns to achieve its goals. Now that the mob is in its final throes, it won't be able to do either for much longer.

MOB BLOG #9:

The Best Mob Story

The following story appeared in the New York Daily News:

Colombo's bad boys go on trial

BY THOMAS ZAMBITO
DAILY NEWS STAFF WRITER

An infamous piece of Mafia history - the 1971 hit on Joe Colombo - will be resurrected this week when two of his sons go on trial for allegedly carrying on the family business.

Anthony and Christopher Colombo are accused of extortion and loansharking - threatening bodily harm and worse to debtors - as part of a racketeering conspiracy.

Pretrial hearings show the sons learned a few lessons from their father, who used to stage Italian-American unity rallies where he denounced the Mafia as a myth.

The sons' attorneys have attacked prosecution attempts to mention La Cosa Nostra or their link to the man who gave the Colombo crime family its name - and who was gunned down at a Columbus Circle rally.

"If evidence that Mr. Colombo is the son of Joseph Colombo Sr. and that his father was ultimately murdered ... the jury will readily infer that Mr. Colombo too was involved in organized crime," Christopher's lawyer Jeremy Schneider wrote to the judge.

Federal prosecutors say the Colombos wore out their welcome in the crime family and created a violent offshoot called the Colombo Brothers Crew that wasn't shy about reminding deadbeats of their Mafia ties.

The defendant dropped the Colombo name to "help instill fear in loansharking victims," prosecutors Lisa Baroni and Jason Halperin wrote in court documents.

Christopher Colombo, 45, has also displayed his father's sense of showmanship, appearing in a short-lived HBO documentary called "House Arrest."

What's important about the story is not the current trial or anyone involved. What struck me was that the government wants to use material about their father, material from more than thirty-five years ago, to convict them. Why did it strike me? Because I was there. It wasn't much more than living in the moment for me at the time. Now, I've come to see the time leading up to the end of Joe Colombo Sr.'s life as the best mob story of modern time. I've even written a screenplay about it.

If you went back far enough, Joe Colombo was unlikely to ever be boss of the Profaci Crime Family, let alone the one who would be dominant enough to have its name changed to his. He was a good soldier, an earner, a standup guy, but not in the dynamic way that other members did. Then he got a bit of luck. I've been told that luck is preparation meeting opportunity. Joe got that opportunity when Profaci died and his inept relative, Joseph "The Fat Man" Magliocco got the nod as boss. Fatso was weak and malleable, so when Joe Bonnano proposed they kill a couple of mob bosses, including Carlo Gambino, and rule the underworld, he agreed then palmed the job off to one of his underlings: Joe Colombo. It didn't take long for Joe to realize the Fat Man was a fat head to go along with something so dumb, and informed Gambino of the plot. Magliocco died of a heart attack, Bonnano fled, and with Gambino's support Joe Colombo became the next boss of the Profaci Family.

Joe actually grew into the role and became a pretty decent boss, smart, forward looking, and ruthless when he had to be for the next six or seven years. Then the best mob story in modern times began.

One day Joe was informed that his eldest son, and his pride and joy, Joe Jr., had been arrested by the FBI on charges of melting down U.S. coins for their silver content. Joe believed the charges were trumped up and that the government was trying to get to him by falsely accusing his son. Infuriated, he ordered those in and around his real estate business to print up makeshift signs that the FBI was persecuting Italians. He then led a caravan to the front of the FBI Building in Upper Manhattan and began picketing. After a couple of days of picketing and shouting by a small group of Colombo's people, the media picked up the story. Before long, picketers and media coverage multiplied until the nightly marches took on a circus-like atmosphere: legitimate Italians who felt that the government had stereotyped them marched with signs and yelled alongside real mobsters. Other mob bosses gave permission for their people to picket too. In fact, many mobsters were actually ordered to march. Joe Colombo led them all from the platform of a truck, yelling things like "The FBI persecutes Italians," but always punctuated by "We're Number One," over and over again. As a writer, it is nearly impossible for me to relate the heady feeling of power Joe instilled in everyone, even as FBI Agents spit down and threw water on us all. Small skirmishes broke out with police. Newspapers, like the Staten Island Advance, that wrote bad stories about the picketing had their trucks overturned. In a big win for Colombo, New York Supreme Court upheld the right of the crowd to picket.

It was a short leap from simple picketing to the formation of an organization, the "Italian American Civil Rights League," headed by Joe Colombo Sr. himself. Chapters of the League opened all over the city, most run by mobsters. Members joined by the thousands: doctors, mob guys, priests, mob guys, housewives, mob guys, politicians, mob guys. Governor Nelson Rockefeller was an honorary member. All over the city, signs, jewelry, pennants, all read "#1." Joe Colombo became a national hero to many. He was named Man of the Year by one organization, was profiled in magazines, and appeared on television interviews with Dick Cavett and others...all the while denying any participation in any criminal organization and running on a day to day basis what was by that time known to law enforcement as the Colombo Crime Family. As his profile grew, so did Joe's power. He forced the U.S. Attorney's Office to publicly announce they would discontinue the use of terms like "Mafia" and "Cosa Nostra." He demanded Paramount eliminate those same terms from their upcoming film, "Godfather," and got it.

He had an Alka Seltzer television commercial removed from the air because he believed it was offensive to Italians. Sinatra and the Rat Pack did a huge fundraising concert for the League at Madison Square Garden. That summer he conducted an outdoor First Annual Unity Day Rally at Manhattan's Columbus Circle that drew almost fifty thousand people, from Italians who closed their businesses for the day, FBI Agents, hot dog vendors cashing in, media people, politicians and entertainers on the podium, kids, mobsters, grandmothers. For those of us who were there, it is one of the most memorable celebrations in our lives. The rally ended with a march from Columbus Circle to the FBI Building on Third Avenue to continue picketing.

But the high profile also brought a downside: heat from the FBI. Mobsters who marched became FBI targets. Acting Genovese Boss Thomas "Tommy Ryan" Eboli was shaken down and strip searched by customs when he returned from a trip to Italy. Other bosses felt the heat and determined that Colombo was profiting from the League and they weren't getting any of it. They "asked" Colombo to step down as head of the League and let some legitimate figurehead fill in. Joe refused. He really believed that without him at the helm, rallying support and leading the fight to intimidate enemies, the League would collapse. To make matters worse, "Crazy Joe" Gallo was released from prison after serving a stint for extortion. Colombo had inherited the Gallo-Profaci War and had pretty much tamped things down by that time. Without his brother Larry, who had died of cancer, to keep him under control, Gallo went straight after Colombo, demanding what he considered his due. Colombo's peace offering was rejected. Battles between the factions broke out in the streets of Brooklyn. Crazy Joe went after Colombo operations. The other bosses demanded Colombo step down from the League. He refused again. Orders went out for underlings and associates of other crews to abandon the League.

By the time the Second Annual Unity Day Rally was scheduled at Columbus Circle, a struggle was in full force between Colombo and Gallo. Colombo men placed signs in the windows of Brooklyn stores announcing they'd be closed the day of the rally, only to be removed shortly thereafter by Gallo's men. Though severely outnumbered, Gallo obviously had the support of Carlo Gambino, who, by that time, while there was no boss of bosses, was the most venerable of family bosses, and therefore deferred to by the others. I remember, as the rally approached, being summoned to Bensonhurst's Ravioli Fair by its owner, an old highly placed pal, who has since passed on.

"The rally is coming up next week," he said. "Make sure you don't go."

"I had no intention of going," I replied.

"You're not listening to me," he said, annoyed. "I said, *make sure* you don't go."

"I heard. I'm not going."

He repeated the make sure thing a couple of more times. I left thinking he'd gone senile. I thought sadly that it wouldn't be long before he didn't recognize me any more.

The following week the rally took place. Joe Colombo had decided that this would be his last hurrah as head of the League, and would indeed step down afterward. Attendance was down about sixty percent. The cheers, as I watched television coverage, seemed forced and somewhat defeatist. Then Joe stepped up onto the stage. A black man with news credentials and a camera hanging from his neck stepped behind him...and shot him in the head. The black man, Jerome Johnson, was set upon and murdered on the spot. Since Joe Gallo had befriended blacks while in prison, it was speculated that he had sent Johnson.

Joe Colombo, paralyzed, lingered for seven years before succumbing. As Colombo had predicted, without him the League collapsed. Joe Gallo was later murdered in Umberto's Clam House, in Little Italy.

Later, when I was writing the screenplay, living through the events again, I was surprised at how short a time encompassed them. I called other old pals who also lived through it. To a man, they all answered that it was somewhere around three years. Amazingly, everything from Joes first night of picketing the FBI Building with makeshift signs to his being shot in front of nearly twenty thousand people took place over an event-filled, fast moving fifteen months.

Are there any modern mob stories that match the impact of this man who tried to live in two diametrically opposed worlds and paid for it with his life? Any other mob story that demands a filmed version? I don't think so.

MOB BLOG #10:

Lansky and Miami

There was a stage play going on in Los Angeles, directed by Joe Bologna, called "Lansky." It focused on Meyer's battle to stay in Israel under the Right of Return policy for Jews, and was favorably reviewed by at least one member of the Lansky family, Mark Lansky, who is in the process of writing a book about his cousin. There have been dozens of books about or including Meyer Lansky, films that presented parts of his life...the early years, his role in Havana, his relationship with Lucky Luciano and the *Unione Siciliano*...and countless stories and myths about the man. He's alternately been called the brain of modern organized crime, its CEO, a cold blooded killer, and a member of the fabled Commission of mob family leaders. He was some of the first, less of the next two, and none of the third. But whatever you think of Meyer Lansky, no matter how bad you think the man was, in the course of his life he left his mark in a number of places both here and in Cuba, but none as lasting as in South Florida.

Lansky was a genius. Numbers spun around his head like a roulette wheel and always came up with the right numbers. From his youth, when he'd first encountered crap games in the alleys of the Lower East Side of Manhattan ghetto that his Polish-Jewish parents had emigrated to from Grodno, Russia, he'd been able to calculate odds and find a way to turn them in his favor. One way of doing that was foregoing the daily routine of a twelve to fourteen hour workday for the freedom of the hoodlum's life. He'd do just about anything to survive, and as a small man fought doubly hard to earn the respect of other young thugs he'd come across, like Bugsy Siegel, Albert Anastasia, Lucky Luciano, and Frank Costello, who would become lifelong friends and business partners. In that diverse group, where each member brought a significant and unique talent...Bugsy was the warrior, Lucky was the manipulator (*that's why he became boss*), and Costello was the diplomat. Meyer was the financial brain. His was the brain that brought gambling in Miami, New Orleans, the Bahamas, and Cuba to the mob. He was even invited by Cuba's strongman Fulgencio Batista to sit on the gaming board of his country. For a time, Meyer really was a CEO, using his executive power to clean up Cuban casinos' crooked gambling and draw players from the States in record numbers...especially to the Nacional, a hotel that still stands in Havana, where he and his partners had a substantial ownership position.

Cold blooded killer was not what Lansky was about. Surely, in his early years, he may have accumulated a notch or two in his belt, but just as easily might not have. Once he'd partnered up with Bugsy Siegel to form the Bug and Meyer gang, he didn't have to. Meyer stepped into his first leadership position and ran it with his brain....a brain tutored by another Jewish gangster actually nicknamed "The Brain," Arnold Rothstein.

Bugsy was, as previously mentioned, a warrior. He'd kill fast and hard, and would not hesitate to use those talents to protect his friends and their earning potential, or to remove a thorn in any of their sides. Since a mob rule has always been that one cannot kill his boss and become boss, it was Bugsy, along with his Jewish cohorts, like Red Levine, who eliminated both Giuseppe "Joe the Boss" Masseria and Salvatore Maranzano to make way for Lucky to take overall power (*that rule kept John Gotti from being recognized by the Commission a half-century later*). Lansky was not among the shooters. Instead, he was expanding the financial interests of his partners with the millions they'd made from Prohibition. While known for his gaming business prowess, Lansky also used their overflowing funds to invest in land, nightclubs, hotels, and anything else that made sense. Much of that investment was in South Florida.

The biggest erroneous story about Meyer Lansky was that he was part of the now fabled Commission of organized crime. Nothing could be farther from the truth. To understand why Meyer never made it to a seat on the Commission, is to go back to the murders of Moustachio mob bosses Giuseppe Masseria and Salvatore Maranzano and the subsequent murder of more than sixty more Sicilian old timer Mafiosi from September 10th to the 11th, 1931, in what is now known as the "Night of the Sicilian Vespers." The Moustache Petes, as they were called, had lived and died for vendettas during their rule; for wars between themselves and those of other towns and regions of Sicily. Those continuous battles cost a lot of profit to everyone involved. They also refused to do business with anyone except other Sicilians. Mainland Italians were as bad to them as Jews or Irishmen. To a group of younger, more Americanized gangsters, made up of men like Lucky Luciano, Frank Costello, Bugsy Siegel, and Meyer Lansky, not only didn't the Moustachioes rule make sense, but something had to be done about it. With Bugsy Siegel in the lead, dozens of old timers across the country were murdered.

Little Davey Petillo, who later went to prison with Luciano on the prostitution charges brought by Thomas Dewey, was a young man who looked like a kid at the time of the Vespers. When a top Moustachio escaped the first round of murders, Little Davey was dispatched to the Mafioso's city. He set up a shoe shine box outside the boss's club and ingratiated himself to the Sicilian mobsters with glossy spit shines. When the extra cautious boss finally put a foot out for Davey to shine, the boy pulled a pistol from his shine box and shot both the boss and his bodyguard to death.

When the smoke cleared, and the new order was ready to go to work, Lucky Luciano surprised everyone by claiming that though all ethnic groups would be welcome to do business, the *Unione Siciliano* would reign supreme. He divided the *Unione* into five families under Sicilian rule, and assigned other ethnic associates to Sicilians who would act as their "liaisons." To Bugsy Siegel, who had done the heavy lifting in murdering Masseria and Maranzano, this was unacceptable. When he left for the West Coast, it was to be his own boss, not, as commonly thought, to establish mob outposts. For Lansky, who was only interested in making money, it didn't matter what status he did or didn't receive. He would accept one of his closest friends, Vincent "Jimmy Blue Eyes" Alo as his man in the mob (*notice that the Lansky character's man in Godfather II was named Johnny Ola, Alo backwards, as was the relationship portrayed*). Lansky was forever an associate, not member, of the traditional mob, though he remained a trusted advisor to the mob's hierarchy throughout his life, a life spent in a large part in South Florida.

There are a lot of businesses and structures in Miami and the greater South Florida area that owe(d) their existence to Meyer Lansky. To this area that catered in large part in early- to mid-Twentieth Century years to vacationers and escapees from cold northern states, Meyer brought organized gambling: crap and card games, horse betting, and slot machines. With gambling came bigger hotels that brought national celebrities and beautiful showgirls. As South Florida grew it needed an economic infrastructure to support vacationers' paradise: wholesalers, hotel workers, grocers, haberdashers and women's clothing salespeople, police, and, especially, restaurants. Some world famous hotels like the Eden Roc and restaurants like the Forge owe their very existence to the foundation that Meyer Lansky and his organized crime cohorts set down.

Hospitals expanded with Meyer Lansky donations. Mobsters and Lansky front men for businesses like the Singapore Hotel threw money around like it was confetti, making locals well to do and leaving a legacy of extreme public tolerance of mobsters that remains today. South Beach embraced a small time gangster wannabe, Chris Paciello, until he turned rat when prison loomed. Chances are if Paciello returns to Miami tomorrow, locals and celebrities will embrace him just the same. South Florida has grown up with a live and let live attitude.

Part of that is because of Meyer himself; the man he was when he was not scheming how to wash money or bury it in Swiss bank accounts.

Meyer's cousin, Mark, who Meyer always referred to as his "little nephew," tells of an incident in which members of the Lansky family were having dinner at the Embers restaurant, in Miami Beach. Behind Meyer, at the next table, a man that he had never met went on and on to his party about how much of a pal he was with Meyer Lansky. All of the family members in Meyer's party ate and drank with knots in their stomachs, wondering what their fabled gangster patriarch would do. When their meal was done, Meyer approached the liar behind him. The Lansky relatives held their breaths. The man turned ashen. However, instead of berating the man, as he certainly had the right to do, Meyer graciously stuck out his hand and greeted the man as if he were a long lost friend; said it had been a long time, and asked how he was, elevating the man in the eyes of his guests and making him beam with, albeit surprised, pride. That was the kind of good feeling toward the mob that Meyer Lansky infused into South Florida's culture, including Hollywood, which had been the early sight of his largest gambling operations, and Hallandale, which at that time was often referred to as "Lanskyland." That generous gesture toward man at dinner was typical of the man he was.

Of course not all of Miami's mob history is peaches 'n cream and full of good will. There were bodies that happened to turn up every now and then, and there is one story, true or not, which stands out as an example of the violent undertones that weren't far from sunshine and palm trees. The story is that Meyer's close pal and mob go-between, Jimmy Blue Eyes, was approached by an acquaintance who pitched him on the idea of opening an informal café or diner-type eatery that would import New York newspapers for the overwhelming number of visitors to that area who seemed to be lost without knowing what was going on back home. After all, it was not a time of cell phones or a 24 hour television news cycle. Blue Eyes agreed to finance the operation, but with one stipulation: there would be one table set aside for him in a corner that no one else would ever be allowed to sit at. The café became an instant success. No one visiting Miami Beach from the north didn't breakfast or lunch there and read the news from New York,

Philadelphia, or Boston. Lines formed to get in.

One day, Blue Eyes passed a queue of waiting diners and stopped dead in his tracks. "What the f_ _ k is going on?" he angrily asked his partner, who explained that he was so overwhelmed with business that he'd sat a group at the table. He gulped more of the coffee he drank all day to keep him hyper enough to handle the business then swore the people would be leaving soon. Blue Eyes left and returned later, when that meal's rush was over. He ate and drank while his partner continued to apologize, swearing that the offense would never be committed again. "I'm sure it won't," Jimmy Blue Eyes replied. A short time later the restaurateur collapsed and died from a cup of coffee laced with arsenic. Blue Eyes, a silent partner, laid out more money when he sympathetically purchased the eatery from the dead man's wife for a new partner of record to run.

Long after Meyer Lansky's most active days in the gambling business were over, and after F.B.I. Director J. Edgar Hoover had passed away, the Feds jumped all over him for tax evasion. Maybe they knew that Lansky had blackmailed Hoover to lay off the mob for too long (*Lansky and Genovese privately claimed to have proof of Hoover's homosexuality; photos taken in a Miami motel*); maybe it was for headlines. Whatever the motivation, the aging Lansky tried to escape to Israel, depending on that country's Right of Return policy for Jews to protect him from American charges. Sand, sunshine, and the sea reminded him of his beloved Miami Beach. He was a confident and happy man as he fought to stay in Israel. The problem was that Israel owed more to the U.S., which financed and protected its very existence, than it did to any Jewish gangster. Meyer was returned to Miami in 1972, when he was seventy years old.

Lansky's last years were spent in Florida. He was not just an important part of Miami...a true King of Miami...but the city was an important part of him and his family as well. He lived with his second wife, Teddy, in Miami Beach; one son, Buddy, ran the switchboard at the Hawaiian Isles Hotel; Sandy, his only daughter, lived close to him; a stepson, Richard

Schwartz, murdered a relative of a mobster at the Forge restaurant and was later murdered in revenge. Had Lansky truly been a Commission member, as he was believed to be, he could have saved the lives of both his stepson, Richard, and his friend and partner, Bugsy Siegel.

Meyer Lansky was indirectly a contributor to America as well, having been the go-between for Lucky Luciano to order longshoremen to protect the U.S. docks against sabotage and helping with the invasion of Sicily in WWII; having broken up Nazi meetings in New York by sending in a crew to break heads; by indirectly having his family produce a foreign service diplomat at the United Nations, who he was infinitely proud of, and a CIA Agent. His last days were spent modestly and increasingly ill, with his greatest pleasure coming from walks with his beloved Shih Tzu, "Bruiser." There was no evidence in his life of the hundreds of millions of dollars he is purported to have stashed away. Meyer Lansky succumbed to lung cancer in 1983, at the age of 81, and is buried in the place that was most important to him throughout his adult life: Miami.

Sonny Girard

MOB BLOG #11:

The Ten Commandments

of the

Sicilian Mafia:

A Tongue in Cheek Look at a Document

Recovered by Caribinari During the

Arrest of a Mafia Boss

In 2007, Salvatore Lo Piccolo and his son, Sandro, were captured by Sicilian police. The senior Lo Piccolo was the presumed replacement of Bernardo Provenzano as Mafia leader, since Provenzano had been captured after years on the lam. Lo Piccolo was determined to revitalize the battered Sicilian brotherhood by initiating more cooperative projects with members of the Neapolitan Camorra and the Calabrian N'drangheta. Another idea he had was to develop a "Ten Commandments of the Mafia" as a sort of Constitution for his fledgling membership to obey. Is this guy kidding?! And they made him boss?

Anyway, that list, not carved in a stone tablet, was captured along with Lo Piccolo, and has since been published and, sometimes, ridiculed. We take a hard, and tongue-in-cheek, look at it here:

RULE 1

NO ONE CAN PRESENT HIMSELF DIRECTLY

TO ANOTHER OF OUR FRIENDS. THERE MUST

BE A THIRD PERSON TO DO IT.

Not a bad rule for times gone by, but there's an old Sicilian saying that "three guys can keep a secret, but only if two of them are dead." In today's atmosphere of mob bigwigs' rodentious behavior, it would do "friends" well to keep that at the very top of their minds. Also, can that third person be a lawman? I got pinched and thrown in an FBI vehicle with another guy I'd never met. I was as mistrustful of him as he was of me (*maybe more, because he was taller*). We've since become close friends. I credit the FBI with the introduction.

RULE 2

NEVER LOOK AT THE WIVES OF FRIENDS.

In days gone by, when Sicilian women covered themselves in black nearly as much as orthodox Muslims, wore no makeup and pulled their hair into tight angry buns, and ate as heartily and could become as muscular as their mates, this rule must have been made to protect the sensibilities of the "friends" doing the looking. After all, membership should offer some kind of protection. A more reasonable rule today, when women would rather look "hot" than "beautiful," and, in America, are chosen from among the most attractive, would be "No *touch* the wives...or commares (*girlfriends*)...of friends." Of course, that means nothing if you kill her husband. When Vito Genovese fell in love, he had his love's husband tossed off a roof so he could marry her. No disrespect, though.

RULE 3

NEVER BE SEEN WITH COPS.

Duh. This rule is a little too simplistic, especially when bribing police is a mainstay of mob life. It was in New York until the Knapp Commission Hearings, when Frank Serpico ratted out his brother officers who tried to have him killed for ruining their games. When I took my first adult pinch at my home, the detective took me in another room. As a teen we'd taken a few kicks and punches along the way. As the cop spoke, I kept watching his hands, ready to roll with the punch. Never got hit, but did get arrested. When my attorney, Cupie Iovine, who was Crazy Joe Gallo's uncle, showed up, my chest was out and my ears were wide open, expecting compliments on what a stand up young man I was. Instead, he cursed me out; called me more morons, imbeciles, etc. He said the detective told him that he had talked himself blue in the face trying to get me to give him some money to go away. I hadn't been paying attention; too busy watching his fists. Cupie determined that not only was I an idiot, but that I would remain that way for the rest of my life. R.I.P. Cupie.

RULE 4

DON'T GO TO PUBS AND CLUBS.

Lots of luck with that one, Salvatore. If "friends" can't go where the hotties are, you might as well repeal Rule 2.

RULE 5

ALWAYS BEING AVAILABLE FOR COSA

NOSTRA IS A DUTY – EVEN IN YOUR

WIFE'S ABOUT TO GIVE BIRTH.

Not a bad rule...oh, Commandment...to maintain discipline in a group that has lost all its discipline. The problem is in the whim of leaders. One captain in Brooklyn would call out the wiseguys under him in the middle of the night; order them to meet him at this diner or that. The guys, who had all taken a loyalty oath, would show up with pajama bottoms sticking out of the pants they'd hurriedly jumped into, fingering their pistols, and wiping sleep-crust from their eyes, only to find that he'd brought them together to impress the hot looking waitress he wanted to bang. Imagine this: "You pulled me away from my wife, who's gonna fuckin' give birth any minute?"

BANG!

RULE 6

APPOINTMENTS MUST

ABSOLUTELY BE RESPECTED.

Absolutely essential, especially when you have to make one of your guys "swim with the calamari." Imagine standing "Under the Clock," the name of a mob discussion book by William Balsamo, Jr., waiting for your victim to show up. The minutes tick by as a bus stops and ejects passengers, a police car crawls by to observe you waiting too long in one spot, you run low on gas. The hit doesn't feel right. You decide to leave. Makes you want to kill him. Does Sally Lo P think a formal

Commandment might have changed things for the better in that situation? Lo Piccolo, I ask again, what the f_ _k were you thinking?

RULE 7

WIVES MUST BE TREATED

WITH RESPECT.

Are these the same wives we were ordered not to look at? Lo Piccolo's got this thing going on about wives (*wonder what his looks like?*). He even wants to respect the ones you can't look at. Hmmm? Is he talking about the other guy's wife...or your own? Mob life, like all others, has its ups and downs, good and bad, moral and highly immoral...even a known homosexual who was "made" to keep his wealth in *la famiglia*. That means there was some hanky panky going on. One legendary Brooklyn mobster didn't show a hell of a lot of respect for his wife when he began an affair with a wiseguy's daughter (*no respect for daughters? Lo P, you missed that*). Carmine was given a simple choice: divorce and marry wisedaddy's little girl...or die. Not a hard one to decide. One time when Lo P's rule was taken seriously was by a pal who is presently doing time for, among other things, shooting a guy's balls off...then killing him...for having an affair with the wife of his boss who was in prison at the time. Ouch!

RULE 8

WHEN ASKED FOR ANY INFORMATION

THE ANSWER MUST BE THE TRUTH.

Liar, liar, pants on fire. You are not a very specific guy, Sally Boy. Does this include police grillings? Maybe so. You guys had Buscetta (*and, may I mention, a few more lately*), while we've been plagued by the likes of Gas Pipe Casso, Mikey Scars, Joe Massino, Tumac Acceturo, and on, and on, and on. Okay, I get it, you mean among each other. A simple rule is to always tell the truth to your doctor, your lawyer, and your boss (*only in a street sense; not at WalMart*). I'm still here. My guy used to have shit fits when I would admit to having fucked up then say, "Well, how are we going to fix this?" The answer was ALWAYS, "We're gonna lie about it." But that was us lying to them (*whoever they were*), not to each other. You have the right idea, Lo P, but you really should take a writing or communication course in prison.

RULE 9

MONEY CANNOT BE

APPROPRIATED IF IT BELONGS TO

OTHERS OR TO OTHER FAMILIES.

Okay, here's where we have a problem, Sally Boy. I really love and respect you guys on the other side. You were the grandfathers who set the stage for what everyone on this side of the Atlantic ever did. One of the things you did, instead of said, was rob anyone and everyone. We, in the U.S., used to remind each other that after shaking hands with one of you, to remember to count our fingers. You guys are a step too slick. Reminds me of a few of your brothers who settled into a Brooklyn neighborhood. The top American wiseguy, a captain, in the neighborhood, visited with the newly arrived Sicilian, had a couple of espressos and a *spogliatela*, and warned him about distributing drugs in the area...too much heat, and all that. Cousin Sicily swore up and down he'd control his men, that there would be no drugs in the neighborhood. They hugged and kissed...then soon afterward the Sicilian killed the American, *appropriated* his rackets in the area, and moved his narcotics at will.

RULE 10

PEOPLE WHO CAN'T BE

PART OF COSA NOSTRA:

ANYONE WHO HAS A CLOSE RELATIVE IN THE POLICE

ANYONE WITH A TWO-TIMING RELATIVE IN THE FAMILY

ANYONE WHO BEHAVES BADLY AND DOESN'T HOLD

TO MORAL VALUES

Funny, I would have thought there would have been a LOT more people who could not join *Società Onore*...The Honored Society: Eskimos, Hottentots, transsexuals, Siamese Twins, and the ghost of Michael Jackson. Instead, Lo Piccolo seems to accept the aforementioned, and starts his banned list with anyone who has a close relative in the police. How close does that relative have to be? Fat Andy's son-in-law was a hack in the New York State Prison system; Jimmy "The Clam" Ippolito's nephew is the infamous Frank Eppolito of "Mafia Cops" case, in New York. Trusting the relative is one thing; being able to use him is another. Old neighborhoods in major cities like Chicago, New York, Boston, etc., turned out both mobsters and cops, many whom made "green" deals with the neighborhood's wiseguys.

Next, Lo Piccolo excludes anyone with a "two timing relative in the family." Well, then, I guess it's him and Sandro against the world. Can't think of anyone I know who hasn't got an affair in their extended family.

"Anyone who behaves badly and doesn't hold to moral values" is his last exclusion. Is it okay if I call you Sal? I've got a tip for you, Sal, from the American side. Anyone who DOES NOT behave badly doesn't belong, unless, of course, you interpret "badly" not to include stealing, beating, extorting, killing, counterfeiting, etc., etc. I feel sorry for you, bud, you missed your calling. And, with all those churches and monasteries around your area...well, at least on the outside of your lifetime home at Ucciardone Prison.

MOB BLOG #12:

Arrivederci, Little Italy

I remember Manhattan's Little Italy from years ago, when people actually lived there. There were well known regional Italian restaurants too, like Grotto Azurra, Angelo's, and Luna. Each had claims to fame and some kind of attractiveness of its own besides the food. Grotto Azzurra had served food to Lucky Luciano, was downstairs, and was close enough to Police Headquarters for mobsters to mingle with police brass, some of the latter who were on the former's payrolls. Angelo's was upstairs, fed President Reagan, and had been a more well known name for decades. Luna was the first restaurant you saw on your right as you crossed Canal Street from Chinatown, and was where "Crazy Joe" Gallo made the threat that sent him to prison. Chubby's was the best: open all night on weekends, with brasciola, sausage, pork livers grilling in the window, all served with sweet or hot peppers and whisky or wine in a coffee cup. You could meet drunken "friends" from all over New York at 4 or 5 a.m.

DAYS GONE BY STORY: Across an open parking lot from Luna was Marconi's Restaurant, also a popular tourist and celebrity magnet. One night, while Frank Sinatra and Sammy Davis Jr. were dining at Marconi's, they were told that Dean Martin was across the parking lot at Luna's. However each side found out the other was across the lot, when their meals were over they all came out with cannolis, which became ammunition for a duel between these international stars to the delight of residents and tourists. That was what Little Italy was in the good old days.

Besides the numerous Italian restaurants, there were espresso cafes where tourists mingled with residents and mob social clubs with

"Private – Members Only" signs on darkened doors and windows for the general public but invisible "Welcome" signs for pals. The Ravenite became the most famous after Paul Castellano was murdered on orders from John Gotti, but there were so many with innocuous names like the Alto Knights, on Mulberry and Kenmare Streets (where the actual murder in a bathroom that Martin Scorsese portrayed in "Mean Streets" took place), the Chatham Square Association, or the Old Mill Club, that catered to legitimate residents and wiseguys alike. There were also Italian restaurants, bars, even funeral parlors on the Chinatown side of Canal Street: Antica Roma, The Lime House, Bunny's Bar, Bacciagalupo Funeral Home. They were the last remnants of what had become Little Italy at the Turn of the Twentieth Century, when the Irish were moving out and up and the Five Points area was being filled by Southern Italian immigrants; when Paolo Vacarelli called himself Paul Kelly when he took over the Five Points Gang to make the ethnic transition easier.

It has always been the pattern of those on the lower end of the socio-economic urban ladder to move out of a neighborhood to make room for the group on the rung below them. Bedford-Stuyvesant was once home to Jews; the same with Harlem; the Irish left the Five Points to the Italians; East Harlem was Italian before it became almost totally inhabited by Hispanics and blacks. This change, however, is different. This is a change from a vibrant, expensive neighborhood that is an ethnic tourist attraction and slice of what once was and what might have been, to a lesser variety in the patchwork quilt that makes up New York City. The beauty of Manhattan is that you can walk from the Bohemian-style Greenwich Village, to the ever bustling Chinatown, to artsy SoHo, to Little Italy in a matter of a couple of hours. The way it's going, Little Italy will soon be removed from that list. The current demise of Little Italy can only be compared to the decades-long downward plunge of Atlantic City and Miami before their rebirths. Without a beach and ocean views, Little Italy will have no such rebirth.

Neighborhood residents have different opinions of when their area started its downward cycle. Johnny "Cha Cha" Ciarcia, the undisputed unofficial Mayor of Little Italy, believes it began when the James Center of the Children's Aid Society, that spanned Hester Street from Elizabeth Street to Mott Street, was abandoned for commercial use in the 1960s. "The James Center's playground that I used to play in as a kid was sold to make a parking lot," says Cha Cha. "It was a shame then, and set a pattern of nobody giving a flying f_ _k about the neighborhood. They only care about their pockets." He's one of the few diehards who have clung to their roots all their lives. His Caffe in Bocca in Lupo, at 113 Mulberry Street is a landmark. The walls are covered with photos of celebrities who are friends and patrons: Tony Danza, Danny DeVito, Robert DeNiro, and on and on and on. "When God takes me, that will be the end," says a saddened Cha Cha. "My cafe will probably be turned into a dim sum joint."

Oddly, the big sale began when the buildings with stores on the bottom and apartments above were selling for five figures instead of the seven today. Older residents who had raised children on Mulberry Street, or Grand Street, or Hester Street wanted to desert the city for suburban areas. The recently built Verrazano Bridge gave them an opportunity to permanently live in an area that they had taken the ferry during the summers to spend some time in bungalows. It had then been called "the country." The problem was that they were so eager to move and upgrade their living conditions that they sold to whoever offered them as low as five thousand dollars more...usually Chinese. Obviously, loyalty was a word that wasn't in their vocabulary. Few saw what would happen to the neighborhood that had given them so much and looked beyond the pittance.

Those Little Italy heroes sold to Italians who wanted to build the area into a major tourist attraction for Southern Italian-style hospitality. Some, like my dear departed friend, "Joe Carlo" Calabro, talked the talk, cursing out the neighborhood traitors, and walked the walk, refusing to sell a building he had to Chinatown expansionists. Oddly enough, one major hero in the survival of Little Italy was a Jew, Sidney Saulstein, a haberdasher and owner of many properties in both Chinatown and

Little Italy. Though he was married to an Asian woman, he refused to sell his Little Italy properties to anyone but Italians, even if he had to take less money, and made sure he did the same for Chinese buyers on the Chinatown side, helping to preserve the ethnic individuality of each area for decades. Saulstein had the distinction of doing exactly that when he sold to Robert Ianello, "Matty The Horse" Ianello's brother, who built Umberto's Clam House at the location... a seafood restaurant later made famous when "Crazy Joe" Gallo was gunned down there one night. Instead of the killing scaring visitors away, they flocked to the eatery in such numbers that now it has moved to a larger location where it can offer a full Italian menu instead of the limited fried seafood items it originally served (okay, the scungilli wasn't fried. Nitpickers!). That says more about the sanguinary fascination of society than it does about Little Italy. God Bless Sidney Saulstein.

THE FEAST OF SAN GENNARO: In 1927, Neapolitans in Little Italy staged the first Festa San Gennaro in the history of New York. Over the following decades it became internationally famous for food (fried calamari, sausage and pepper sandwiches, zeppoles, etc.) and fun (Ferris wheel, barkers calling to pitch a ball or bet on which hole a mouse will disappear to, card games, souvenirs, etc.). It was the most concentrated Southern Italian experience in the country each September...that is, until political correctness and political pressure brought San Gennaro to its knees...something a Roman furnace and beheading couldn't do to the Saint himself.

By the 1980's, a politically correct shift had brought an inordinate number of non-Italian spots into the Feast. There were always a scattered number of tables or booths that peddled incongruous things: fortune tellers, egg rolls, maybe a tee shirt or two with outsider messages, but suddenly there were Rastafarians with multicolored caps and shirts, falafel, cactus kitchen magnets, and things that I turned my head away too fast to capture in my memory. The feeling was ebbing. Less of the people I knew showed up. Less of the unique feeling that I'd get even in a garlic festival. Less special.

An assault by Mayor Giuliani also threatened the Feast's survival as he relentlessly fought the windmills of organized crime. I haven't been to New York's Festa San Gennaro for years, instead participating in the founding of the first feast by that name in Los Angeles' history. The dedication of a few men, like restaurateur Frankie Competelli, Jimmy Kimmel producer Doug DeLuca, and filmmaker Gregg Cannizzaro combined with the newness of the experience on that coast has resulted in a more pure ethnic experience. How long will that last in L.A. before the PC police gets to it? Who knows? Hopefully, eighty years like New York.

All of those things have contributed to the creeping demise of Little Italy, but none as much as the sellouts who betray their heritage for money. The Manna family of Luna's Restaurant, which includes the mob rat, Nicholas "P.J." Pisciotti, is only the latest. Are they all headed for the Witness Protection Program with him? A Luna's in Iowa or Idaho? It's shameful and it's sad, and all New Yorkers and visitors to New York are the losers. It would be just as sad if Chinatown were lost. Or Greenwich Village. Or SoHo.

But Chinatown, Greenwich Village, and SoHo are not in jeopardy; Little Italy is because of greedy property owners who owed so much to the neighborhood and chose to pay back nothing. Shame on them.

P.S.: There are many "dogs" who have hurt the neighborhood for their own greed. I've collected the names of many of them and was going to list them. However, after some thought, I decided it would only hurt their children and grandchildren, none of whom had any part in the betrayal. The dogs know who they are, and so do others. That's enough.

MOB BLOG #14:

DAGO:

The Joseph Petrosino Story

My background is organized crime. There aren't many crime fighters who I hold in high esteem. For most of my life they were corrupt, enabling those of us in the business of crime to operate with virtual impunity. When I couldn't pay an accuser off to get out of an assault case, the judge took half the money we had offered the so-called victim (*I call him that because he attacked me first, then yelled cop after he'd gotten the worst of it*) to drop the charges. In fact, after my first major adult arrest, my attorney showed up to bail me out. Instead of praising me for keeping my mouth shut, he berated me, calling me every synonym for idiot he could think of. Why, because, he said, the detective told him he had given me every hint he could that I could pay him off to let me go and I hadn't responded. The truth was, I had been to busy waiting to roll with the punch if he slugged me to hear anything he said, and hadn't had the experience yet of that scale of bribery. That's just the way it was. Later, when the Knapp Commission scared most law enforcement to stop taking bribes, they cut the limbs we were on out from under us and walked away mostly unscathed. More recently, when the U.S. Attorneys and FBI Agents won victory after victory against mobsters, I gave more credit to the internal disintegration of the mob than to good police work. Without scumbags trading other people's families and freedom for their crimes, how many cases would the Feds have successfully prosecuted?

However, there is one lawman from long ago that I've come to greatly admire; so much so that I've recently completed a screenplay based on his life. The name of the screenplay: "DAGO." His name: Giuseppe

"Joe" Petrosino.

By the time the great wave of poor Southern Italian immigrants landed in New York at the turn of the Twentieth Century, Joe Petrosino had been there for nearly thirty years. He'd arrived in New York from Padula, Italy in 1873, at 13 years of age, at a time when a wealthier middle class of Italians, mostly from north of the Mezzogiorno, came to America to springboard their offspring to an even better life. Many were skilled workers or artisans, and tended to live in ethnically mixed areas as they moved up the American ladder, not in the ghettos abandoned by the second generation Irish as the later, poorer arrivals from Italy did. Joe's father was a tailor and opened a Manhattan shop that became successful enough to comfortably support his family.

Young Giuseppe shined shoes outside Police Headquarters, where he developed a friendship with a Captain of Police. That friendship led to his getting a job as a "white winger" or street cleaner, which was controlled by the Police Department at the time. White wingers were named for the white uniforms they wore as they made their way through New York's streets, picking up litter in with small brooms and dustpans and depositing in barrels on wheels that they dragged along. Later on, since crime in the Italian ghetto was out of control and the Police Department was made up of primarily German Jews and Irish, the Police Commissioner bent the 5'7" height minimum rule to admit the 5'3" Petrosino to the force. The latter quickly distinguished himself by his ability to solve crimes that English speaking law enforcement community couldn't. He was quickly promoted to Sergeant by Police Commissioner Theodore Roosevelt.

Though his professional life moved forward, Petrosino's personal life was virtually nonexistent. His insecurities about his looks, his station in life, and, later, a preoccupation with his work kept him from entering into any serious relationships. Danger was another factor that added to his lonely life. Constant threats of murder forced him to move from his parents' apartment to a solitary one in order to protect them.

Petrosino's style was rough. He regularly beat criminals, especially if he felt they would be released without punishment by the courts. On his first day as a detective he beat two men senseless who he caught assaulting a black man. Years later, when he found that one pimp he particularly detested was being deported back to Sicily, Petrosino got him alone in an office on Ellis Island, where the man was being held, and knocked out all his teeth with a ring of keys. His actions were picked up by the press, which saw him as a hero among an immigrant community they feared and believed was criminal in nature. He had no such support from the Tammany Hall politicos, who, more likely to take bribes from criminals than support their convictions, were a constant thorn in his side. Most Italian newspapers also denigrated him and his actions, probably because of their own connection to the community's toughs. At that time, Southern Italian gangs preyed on their fellow immigrants only, since neither group could speak anything but their dialect from the old country. Gangsters, many using Black Hand symbols to strike fear into their *paisani*, couldn't deal with English speaking groups. Italian victims' inability to communicate with authorities kept them from getting protection or justice.

Petrosino was also an innovator in police procedure and methodology that has lasted far beyond his life. He was one of the first to make regular use of forensics in solving crimes. Things that were generally overlooked didn't escape Petrosino's eye. He would dig out bits of substance to determine points of origin of evidence and relations and background of a murder victim. One of his most famous cases took place in the early 1900s, when a body was found in the Italian immigrant section of New York, in a barrel of sawdust, cut up with the cadaver's genitals in its mouth. Immediately, a call went out from the Police Commissioner, of, "Get me the Dago!"

In what was labeled "The Body in the Barrel Case," merely by examining the barrel, its contents, and the possessions of the victim, Petrosino found both the location of the murder (*a Sicilian café frequented by criminals*) and a relative (*a Sing Sing inmate serving time for counterfeiting*) who supplied the perpetrators and motive for the murder. He also did a lot of undercover work to gather criminal intelligence in Italian communities in and out of New York City. He might pass as a construction hand, a bum, or a Hasidic Jew.

His rate of crimes solved in Little Italy, where few police even spoke the language and had to deal with a wall of fearful silence, was especially high, though he was plagued by a turnaround court system that regularly had the criminals back on the street almost before they could post bail. Frustrated by the system, he begged to be sent to Sicily to investigate whether many of the criminals had warrants that he could use to deport them. Over a period of years he was turned down time and again, mostly because of budget considerations and a lack of understanding by politicians of the impact criminals were having on the Italian immigrant community.

Personal law enforcement success, like single-handedly rescuing the kidnapped thirteen year old daughter of an extortion plot victim by sliding down a rope thrown through a skylight, brought not only more adulation from the American press and continued derision from the Italian newspapers, but numerous death threats. He made important enemies like "Lupo The Wolf" and Vito Cascio Ferro, who would later become one of history's most important Sicilian Mafia dons, and who carried Petrosino's photo with him as a reminder of his vow to personally kill the detective by his own hand. Ferro's and Petrosino's lives intertwined in a way that would eventually bring a fatal confrontation for one or the other.

Petrosino also made powerful friends, including Vice President Theodore Roosevelt, who, as New York Police Commissioner, had promoted Petrosino to Detective Sergeant. Further appointments made him New York City's first Italian Detective Lieutenant and the head of "The Italian Squad," made up of Italian police who would be able to communicate with immigrant victims and identify criminal elements in their area.

In the early part of the Twentieth Century, before Lucky Luciano and pals had put the "organized" into "organized crime," Italian ghettos were plagued by four major crime problems: anarchism, Black Hand extortion, prostitution (*Sicilian hoodlums would write to the old country saying they needed a wife, then beat the supposed bride when she arrived and pimp her off*), and counterfeiting. During one months-long undercover investigation while on loan to the U.S. Secret Service, Petrosino worked as a tunnel digger and lived in a rooming house with suspected anarchists in New Jersey. During that time he discovered that there was a plan to assassinate President McKinley.

Anarchists had already murdered King Umberto, of Italy. Joe notified Vice President Roosevelt, who arranged a face to face meeting with the President at the White House. McKinley refused to take Petrosino's information seriously, stating that anarchist assassinations happened overseas, but not in the U.S., and that in general people loved him. Why, if Americans didn't like the job he was doing, they could always vote him out of office. There was no need in this country to murder any President, he insisted. President McKinley was later assassinated by an anarchist while giving a speech in Upstate New York. Petrosino sadly attended the funeral for the President, but remained a close friend and supporter of Theodore Roosevelt throughout his Presidency.

He also became a friend of legendary opera singer, Enrico Caruso, when the latter became the victim of a Black Hand extortion plot. Caruso, fearing for his life, reached out for Petrosino. The detective supplied bodyguards for Caruso while he investigated the plot. Eventually, he found the conspirators, put the fear of death into them, and had them deported back to Italy.

In spite of all his high profile exploits, the body in the barrel became Petrosino's signature case. The Jewish Commissioner at the time was so ignorant of not only Italian culture, but his own, that he believed *"INRI"* on the victim's crucifix indicated some secret organization or cult killing.

Petrosino discovered the murder was part of a counterfeit money deal. His experience in working with the Secret Service on counterfeit investigations helped him track down the conspirators, which included his sworn enemies, Lupo The Wolf and Vito Cascio Ferro.

Arrests were made, but bail was made while Petrosino was off chasing another criminal who had fled the city. By the time Petrosino returned, Vito Cascio Ferro had disappeared, on his way back to Sicily, and the man believed to be the actual murderer, Tomasso Petto, had substituted a look alike for himself at the re-arrest if the crew and had also run away.

Joe Petrosino was not just a gung-ho crime fighter, but a man of justice. When he found that a man had been sentenced to die in the electric chair for a murder he hadn't committed, he found out who the real murderer was and tracked the man all over the country and into Nova Scotia as the latter moved from place to place in an effort not to be discovered, at least until the wrongly accuse man had been disposed of and the case officially closed. The chase ended with Petrosino delivering the real killer to authorities a week before the innocent man's execution. The detective also wound up with pneumonia as a result of terrible weather in Nova Scotia and other cities during his efforts to right the wrong.

In 1908 Joe Petrosino finally married. Thirty-seven year old Adelina was a childless widow who worked in her family's restaurant, and within a year of their wedding bore him a daughter. It was the high point of Petrosino's life, as he'd hurry home each day to marvel in his infant offspring. He cut back on his work hours to spend time cuddling the baby in his arms. At that same time, the investigative trip to Sicily he no longer wanted suddenly materialized. Three months after his daughter was born, the dutiful Petrosino departed under an assumed name on a supposedly secret mission to discover those warrants and to pay informers to supply him with ongoing information once he returned home.

While Petrosino was on the ship to his first stop, Rome, on his way to Sicily, his mission was leaked to the press by a Police Department superior. His cover blown, Petrosino continued on to Palermo, where he incurred opposition from the authorities as well as danger from Mafiosi. He refused police bodyguards because he didn't trust them. One night a man approached him as he ate in a small restaurant near the hotel he was staying at. He hurriedly left for a local train station's piazza, where he was shot to death. A gun and his derby lay by his bloody body. Legend has it that Don Vito Cascio Ferro, who had become the most powerful Mafioso in Sicily after having been run out of the United States by Petrosino's relentless pursuit, had been told of his nemesis' location. He dispatched someone to lure Petrosino to the deserted station with a promise of information. At the appointed time, he left a dinner party with top Palermo politicians, went to the piazza, murdered Petrosino himself, and returned to the dinner. Joe Petrosino had only gotten to spend three months with his precious daughter before being dispatched to Sicily, where he died.

The reaction to Petrosino's death in the U.S. was pure outrage. Calls were made by newspapers and politicians to deport all Italians, overlooking the fact that Joe Petrosino was himself of Italian descent. Joe's coffin arrived in New York by ship from Sicily nearly a month after his murder. His funeral procession, begun at St. Patrick's Church on Mott Street after a Mass by Joe's old friend, Bishop Lavalle, drew more than 250,000 mourners following from Lower Manhattan's narrow streets uptown to Fifth Avenue, keeping other movement in the city to a crawl. To this day, Lt. Detective Joseph Petrosino is the only American detective ever killed overseas in the line of duty, and is remembered in Lower Manhattan with a statue of him that stands guard in a tiny park that bears his name, and is just steps from the old police headquarters on Grand and Baxter Streets.

Though Giuseppe "Joe" Petrosino fought the forerunners of my friends and associates, his name is forever linked with organized crime, and, due to his exploits in defense of a victimized Italian immigrant community, he is a figure deserving of admiration...even by me.

MOB BLOG #15:

The Family Capone

I've always had a special place in my heart for Al Capone, not because of his ruthlessness, his fame, his fortune...certainly not his death from syphilis...but because we lived around the corner from each other. Of course, this was decades apart, but Capone was born on January 17, 1899, in a small house on Navy Street off Sands Street, facing the entrance of the Brooklyn Naval Shipyard, around the corner from Sands Street around the corner from Navy Street, where I spent my early criminal-forming years also looking at the entrance of the Navy Yard.

We also attended the same elementary school, P.S. 7, a stereotypical old fashioned red brick schoolhouse that might have been on the cover of a greeting card or on the pages of the Saturday Evening Post. We both wound up in South Brooklyn too; Al on Garfield Place, me on President Street. The only difference between us setting out on our similar criminal paths was his later move to Chicago...and, of course, his extraordinary level of success. I also didn't die of syphilis...at least, not yet.

Big Al and I also had the fact in common that both our fathers were legitimate working men. Al's father, Gabriele, was a barber by trade, who arrived in this country during the great wave of Italian immigration, in 1894. He traveled to America by steamer from Castellamare di Stabia, a town in the Campagna province of Italy, sixteen miles south of Naples. The fact that Capone was Neapolitan is important to note, in that the leadership of Italian mobs at the time was primarily made up of Sicilians, and prejudices between the two groups was a brutal factor in daily life. In light of that, Capone's dominance of crime in Chicago enhances his accomplishments. While most illiterate immigrants were forced to take jobs as laborers, Gabriele was able to find work in a grocery store until he accumulated to open his own barber shop. Al's mother, Teresina, who bore nine children, took in sewing piecework to provide extra money in addition to caring for her brood. Women's Lib had obviously not been born yet.

Alphonse was the fourth of Gabriele and Teresina's nine, and the first to be conceived and born in the United States. While plenty is known about Al Capone, even before he earned the moniker "Scarface," little is known about six of Big Al's siblings, the exceptions being his older brothers, James (*Vincenzo*) and Ralph (*Raffaele*). The remaining brothers, Frank (*Salvatore*), John (*Erminio*) Matthew (*Amedoe*), and Albert (*Umberto*) were all part of the Capone crew and had various moments when they were more visible in the public eye. Regardless of what any of the brothers did, they would never come close to their brother, who had come to be known as "Scarface" Al Capone.

Al's infatuation with crime began after his family moved to Garfield Place, in South Brooklyn, which was a hotbed of gangs, not like street gangs today, but men associated with various criminal enterprises and young people hanging out together who would eventually become assimilated into the older groups. Grown leaders would keep an eye on the young men in their neighborhoods and pluck the ones they considered worthy of becoming a member of their crew. It was a system that dated back hundreds of years in Southern Italy and Sicily, and was the basis for the organized crime structure that formed in 1931 and has lasted until today. In Al's area, the recognized top man was Johnny Torrio, a refined gangster who presented a model for future mobsters of good and legitimate appearance, a clear and rigidly kept division between home and criminal life, and the importance of friends and alliances in moving up and maintaining positions of power. Al Capone became one of his better students.

When Torrio left for Chicago, he recommended Al to his successor, Francesco "Frankie Yale" Ioele, a mobster as brutal as Torrio was refined, as respected and feared as Torrio was admired and loved. The recommendation was for the eighteen year old Capone to tend bar at Frankie Yale's Coney Island bar, the Harvard Inn. It was at the Harvard Inn that Al earned the moniker that would haunt him all his life. While serving drinks at a table, he insulted the sister of one Frank Gallucio. The two men got into a fight and Gallucio cut Capone's face before running out with his sister. The incident led to a sitdown called by Gallucio's man, Lucky Luciano, where the latter and Frankie Yale agreed that Capone had to apologize for the insult. As a result of the brouhaha, Yale took young Al under his wing and taught him the brutal side of life that Torrio hadn't, and which Capone would later become known for. Now Al would become involved in extortion, shylocking, and other illegal activities. Alphonse Capone was now a gangster.

After fathering a son, Albert, who he infected with syphilis at birth, Al married the boy's mother, Mae Coughlin. It was only when the diagnosis of VD in the child, who they called Sonny, was presented to him that Al admitted he'd contracted and been treated for the disease before conception. In an attempt to be a good family man, Capone moved to Baltimore, where he worked as a bookkeeper for a construction company. The death of his father at the early age of fifty-five hit Al hard. Johnny Torrio, who had easily moved up the mobster ladder in Chicago, offered Al work if he'd join him in the Windy City. Possibly for a chance to be close to his surrogate father, Al took Torrio up on his offer and brought his family north.

The situation Capone found was one where Big Jim Colosimo was getting too big for his boots. He had a huge prostitution business and a café for the rich and famous, but instead of taking his money and living a disciplined life, he was a drinker, gambler, and womanizer, divorcing his wife for a younger woman. Frankie Yale saw this as a weakness and made short work of Colosimo, who had the largest funeral Chicago had seen to that time. Yale made one error, thinking he could take over, but encountered a brick wall in Colosimo's second in command, Johnny Torrio, whose philosophy of becoming a big man by the number of friends one has, not enemies, had solidified his position to take over as Chicago's rackets boss...and keep it. Torrio's right arm: twenty-two year old Al Capone.

In time, Al's business acumen and brawn earned him a partnership in Torrio's business, consisting of whorehouses, speakeasies, and gambling joints. Al managed the Four Deuces, a combination brothel, gambling hall, and speakeasy that also served as Torrio's headquarters. Capone brought his brother, Ralph, from New York to assist him with his expanded duties. Soon after that, he brought Mae and his son, his mother, Teresina, and all his siblings except Vincenzo, who had left home and wasn't heard from since then, to Chicago. Outside of Vincenzo and Gabriele, who had passed away, the Capone family was together once more.

Al's older brother, Salvatore, or Frank, as he was called, was a favorite of his. Frank was the tallest, best looking, and most refined of all the brothers. When Al moved his headquarters to the Chicago suburb of Cicero, after Torrio had retired to Italy and Chicago authorities were in one of their anti-hoodlum moves, he appointed Frank to be his liaison with Cicero's political machine. When elections rolled around, Capone henchmen kidnapped the opposition's election workers and spread violence across the area. The Chicago Chief of Police decided to teach the Capones a lesson. With a group of around eighty cops in plain cars, he entered Cicero using the excuse that he was protecting workers at a Western Electric Plant. When he spotted Frank Capone crossing the street, the car stopped so quickly that the rear cars almost piled up on each other. The police emptied their cars and started toward Frank with guns drawn. Frank realized what was happening and drew his own pistol...but too late, as the police riddled his body with bullets.

Al was so incensed that he retaliated by outright stealing ballot boxes, kidnapping a number of election officials, and murdering one. Capone won his political victory, but had now become a public figure and a target for law enforcement and other gang leaders, like Dion O'Banion and Bugs Moran. Once again, the death of a family member drove Al

Capone into a change of direction. He tossed the lessons of Johnny
Torrio out the window and adopted the brutality of Frankie Yale. For
every attack on him he struck back with a greater level of violence.
Everyone remembers the St. Valentine's Day Massacre of Moran's men
in a garage. Capone's violent years have been chronicled over and over
in books and film. The only thing that may have been overlooked in that
area is his attempted murder of Elliot Ness. In "The Prodigal Son"
(September, 2008), Tony Napoli documents how his father, James
"Jimmy Nap" Napoli, was sent to Capone by Frankie Yale. Capone
needed an outside shooter to go after Ness. The seventeen year old
Napoli, eager to prove himself, pulled up alongside a car that Ness and
Federal Agent Al Fuselli had just stopped at the curb, stuck a
submachine gun out the rear window, and sprayed the car with bullets.
Ness managed to duck down and crawl out of the car to safety. Fuselli
was killed.

By far, the closest and most trusted of Al's siblings was his older
brother, Ralph, nicknamed "Bottles," who was the last of Gabriele and
Teresina's children to have been born in Italy. Ralph was the first to join
Al in Chicago, and became his right hand man when he became boss. It
was Ralph who went to work on a Cicero Tribune reporter who had
gone undercover and written extensively about the Capone brothers'
prostitution and gambling operations. It was Ralph who was Al's go
between with his men when the latter did a one year prison term for
carrying a gun, and it was Ralph who was Eliot Ness's first tax evasion
target as he perfected his eventual case against Al Capone. When Al
was released and dying of syphilis on his Palm Island, Florida retreat, it
was Ralph who cared for him and was the spokesman for reporters who
crowded outside each day. After Al's death, Ralph faded into obscurity,
dealing with personal problems like divorce and the suicide of his son.
Ralph Capone died in Mercer, Wisconsin of a heart attack at the age of
eighty.

In another similarity between this author and Big Al, the latter's oldest
brother, Vincenzo, who the family called by the more American version,

James, seemed to carry the memory of the Italian countryside in his heart, and left the city in 1908, when he was sixteen, to find more open space in the U.S. His only communication for many years was a letter posted Wichita, Kansas, about a year after he'd left home. James traveled the Midwest with the circus, where he practiced long hours teaching himself to become a great shot, probably better than his younger brother, Al, would ever become. He used that marksman skill to the benefit of the United States of America when he enlisted in the army at the breakout of World War I and fought in France with the American Expeditionary Force, where his courage and skill in battle earned him the rank of lieutenant and a marksman medal from the unit's commander, General John J. Pershing. My younger brother left Brooklyn to enlist in the Air Force during the Vietnam Conflict then settled in Cincinnati for a time before moving to Florida.

When discharged from the service, James returned to the Midwest and settled in Homer, Nebraska. In 1919, Homer experiences the kind of flash flooding that is common to the area. James, now living under the name, Richard Hart, in honor of a silent film cowboy of the time, rescued a young woman, Kathleen Winch, and her family. A short time later he and Kathleen were married. Richard Hart worked at various mundane jobs, none of which satisfied his need for adventure. When the Nineteenth Amendment to the United States Constitution was passed to usher in the period known as Prohibition, Richard Hart signed up to become a Prohibition enforcement officer. Ironically, as younger brother Al was making a name for himself as a bootlegger and master criminal in Chicago, older brother, Vincenzo, was running on a parallel track as a lawman, becoming well known because of his expert marksmanship as "Two Gun" Hart. Big Al's brother not only busted stills, but took over law enforcement of all kinds in his jurisdiction, with an exceptionally high percentage of convictions. And, as Al Capone garnered headlines, "Two Gun" Hart did the same, with newspaper leads like, "Two Gun Hart Gets His Man Again" and "Two Gun Hart Brings in Bootleggers." In fact, his notoriety landed him a stint as bodyguard for President Calvin Coolidge. To continue the narrative of similarities between Al Capone and Sonny Girard, my brother also worked for the sheriff's department in a North Florida city before becoming an attorney.

Life began unraveling for Vincenzo/Richard in 1923. He was cleared of all responsibility for an innocent man being shot to death during an incident, but was unable to restore the shine his name previously had. Within a year, local newspapers had discovered and published his relation to the infamous Capone Brothers of Chicago. Thus began a series of moves that took him and his family from one Indian Reservation to another, as far away as Idaho near the Washington border.

He continued to make a lot of arrests, but also had problems with both criminals and authorities. Another murder, this time of an Indian, resulted in an acquittal, but had ruined his career in law enforcement of Indian reservations. He returned to his job as Prohibition enforcement agent in Homer, Nebraska, in 1931. When Prohibition ended two years later, Richard Hart took a low paying job as justice of the peace.

Things worsened for Hart financially over the years. By 1940, he couldn't even pay his electric bills. As a last ditch effort to bail himself out of trouble, he went to ask his brothers for money. Al was out of prison and deteriorating from syphilis. Ralph made sure his older brother was taken care of, and Vincenzo/Richard returned to Homer, Nebraska with enough hundred dollar bills to keep him and his family comfortable. He continued to visit with Ralph and Al, even as the latter's health deteriorated. Hart returned the favor to Ralph after Al had passed away. Hart was called as a witness for Ralph's second IRS trial. Ralph had bought a house under his Vincenzo's name without informing him. Richard Hart lied under oath, claiming he had bought the house Ralph was living in, thereby getting him an acquittal. Vincenzo Capone, A.K.A. Richard "Two Gun" Hart, died shortly afterward in Mercer, Nebraska, at the age of sixty.

"Scarface" was one of the most notorious criminals in a world of notorious criminals at their peak of power. He was also the most famous sibling of a biological family with the last name Capone.

MOB BLOG #16:

Great Mob Movies You May Not Have Seen

If I asked you what the great mob movies are, I'm sure most would run off the Godfather films (*NO, NOT III*), Goodfellas, maybe Casino too. But there are a number of mob genre films around that have not been as widely seen, and really do have a place in a legitimate top ten. Take it from me, someone who's lived the mob life for decades, that if you like mob films, you'll love these:

1) **Once Upon a Time in America:**

   Probably the best mob movie outside of Godfathers I & II, about Jewish mobsters growing up on the Lower East Side of New York, and starring Robert DiNiro and James Woods. It is a period look at mobdom that spans the time of Prohibition through a couple of more decades. Sergio Leone created this masterpiece, only to have it arbitrarily edited down by Fox to allow more showings. Eventually, he bought back the negative from the studio, restored the footage cut, and released it in its entirety as a video. It is now considered a classic.

2) **Mean Streets:**

   Martin Scorsese's first mob film, also starring a very young DiNiro, portrays the gritty, not too glamorous, day to day life of mobster wannabes in Little Italy, New York. It is not as refined as Scorsese's later work, but is about as authentic as any film you'll see about how it was being a young man growing up in the underworld in the Sixties.

3) **Flight of the Innocent:**

   This Italian film (*subtitled*) is a down to earth portrayal of two

Calabrian N'drangheta families in a life and death dispute. A young boy sees his family murdered by another over a kidnapping plot's ransom money and barely escapes with his life. His travels from city to city to find relatives who are part of his family's *cosca* with the money as he is being pursued by the killers illustrates the breadth of Italian criminal organizations like the aforementioned N'drangheta, Napolitano Camorra, Sicilian Mafia, and Pugliese Sacre Corona Unita. The cinematic beauty is in how much of the film is told with a camera without accompanying dialogue. It is a law of film that a page of screenplay translates to a minute of screen time. Flight of the Innocent dispels that theory, with a film that must have had a substantially shorter script. *In Italian with English subtitles.*

4) **Johnny Stecchino (*Johnny Toothpick*):**

Not all mob theme movies have to be serious or bloody. One of the funniest movies of any genre is Roberto Benigni's film about a woman who finds a look alike for her mobster turned informant, Johnny Stecchino, who, true to his name, always has a toothpick hanging out between his lips. She brings the unaware look alike to Sicily to have him killed so that no one will look for her beloved Johnny when they run away. Besides the fantastic perfomances by the cast, especially Benigni, the writing is amazingly funny. After Benigni's stumblebum character arrives in Sicily, he is always talking to people who are talking about something else, yet they always make sense to each other. I've watched this film a number of times, and always found something new to laugh at. *In Italian with English subtitles.*

5) The Sicilian Girl:

In his book "The Thirty-six Dramatic Situations," Georges Polti claimed there are only thirty-six stories in the world, but an infinite number of treatments of them. The story of the Mafia Wars of the 1980s is not new. The story of how two prosecutors, Paolo Borsellino and Giovanni Falcone, took on the Mafia; their efforts and their deaths at the hands of those they sought to destroy, is not new. Viewing that story through the eyes of a major witness is.

In the movie, "The Sicilian Girl," Rita Mancuso, based on the real witness against the Mafia, Rita Atria, grows up in a Mafia tradition in a small village in Sicily. Her father, Don Michele, is a local don whose influence extends from the village throughout the surrounding countryside, and is known as a fair and magnanimous protector of the populace. Part of his gentle side is that he dotes on his daughter, Rita, whose energy and spirit put her at odds with her mother. On the other side, Don Michele orchestrates and participates in murders to enforce his decisions. Rita's life comes apart as one person then another deserts her; first her dad is murdered then, a few years later, her brother.

When Rita finds that the engineer of those deaths is, Don Salvo, a man she always called uncle, she turns to the authorities for revenge, presenting them with detailed notes she's kept for years on Mafia activities, from drug dealing to murder, in her village. Once her betrayal of the Mafia is known, her fiancée shows his loyalty to Don Salvo over any to her and her mother chases her away. The prosecutor, who represents the real Mafia prosecutor, Paolo Borsellino, brings her to Rome with a new identity as he prepares for a maxi-processo trial against those she's tied to crimes. He becomes her only friend, but, like the real Borsellino, is assassinated by a bomb placed in his car.

In the end, a large number of Mafiosi are convicted because of her.

The director, Marco Amenta, who had previously produced a documentary on Rita Atria's life, did a masterful job of condensing that child of his into a streamlined Shakespearean dramatic version. Yes, the cinematography sometimes seems too dark, and one or two small glitches in acting or dialogue that stop the trained viewer, but they do not balance the steady theme a film needs to be successful or the tying up nicely the various supporting characters so they are understood. It is a thoughtful film that should be watched more than once to fully absorb the meaning of Mafia in Sicily; of how it permeates the psyche of Sicilians so deeply and sometimes subtly that their states of being are dominated by it. Parallels are also drawn by Amenta between the seventeen year old Rita, growing up in a Mafia environment, and the prosecutor's seventeen year old daughter.

The performances of the actors are also realistic, especially that of Veronica D'Agostina, who portrays Rita's anger and frustration flawlessly. She brings out the constantly growing isolation and sadness with perfection. Marcello Mazzarella, as Rita's father, Don Michele, is eminently believable as a Mafioso who is not a one dimensional man of honor, but someone who can be as tender and understanding as he is vengeful. In contrast, the film's villain, Don Salvo, is so one sided that he conveys a murder by innocuous conversation. Lucia Sardo, as Rita's miserable disposition mother, brings understanding of her own suffering at the end.

Roberto Saviano's acclaimed book and film about the Napolitano Camorra, "Gomorrah," shows the lowest of all the Camorristi and those in their circle of friends and family. It is a film that falls flat when it comes to understanding the structure of organized crime around Naples and its emotional impact on everyone in its sphere of influence. "Gomorrah" is a Bloods and Crips film set in Italy. "The Sicilian Girl" is heads above that. It's a terrific film that should not be missed. *In Italian with English subtitles.*

If you haven't seen these films, you've missed some different aspects of mob life and history, fiction and non-fiction, presented in a highly entertaining and memorable way.

MOB BLOG #17:

Why So Many Rats Today?

A while ago, when Joe Massino, boss of the Bonnano Crime Family, rolled over and began cooperating with the Feds, someone I know who was close to Joey asked me how he could do something like that. My response was to say that the phrase "wiseguys" wasn't put together carelessly. I'm sure, I said, that "dumbguys" had never even been considered. That term, "wiseguys," didn't mean that people with that moniker were geniuses, but that they were slick, sharper to see opportunities than most people; had a ruthless sense of how to survive best. I told my friend that if he thought back over the last two decades, he'd see that working with the authorities had more upsides than downsides. I asked how many men who had testified against the mob since Joe Valachi had been caught up with and killed? He said, "None." I seem to recall one, but can't remember who, and can't even be sure I'm right. In either case, it's little or none.

There have always been rats in the mob. They were harder to identify because they were virtually all "dry snitches," which means they provided information without ever being exposed or having to take the stand and testify. Many times they were the highest ranking members, like Lucky Luciano, who used the authorities to reduce a case or solve a personal problem. Lucky Luciano had his rodent cherry cracked when he was just a young drug peddler in the Five Points area of Little Italy. Arrested without the heroin on him, he led the cops to where he had stashed it; working a deal for a softer charge. He reached back into his rat bag when Meyer Lansky and Bugsy Siegel were at odds with Waxey Gordon, in what was then called "The War of the Jews." Fearing that the war would break into a hot shooting one, with Siegel leading the charge, Luciano and Lansky sent Meyer's brother, Jake, to the Feds with enough Gordon's financial records to send Waxey away on tax charges. Quiet. No one in the streets knew. War over. Poor Gypsy Rose Lee had to attend all those parties without Waxey by her side. Boo hoo.

Those kind of dry snitch events are hard to document, since no one came forward to leak those crimes. However, from experience, I am absolutely positive there was much more going on and usually at higher mob levels than we can imagine. For mob leaders, it was, and remains, "Do as I say, not as I do." And, as time went on, at least three of my own experiences had higher ups looking the other way about proven rats that were making money for them. Two of them went to prison when the informants they protected for money testified against them.

That doesn't mean that there weren't men who were real men in those days. I would say that the great majority were. They came out of the same ghetto environment that the great prizefighters of the day did. Each was fighting his way out of poverty by putting up his body as collateral. Boxers subconsciously said, "Beat my face and body, but I'm not going back there." Mobsters said the same thing, but put their lives and freedom on the line. Becoming a rat was unthinkable, and truly despised, not just with empty words to make them look good. A prime example is a well known story about the "Lord High Executioner," Albert Anastasia. Willie Sutton was a bankrobber who was known more for his escapes from prison than his actual robberies. One day, while Sutton was enjoying a hiatus from his latest incarceration, a haberdasher named Arnold Schuster spotted him and informed police where to catch him. The clothing salesman got a lot of good citizenship publicity. Unfortunately for him, some of it reached Anastasia. Despite the fact that Albert knew neither Sutton nor Schuster, he exclaimed, "I hate rats!" and ordered the latter eliminated.

On a more basic, day to day, level, in the old days, before mass communication and the Witness Protection Program, and with leaders like Anastasia around, if someone testified against a mob figure then ran away, a local boss could pass off a story about how the turncoat was tortured then dismembered and fed to animals at the nearest zoo. Other potential turncoats sitting on the fence shook in their shoes and took a jail term instead. Today, the stoolpigeon gets a book and/or film deal, does interviews with Barbara Walters, and has photos released of him lounging by a pool with palm trees in the background. The fact that a lot of what they say in those interviews is self-serving, gratuitous bullshit means nothing to the interviewers, law enforcement, or the public.

Henry Hill, for example, never told Nick Pileggi about how he was despised by most mob guys but given some modicum of respect because Paul Vario loved him and cast his wing of protection over him. The expression commonly used about Henry at the time was, "You respect a dog for its master." Instead of that side of the story, he wove a tale of how well he was respected by all. The "facts" he told Pileggi and other interviewers was what they wanted to hear, about how the mob turned on poor him, also means nothing. The truth is that he turned on everyone because he was a junkie and a punk, and decided to trade former friends' families for his own. Paul Vario, for example, got Hill a no-show job for him to get out of prison and into a halfway house. Hill testified to that fact, which sent his former father figure to jail, where he moaned about the betrayal until he died...in prison. The fact that he tells interviewers what they want to hear makes him a media darling. In the early 1990's I appeared on Geraldo Rivera's show, with Hill brought in via satellite. I challenged his lies. His only defense was to nervously stammer that I was wrong. I was never invited back, while he's always been Geraldo's mob expert pet and has appeared numerous times over the years.

The truth is that government tactics and pressure get too much credit for destroying the mob. It has destroyed itself both by natural causes, as the ghetto areas that spawned traditional mobsters are gone. Little Italy is now restaurant row. East Harlem, which produced many mob legends, is reduced to one famous restaurant, Rao's, and a couple of social clubs for some of its geriatric neighbors. South Brooklyn is trendy Carroll Gardens. All the other ghetto areas have been turned over to those other ethnic groups at the bottom of the social and financial ladder.

Young wannabes grow up in suburbs. They can shoot, but they won't be shot at. A former partner of mine used to say, "Everybody can be a toughguy if the shoe fits. It's when the laces get tight that you see who screams." When these young mob hopefuls grow up, the shoe fits comfortably. They have nice homes, girlfriends, cars, and MTV. There is no one that they "needed" to stay alive as they grew up. They have no loyalty experiences in their background. They need their MTV. When the gates clang behind them, those laces tighten quickly and they scream. Older wiseguys feel like jerks when they realize that their co-defendants are likely to have palm trees instead of jail cells, and rush forward. Joe Massino might be the first official boss to roll over, but the recent past is filled with high ranking members who have chosen rolling over to standing up: Jimmy "The Weasel" Frattiano, Acting Boss of L.A.; Ralph Natale, Acting Boss, of Philadelphia; Underboss, Sammy the Bull, of New York; Lucchese executives Gaspipe Casso, Little Al D'Arco, and on and on and on.

Another problem for the mob is its Americanization; the idea that the only goal is money. Years ago, believe it or not, there was a thread of honor that ran alongside the thread of crime. As time went on, the crime should have been discarded, with the code of honor dictating a tight, secret organization, much like the Masons, which circulated money among its members. The "Me Generation" has taken over. A number of years ago, a partner of mine died. The brass called me in to find out what he had going; what profit was out there to be had. One of the things we had our fingers in was to maintain order in a huge operation. The big guy asked how much was made from it. I answered, "Nothing." He said that if there was no money coming out of the place, we should step back and let someone from another crew go in. I replied that there was no responsibility for him, since I handled all the beefs, and that we had maintained our position of authority there to guarantee that we had jobs for our guys coming out of jail. His answer: "Fuck the guys in jail." That kind of thinking, or lack thereof, explains a lack of loyalty even further. For years, guys have gone to prison with zipped lips, many times to protect others. Unless they are bosses, it is a rarity that any of their families get a cent; that they get any money themselves for commissary. In fact, more times than not, money is stolen from operations they had going when they went to jail. The Government didn't do that. Add all the corrosion from the inside-out and you'll see why there are so many rats and the mob is gasping its last breaths.

Twenty years ago a friend of mine from Jersey said that one day there would be a time when a bunch of mob guys would be standing on a corner when they saw another mobster coming, and one would say, "Shhh, don't talk, he's a stand up guy."

That day is now.

P.S.:

A current example of the case I've made is that of Chris Paciello, a Staten Island "toughguy" until he faced prison time. Paciello has had a book written about him, a television movie about him done too. As of this writing he has relocated in Los Angeles, mingling with entertainment figures like the cast of HBo's "Entourage," excited by his past. Some may have been patrons of his hot Miami nightclub. Some will probably wind up in his bed.

Paciello came to mind today because of a recent article by Richard Johnson published about him, one that also involves MySpace.com, in the New York Post:

MYSPACE MISERY FOR MOBSTER

*January 15, 2007 -- WHILE Brooklyn mobster **Chris Paciello** tries to start a new life in Los Angeles, having served six years in prison for a 1993 murder, there are plenty of former friends from Bensonhurst who wouldn't mind if he got run over by a truck.*

*Paciello was a government witness - along with such pals as **Fat Sal**, **Applehead** and **Skeeve** - who helped send a dozen of his old associates behind bars, including **Alphonse** "Allie Boy" **Persico**, the acting boss of the Colombo crime family.*

"Paciello is a no-good snitch, a rat, and a selfish [bleep-bleep]er," says a Brooklynite surprised that Paciello didn't undergo plastic surgery and enter the witness-protection program.

*Always quick with his fists, the handsome Paciello was Miami's nightclub king 10 years ago and dated the likes of **Madonna**, **Jennifer Lopez**, **Sofia Vergara** and models too numerous to mention.*

Now, one of his enemies has set up a phony MySpace page bearing Paciello's likeness and his (made-up) words: "For some reason everyone in Miami and Hollywood thinks I only ratted on four people." The entry then lists five "Springville Boys" from Staten Island he actually helped put away for sentences ranging from 3 to 10 years.

*"I also took the stand against **Eddie Boyle** [a high-end bank burglar associated with the Gambinos] and **Tommy Dono** from Brooklyn. I provided information on **Tommy Reynolds** and **Fabritzio** "The Hurter" **DiFrancesi**, now serving 30- and 36-year sentences.*

*"I also snitched on my best friends from Brooklyn who I grew up with my whole life, **Rico Locasio**, 5 years, and **Dom** "Black Dom" **Dionisio**, 16 years."*

A law-enforcement source says this account is accurate: "Paciello would have testified in a lot of other cases, but the majority of defendants pleaded guilty and there were no trials."

The MySpace hoaxer points out that even after all his cooperation, Paciello was sentenced to 10 years: "As I cried in the courtroom, the prosecutor said he would appeal the sentence. A few weeks later, I got a 7-year sentence. Basically what I'm saying is I could not do an extra three years . . . I'm a selfish rat [bleep-bleep]er."

All I can say is, "Kudos to the MySpace mischief maker.

MOB BLOG #18:

"Turning Mob Myths, From the Inside and Out, Inside-Out"

Because of the secretive nature of organized crime, there have been many myths propagated by insiders for a variety of reasons and outsiders because they didn't know any better. Some have been so ingrained in the public consciousness that gangsters themselves now believe them. I have no reasons to lie and, as a former inside player in that world, know better, so I'll affirm or debunk some of those myths honestly and accurately for you here.

MOB MYTH #1: Everyone must "make their bones" by murdering someone before they can become a made member of the mob – FALSE.

You don't have to be an insider to count. For example, the number of made men the FBI claims are in all five New York Families runs anywhere from one to three thousand, depending on who's counting and how much more funding they're looking for. Now find the substantially lower number of mob-related murders, at most in the low hundreds that have taken place in the last two decades and are not related to a war, like the last Colombo Family conflict of the Early 1990s. Those war figures are discounted because most of the successful hits are by guys who are already made. Now take into account the fact that there are guys, the "workhorses," walking around with double digit notches in their belts. One former pal died with a mere eleven dead bodies to his credit; another, an astonishing forty-nine. As a matter of fact, when he was sentenced and the judge mentioned that he was to be sentenced for forty-eight murders, he corrected the judge to make sure it was an accurate forty-nine he'd go to prison for. After considering those figures, it would be virtually impossible for every made man to have killed someone.

From the inside, it's almost laughable that every "goodfella" left a body somewhere. I've known some that couldn't kill a rubber duck. They were given the honor of membership to keep them...and their assets...within a particular family. Rules are that if the crew one is associated with won't propose him for membership another family can. Big earners are not turned over to another family under any circumstances. Money overcomes principal in the legitimate world, why not in the mob? One reason Albert Anastasia was murdered was because he was thought to have sold "buttons" for fifty grand apiece. In the 1950s, that was a lot of scratch. After Albert was gone, his successor, Carlo Gambino, had "the books" closed for decades. A more recent, but very telling, story has it that a proposed member who was bothered by never having fired a gun decided to take a few shots into a tubful of water. Embarrassment replaced experience as the bullet ricocheted around the porcelain and into his body. He got made anyway. Remember that the next time some unlikely hood intimates he's a killer. Chances are if he's trying to make you think he is, he isn't. An old Sicilian saying goes: *"Those who say, do not do; those who do, do not say."*

MOB MYTH #2: Once in the mob, you can't get out – FALSE.

Aside from becoming a rat and joining the Witness Protection Program, there are ways for both associates and members to get out of the mob, if not totally, at least in effect. One happens when someone is "put on the shelf." Most times it's not by choice. On the other hand, sometimes it is. During the 1931 "Night of the Vespers," when more than sixty Sicilian "Moustache Petes" were murdered to make way for the new order of Americanized organized crime, led by Lucky Luciano and pals, one of the followers of the old order was also shot, but survived. Through a relative aligned with the young crowd, the shooting victim pleaded not to be shot again. He was not of a mind to seek revenge, he said, and begged to be "put on the shelf," where his button status would be suspended. If granted that wish, he swore to work legitimately for the rest of his life, which he did. More recently, a few big name made guys who were at odds with the leadership of their crew were all placed on the shelf instead of becoming targets. That meant that they no longer had the backup of their family in disputes with those from others. They would be automatic losers in beefs with other mobsters. It might have been uncomfortable, but, on the other hand, may have been a gift in disguise, leaving them to rein in any mob community activities that might have landed them in prison again.

I was fortunate enough to do part of my federal time with my direct mob superior. I told him I'd written a novel, and didn't want to do anything in the streets anymore. I saw the handwriting on the wall and that we, as a way of life, were finished; that there was no one left on the outside to trust. Besides, I said, I thought I'd earned it. I mentioned a so-called friend of ours who was a crybaby through his whole prison time. I pointed out that this guy would go right back to his old life, but would never do time again. His ace in the hole would be information. Not for me. That, I said, didn't leave me many choices. He agreed to put me on what would parallel the injured list of a ballclub with one caveat, that if I decided to go back to the streets, it would be back to where I'd come from; no jumping horses. I didn't go back; didn't jump horses; remained friends until he passed away. Of course, there are a couple of other ways of effectively being released from obligations: distance, illness (*real or feigned*), alcoholism (*exaggerated so no one thinks of depending on you*). Yes, there can be life without dishonor after a life of crime

MOB MYTH #3: You must be one hundred percent Italian to be made – FALSE.

It started out as only Sicilians being "straightened out" when the organizations were controlled by Sicilian Moustache Petes. Before 1931 and the Night of the Vespers, Sicilians were killing other Sicilians because of vendettas from the old country and because there were old time rivalries from one town or region to another. That all changed when the new order was formed by younger, more Americanized gangsters like Lucky Luciano, Frank Costello, Vito Genovese, etc. At that time a rock solid requirement for membership was that one's family tree, on both sides, had to be traced back to Sicily or mainland Italy. That rule remained in effect for around a half century. But, as Italian ghettos disappeared, so did the number of those qualified to join. After Carlo Gambino died and the "books" were opened for new members to bolster every family's depleted ranks, the Italian heritage requirement was modified, so that one's father only had to have Italian/Sicilian roots. I knew it to be accurate when "Fat Patty" Catalano, who had previously been "knocked down" for membership because of a German-American mother, was finally given his "badge."

MOB MYTH #4: Mob bosses hire outside killers for certain jobs – FALSE.

I watched a documentary recently on a guy dubbed "The Iceman." I loved the persona of this guy as he described a variety of murders he'd committed. Very matter of factly; almost rehearsed. No doubt he'd murdered a number of people; there was enough evidence of that. However, when he began claiming he'd been hired a number of times by mobsters, at least one a close friend of mine, to kill for figures in the high thousands, I laughed. Fact: Top level mobsters are the cheapest SOBs around. One was even nabbed trying to beat a bridge toll; another friend used to steal cigars from a diner on his way out. Yes, they'll throw money around for girls, cars, clothes, food, booze, and other entertainment or luxuries, but to pay for something they can get for free? I don't think so. Killing is easy. Kids do it. So do women. Every mobster of any stature has underlings who would pay them for a chance to prove themselves by killing someone. The higher up the mob guy, the more underlings and the more free opportunities to eliminate those targeted. Would he bypass the freebee and pay fifty or seventy-five thousand dollars to an outsider? Answer that one yourself. One of the people the Iceman says paid him was a dear friend of mine. He had a crew under him that was second only to Murder Incorporated. Would he pay the Iceman? C'mon.

MOB MYTH #5: Married mobsters all have girlfriends – MOSTLY TRUE.

What are the biggest factors in anyone cheating on a spouse? Accessibility and opportunity. Mobsters have an accessibility to women that is only matched in Hollywood. Females are attracted to the danger and power they associate with organized crime. As a matter of fact, a large number are attracted to any kind of bad boy, from drunks to motorcycle gang members to ex-cons. We used to have a bar in Brooklyn where some of us were periodically arrested on a nonsense charge just for the irritation factor. Each time, the newspapers would run articles about the mob figures rounded up in that bar. The next weekend, the bar would overwhelmingly be filled with females from as far away as New Jersey. One even rode from the Garden State to Brooklyn on her bicycle, just to meet gangsters. I also learned not to speak well of any of my associates to any female. Legitimate guys attracted to mobsters would go home with stories of how wonderful they were. By the time wifey met hubby's ballyhooed mobster pals she was ready to drop her drawers and jump in the sack with them. Sometimes many sacks. They were affectionately known as "wiseguy humps." Power brokers in any business have groupies, usually associated with their profession. Mobsters and Hollywood players get them from every walk of life.

Opportunity means having time on your hands to play around. That's what makes housewives such easy targets for smut novels and movies. A lot of that writing is fantasy; a lot of it is true. The infamous Alice Crimmins had enough time to bed her kids' barber, the stock boy from her local supermarket, the cop on the beat, etc. And, Alice was not alone. Mob guys have time on their hands. Add that to the access and the fact that they don't want to expose their wives to much of what they do and you've got a recipe for chronic cheating. At least it was that way years ago. Today, it seems, mobsters can't keep anything secret...even incriminating stuff. Unfortunately for most wiseguys who cheat, they fall in love, and the overwhelming number of those who cheat actually wind up with two wives. They assume a second set of obligations. They have to put up with double nagging. And, they disclose business secrets about themselves and others that they would never let their wives know. They're simply, in my opinion, out of their minds. Some *commari*, or, girlfriends, even wind up going to prison as a result of their new partnerships. Of course, there are those, few and far between, who are solid family men, not just to their mob families but to their biological ones as well. Hats off to them for loyalty, respect, and, most important if you are in that life, limiting an unnecessary vulnerability. Same with Presidents of the U.S.

MOB MYTH #6: Mob bosses are loyal to their troops – FALSE.

People think of *la famiglia*...the family...as a vertical structure that insures loyalty up and down the ladder. Not so. Mob loyalties are more horizontal than vertical. Of course, there's always the "me" factor, which outweighs any loyalty at all, but the tendency, once someone is initiated into traditional organized crime, is to become part of a caste system. Typically, when a wiseguy goes to a sitdown for some underling or associate's beef, the first thing he will do is invite the wiseguy representing the opposition outside. That's where the deal is made: *"Fuck them both. I'll make my guy pay; you tell your guy he lost, and we'll cut up the money."* That same conversation goes on when captains are representing wiseguys and when bosses are representing captains. Loyalties are horizontal. A captain will sooner side with another captain, who might wind up in a higher position one day and be a good connection with that crew, than with the guy under him, who he can silence with a word. Same with bosses. Why do you think there's a rule in place that you can't kill your boss and become boss. Horizontal protection of position. That's why John Gotti was never recognized as a real boss by Chin and others. Can't kill your boss and become boss.

MOB MYTH #7: Mobsters hate rats – SOMETIMES.

Only when they're not profiting from them. Balance two things on a scale: $$$$ - rat, $$$$ - rat, hmmm, $$$$ - rat? $$$$ will win more times than not. Sadly, I've seen this myself too often. It didn't mean much when I was really young and heard a famous mob captain make excuses for a business owner who was called a rat, because he was making money with him. As time went on I occasionally heard those same kinds of charges and excuses made by others surrounding me. I sort of dismissed them because I had no direct involvement with those guys, and thought that the term rat might have been thrown around too easily. Then the experiences got closer.

One of my associates out on Long Island told me he had a guy who was dealing in "paper." In those days, "paper" meant stocks and bearer bonds that male and female workers in banks or Wall Street brokerages were stealing from cages and selling to street guys for a small percentage of the face value. Ten hundred-thousand dollar notes might put ten grand in their pockets. Some were girls just happy to make a mobster they were bedding happy, and got a television at best...along with their romps between the sheets. Those papers were turned over to only one or two central guys for around ten percent who had connections in Swiss banks that would in turn give no-questions-asked loans of up to seventy percent or so. The Swiss bankers would stash the paper in their vaults and own the stocks or bonds at a profit of thirty percent when the loan defaulted. Everyone made money. So, at my associate's behest, I went to meet his connection.

When I sat down, the paper broker started shooting his mouth off about how he had millions of this and millions of that. No one had that kind of volume unless they were ripoff artists or stool pigeons. I asked who knew him; someone I could verify his reliability with. After a while, he asked if I'd heard of Joe Colombo; he claimed they'd been in prison together. I said it sounded familiar and that I'd get back to him. Joe went ballistic, especially since he'd never been in prison, he said. I went back to find the guy, who'd disappeared. Fast forward a couple of years, and I found a close friend of mine in deep conversation with the same paper broker. I called him outside and told him the story. His response was to tell me the guy was really a good guy and he was making money with him. He begged me not to say anything to anyone, and I didn't. The broker eventually took the stand against him and seven others. They all went to prison.

I brought another wiseguy pal actual court minutes of an associate of his testifying against someone else at trial. His response was to say, "He won't rat me out if he wants to live." The fact that the guy had testified against someone else meant nothing. $$$$ had once again overcome the rat factor. His pal eventually sent him to prison also. It happened again when a wiseguy in the Bronx went to bat at a sitdown for a guy on the run after he'd actually brought police into a mob club where stolen merchandise was stored. The wiseguy's plea: "I'm making money with him." Sounds ridiculous, but each story is one hundred percent true. $$$

MOB MYTH #8: The FBI destroyed the mob – FALSE.

At the beginning of Mel Gibson's film, "Apocolypto," there is a printed statement on screen to the effect that no great civilization has ever been defeated from the outside until it had already decayed on the inside. Same with the mob. Unlike the Sicilian Mafia, the American mob, wrongly dubbed La Cosa Nostra by that idiot, Joe Valachi, was doomed the minute it set foot on United States soil. First a word about the name. As a young man, I had heard the term *cosa nostra*, with lower case letters, to mean this thing of ours that has no name. When Valachi, semi-literate boob that he was, testified before the Senate Committee on Organized Crime, he mistook the lower case *cosa nostra* for the proper noun *Cosa Nostra*. It was immediately seized upon by the media and authorities, and so permeated the culture that by the Nineteen Nineties even top mobsters like John Gotti were using the term as if it were the official name of the mob.

To realize why the mob was doomed here in America is to understand history. Every immigrant group to enter the United States had organized gangs. The Irish had gangs like those portrayed in Martin Scorsese's film, "Gangs of New York." Eastern European Jews had the

Bug & Meyer Gang, Murder Incorporated, and Lepke & Gurrah. Each group viewed crime as a vehicle to take them from poverty to affluence. The Sicilian/Italian was the only one to view it as a way of life, to be handed down to their sons and their sons' sons. They had a tradition that went back some eight hundred years on an island that was constantly run by invaders that spoke a different language and had little or no interest in the Sicilian people. There was no justice. To find justice, a sub rosa government was formed: the Mafia. Like all governments, this one had to tax people to survive, which in this case came in the form of theft, extortion, kidnapping, and other rackets. When Sicilian immigrants came to America they found the same conditions. The local governments were run by people who didn't speak their language and had little or no interest in their well being. Italians were considered scum by the reigning WASPs, Irish who had emigrated to the U.S. a half-century earlier, and German Jews who had also been in America for decades. They needed justice. The Mafia gave it to them.

Had it not been for Prohibition, Sicilian mobs would have vanished by the mid-Twentieth Century. But the enormous revenue, power, reputation, and businesses that illegal booze had given to them carried the mob for another half-century. What no one realized was that this is not Sicily, and as new generations grew Americanized the need for justice was no longer in their hands. The tradition was gone. The immigrant ghettos that had turned out true toughguys no longer existed. Historically, when Italian gangsters were at their peak so were Italian prizefighters. Each group was fighting its way out of poverty, one by anteing up its life and freedom, the other by having its body pummeled. Look around. Name some Italian champs today. Can't? What does that tell you? If one group is gone, so should the other. The ghettos are gone for Italians. The tradition doesn't exist, and has in fact been perverted, where the old code of honor that ran parallel to criminal activities has been discarded and the latter clung to. Had the opposite occurred on the inside, maybe the there would have been no destruction from the outside. Toughguys today are not so tough. They don't grow up in conditions that build loyalty or inner strength. Instead, they grow up in suburban areas and are as spoiled rotten as any American youth. A former partner of mine used to say that everyone was a toughguy as long as the shoe fit; it was when the laces got tight that you saw who screamed. Add that to the American obsession of money over honor and the demise of organized crime became inevitable, FBI or no FBI.

R.I.P. *cosa nostra.*

MOB BLOG #19:

The Real Story of Bugsy Siegel

The story of Bugsy Siegel is about as familiar to American organized crime watchers as that of Al Capone or John Gotti. There have been books about Siegel. There have been movies, like "Mobsters" and "Bugsy" that featured him. I've read just about every one of the books and seen every one of the films. I've also watched the documentaries about him or that featured him in telling the story of one of his cohorts, like Lucky Luciano, Frank Costello, or Meyer Lansky. What I haven't seen is the real story of the man. I've seen the events over and over, but have not found one book, movie, or TV show that has understood what Benjamin "Bugsy" Siegel was all about. How do I know what those authors and producers did not? I wasn't old enough to be there, but my friends were there and my friends told me things. Now, I'll tell you.

The beginning of modern organized crime in America is widely attributed to four men: Charles "Lucky" Luciano, Frank "The Prime Minister" Costello, Meyer Lansky, and Bugsy Siegel. Each of them had a role in laying the foundation for the mob's existence for another half-century. The most widely known was the top executive, Lucky Luciano. His story is no secret. He came up in the ranks of Joe "The Boss" Masseria, a Sicilian immigrant thug who was at constant war with his main Sicilian rival, Salvatore Maranzano. Both men were old school, "Moustache Petes," who ignored profits for murderous vendettas. After Maranzano's men kidnapped Luciano and beat and cut him before leaving him for dead, he agreed to set his current boss, Masseria up to be killed. A long standing Sicilian/Italian mob rule was that one could not kill his boss and succeed him. That is why John Gotti was never recognized by the Commission as the true leader of the Gambino

Family, having very publicly and obviously had Paul Castellano murdered. Genovese Family members were actually indicted for a plot led by their leader, Vincent "Chin" Gigante, to murder John. Luciano, in a much less media driven day, got around this by handing off the dirty work to Bugsy Siegel, who, along with Red Levine and other Jewish gangsters, shot Masseria to death in a Coney Island restaurant while Luciano was conveniently relieving his bladder in the bathroom.

Luciano later had Siegel and his Jews murder Maranzano too, and name himself boss of both sides of the conflict. Luciano was a weasel. He had proven it earlier by leading police to a stash of heroin to avoid an arrest and later by sending Meyer's brother, Jake Lansky, to the IRS with business records of fellow mobster Waxey Gordon, to avoid a brewing "War of the Jews." He finally elevated weaseldom to its peak when he got out of his prison term after helping clear the way for U.S. forces to invade Sicily and drive out the Nazis, while leaving his co-defendant, "Little Davey" Petillo to serve out his entire sentence in prison. Weasel.

Costello and Lansky had different positions in the formation of modern organized crime. Costello was a diplomat. He mingled with businessmen, politicians, and judges, and never really thought of himself as a mobster. He was good looking and smooth as silk, blending into high society much more easily than into the circles of mob underlings. The clubs he frequented were El Morocco and the Stork Club, not Mulberry Street social clubs, with neighborhood gamblers, toughs, and murderers playing pinochle and drinking espresso brewed in beat up Napolitano maganettes. Diplomat.

Meyer Lansky, as the third leg of the mob's four-legged stool, was a businessman, more at home with an adding machine than a machine gun. He was brilliant with numbers and with seeing business possibilities that enriched the mob over decades. He set in motion business interests, like gambling in Havana and investments of union pension funds that kept organized criminals rolling in cash for decades. Businessman.

That brings us to Siegel, the man portrayed by historians and filmmakers as a bloodthirsty maniac. The truth was that Siegel was the only true warrior in the quartet that founded modern organized crime. Did he murder? Absolutely? Did he have a mean temper? Yes, indeed. And that temper combined with a cold hearted ability to murder as needed to protect his and his partners' interests to give him a reputation that would make generations think of him as a cross between Jack the Ripper and Dracula. No blood dripping from Siegel's lips, unless, of course, he was in a wild bout with the love of his life, the closest thing to a female mobster, Virginia Hill. That maniacal image of Siegel is the first misconception about the man. <u>Warrior.</u>

But, how Siegel is understood or misunderstood in his bloodletting activities is an unimportant distinction. Remember, sticks and stones can...blah, blah, blah. What is important is to understand the relationship between Bugsy and his mob brethren AFTER he's killed Masseria and Maranzano to form a new organization, or syndicate. One of the beefs the younger group, which Siegel was an integral part of, had with the old Moustache Petes was that they would only do business with Sicilians, and, in the extreme, only trusted those who originated from the same Sicilian areas they did. Jews, Irishmen, even Neapolitans like Costello were not welcome. To the young Americanized Sicilian gangsters like Luciano, money had no ethnic preference. Green was green, and they'd take it from or make it with anyone, anywhere. To Bugsy Siegel, that meant that he and his partners would be equals once the Moustache Petes were eliminated. But power corrupts, and once Luciano's plan to form a more modern mob had been accomplished, he announced that there was this centuries-old Sicilian thing, at the time based on what was known as the *Unione Siciliano*, and that non-Italians had to have a Sicilian/Italian made guys to be their liaisons to the newly formed Commission of bosses from around the country.

To Meyer Lansky, who was interested in money and not official mob position, that edict by Luciano meant nothing. His long time close friend, Vincent "Jimmy Blue Eyes" Alo, became "his man." Lansky never sat on the Commission, and couldn't give a crap less about it. In fact, until recently the remaining old time Jewish mobsters and their offspring...guys like "Max the Jew" Shrager (*father of luxury hotel owner, Ian*) and the Jacobson brothers, Sam and Ralph, the latter who murdered the black owner of Conrad's Cloud Room, the hot Queens nightclub...all answered to the Genovese Family, which is the descendent of Lucky Luciano's crew after the re-organization of the mob. On the other hand, to Siegel, the warrior...the one who had done all the heavy lifting to put the Sicilian weasel and the Neapolitan diplomat in power...it sucked, and he would have no part of it. He would be his own boss and not take orders from any greaseball who was half the man he was. He would go somewhere to get away from the New York Italian-run mob...not to cut ties, as much as he despised them, and not as a point man for Luciano and Lansky, but to run his own show...and put three thousand miles between him and his pals. He set out for California, where he would be his own boss.

Again, all the events surrounding Bugsy Siegel's wild romance with Virginia Hill and his founding of the Flamingo Hotel have been beaten to death in books, films, and TV. Everyone knows how the Flamingo cost millions more than it was supposed to and how the opening was a disaster. That's where the common understanding of events, particularly Siegel's murder, diverts from the truth.

A number of years ago, I had a good friend named Joe Stassi, who was known in mob circles as "Joe Rogers." Who was Joe Rogers? Joe was like a grandfather who had been a feared killer in his early days, most notably for arranging the murder of Dutch Schultz on Luciano's orders, who became the representative for the mob in Havana during its heyday. In his book about the mob in Cuba, "Havana Nocturne," T. J. English writes about weekly mob summit meetings in Havana, "These meetings took place on Thursday or Friday at the Miramar home of Joe Stassi, the gravelly-voiced Mafioso...Stassi's home was located on a winding, well-hidden road...not far from the site of Lansky's highly anticipated Hotel Riviera...with Stassi presiding as a kind of go-between for the various parties in attendance...along with Meyer, and sometimes his brother, Jake, the participants included [Santo] Trafficante, the Cellini brothers...others in attendance were a collection of men...most with experience in the casino-gambling business – who filled out the lower ranks of the Havana mob." Joe Rogers was the ultimate insider...and Joe Rogers was my friend.

One day, during one of the sessions where Joe would relate stories to me of past mob events the talk turned to Bugsy Siegel. He said that all the stories about Siegel being killed because of his having lost the mob's millions were bullshit. "If you check the numbers," he said, "you'll see that the Flamingo was already in the black in March. Ben got killed in June." He went on to explain, with great authority, that after the money started coming in and Luciano and the others who had sunk millions into the hotel could breathe, they sent a message to Siegel to come back East for a meeting. According to Joe Stassi, what they wanted was to give Bugsy a dressing down followed by them demanding more points in the profits they could already forecast. If it had been Meyer Lansky or even Frank Costello, they would have jumped on a plane, listened to some harsh words, and given up some more money in what had already shown would generate untold amounts of profit. Bugsy Siegel had another approach, more in keeping with his warrior's persona. "Bugsy sent back a message," Joe Stassi said. "The message was 'Fuck the WOPs!' That was why he died."

Do Bugsy's real motives for going West or the real reason he was killed matter? Sometimes popular belief or fictionalized accounts are better than the reality. In Martin Scorsese's "Goodfellas," Paulie Vario, the Paul Sorvino character, is portrayed as a quiet, dignified, man of few words. In reality, Paulie Vario, who was also a friend of mine, was as loud as any mob guy you could ever find. His men used to call him "Magilla Gorilla." However, in the film, Sorvino's restrained performance worked much better as a foil for the violent antics of his crew than the reality of the man. On the other hand, the real story of Bugsy Siegel's strained relationship with New York's mob leaders *before* the whole Vegas fiasco and the real story of why he died are much more compelling than the misunderstood events portrayed in every book and film to date. It is the real story of Benjamin "Bugsy" Siegel, thanks to Joe Stassi.

RIP my friend.

MOB BLOG #20:

"When We Were Kings"

*A contemplative look back at the good old days of mobdom, brought on
by the half century anniversary of the infamous Apalachin Convention.*

Traditional Organized Crime was born out of poverty and necessity.
Historically, though every ethnic group in America has or has had its
share of gangs or organized criminal groups the mob, as we know it has
its roots in "The Two Sicilies." That phrase is not used in modern times,
but at one time the description encompassed not only Sicily (Mafia), but
the entire southern region of Italy's mainland, which included
Campagna (Camorra) and Calabria ('Ndrangheta). While Sicily is known
to have been inhabited by foreigners...Greeks, Moors, Spaniards,
Bourbon French...the entire southern region suffered the same fate.
There was no government of the people, by the people, and so on and
so forth. The population was at the mercy of foreigners who for the
most part didn't even speak their language or give a crap about them.
There was no way to get justice except for a sub-rosa government of
local toughs who would enforce their longstanding rules of honor and
general behavior. To be effective, that underground government, like
any government, needed funds. Since it couldn't openly tax its
constituents, it took its taxes in the form of criminal acts: extortion,
kidnapping, expediting business deals.

That tradition of a criminal government was exported to the United
States in the earliest days of the great wave of immigrants who landed
here from Southern Italy/Sicily and Eastern Europe. The Italian/Sicilian
immigrants found the same conditions as they had left behind in the old
country. Police and Courts, overwhelmingly Irish, Anglo, Dutch, and
German, did not speak their language and, in fact, looked at them as

scum. They turned to the only group that had given them justice for almost eight hundred years, the criminal gangs known as Mafia, Camorra, and 'Ndrangheta. It was because of that history that Italian/Sicilians saw crime as a way of life instead of as a vehicle from poverty to affluence, as other ethnic groups did. The great majority of the sons of Jewish and Irish mobsters went on to become business owners and public servants. Ian Schrager, former lawyer, Studio 54 owner, and hotel entrepreneur...not to mention rat...is the son of one of Meyer Lansky's biggest numbers bankers. The twisted path that took him to prison was never one laid out by his old man. During that same time Italian captains and higher were pulling their sons out of college to induct them into their "thing." One, in particular, will spend the rest of his life in prison because of that unscheduled day off from school.

On the other hand, while Italians/Sicilians dominated crime...and for those who take offense in that, remember I didn't create it and won't rewrite history to cover it up...they also brought a Mediterranean lust for life, including food, style, etc., that, despite the danger to life and freedom, made being part of that subculture exciting, fun, and often glorious...not just for us, but for everyone close to us. Those were the days when we were kings.

I've been in Little Italy restaurants where I could spot tourists looking around for mobsters. They'd huddle and try to discreetly point with their eyes toward someone they thought was a wiseguy. As often as not, they would reference a guy from the neighborhood who was a fishmonger, worked for the Department of Sanitation, or manufactured tee shirts for a living. That was because of the Americanized Mediterranean-style of dress and carriage that pervaded Southern Italian neighborhoods. The diamond pinky ring associated with mobsters was worn by just about everyone in urban Italian areas. Silk suits, print ties (no Brooks Brothers rep-stripes, thank you very much), and lock-collar white on white shirts; Italian knits and worsted slacks for casual wear. Shiny Euro-shoes too. When I was doing a book signing at a Los Angeles Barnes & Noble, one reporter mentioned that John Gotti wore expensive clothes and so did I. He wondered why? Was it a peacock thing? I asked him what he got for Christmas when he was a kid. Toys, naturally, he said. I told him that I got socks, a belt (*I can still remember that three quarter inch piece of leather*), a stylish sweater. Expensive clothes were not just something I enjoyed, but a daily reminder of where I came from. He blushed; felt embarrassed. We became friends, and remain so to this day.

Neighborhood treatment was another badge of success to us. Celebrity for us growing up in ghetto neighborhoods wasn't national, but like all politics was local. Being not only feared in our neighborhoods, but respected and looked up to made us local celebrities and a feeling that we were kings. Our legitimate neighbors knew who we were. They knew who had what position, who ran what racket, who the money guys were and who the hitters were. One time the FBI came looking for me at a social club I ran. I was next door in a luncheonette playing pinochle. Crowds of our neighbors crowded around the outside of the club, watching, waiting then dispersing after the Feds had left. Not one person told the FBI I was next door. Fear? No. They just identified much more with me and my guys than the authorities. In fact, they were enablers, and a party to our ability to operate and commit crimes. A parallel can be seen today in Muslim neighborhoods. The average, non-terrorist resident knows who the rabble rousers are, who the foreign strangers who stay to themselves are, and who the recruiters in the mosques are, yet they stay quiet. Like our old neighbors, these "good Muslims" are enablers, and responsible for whatever results from that.

Then there was the money, which made a difference in the lives of family members. By my late teens I was actually making ten times the forty or fifty dollars a week my father made as a factory worker. I was able to take my mother to a nightclub for the first time in her life and watch her cry from happiness, or regret for what she'd missed throughout her hard life. That was the first of many nights out. Her favorite restaurant became the nostalgic Bill's Gay '90s (*gay meant happy at that time*), when previously it was Tads. Carnegie Hall was a thrill, as was meeting the star of the show, Jimmy Roselli. She had sacrificed her whole life for her children and placing a fur coat on her shoulders made me feel like a king. The methods I used to obtain the money were criminal, but, then again, what king ever rolled up his sleeves and worked for a dollar?

Two things make for an active and varied love life. Leisure time and access. No one doubts that street guys had time on their hands. In fact, most time spent away from home was spent wasting time: sitting in a café, playing cards in a social club, going to the movies or ball game in the days when baseball was played on weekday afternoons too. Time to roll in the sack with some bimbo or mistress was just as easy, and had a greater incentive. While time was a positive factor in mobster sex lives, access was incredible. Some of the access came from non-mobsters who came in contact with the real guys. In an effort to look tough by their acquaintance with gangsters, they'd talk the latter up to celebrity status. By the time they introduced their new friends to their wives or girlfriends, those females were halfway into a motel bed with their pals. News accounts of arrests provided even more mob candy. I remember when my friends and I were periodically arrested in a Brooklyn bar where we hung out. Each time the newspapers published accounts of the arrests, the following weekend saw the lounge packed with new females. Some arrived safely with a male who usually went home alone after the girl had attached herself to one of the regulars. One young lady (?) showed up on a bicycle. When told she couldn't bring the bike into the bar she pleaded that she'd come all the way from Jersey to meet the guys. I stored her bicycle in the kitchen until she was ready to pedal back the next morning. It was a part of the life that made us all feel like kings.

More important in this headiness that pervaded this era of mobdom due to others' fear or excitement, was the power of the dollar earned illegally, but not, as you'll see, immorally in our minds. Yes, I could go on and on about the respect in the neighborhood, the front row in theaters and nightclubs, the fawning by legitimate business owners who needed favors, but none of them instilled the feeling of superiority that the cooperation of authorities did. Michael Corleone, in "Godfather II" told a Senator that they were both "...part of the same hypocrisy." Before the Knapp Commission Hearings in New York City (*Serpico*), authorities from local police to judges to the Governor's office all had people on the take; willing to comply with us for a buck. It was commonplace to be stopped for a traffic ticket and, when a cop came to ask for license and registration, hold a twenty dollar bill (*worth a LOT more then*) out the window, say, "My name is Mr. Green and I'm in a hurry," and get waved on by the officer.

Nothing woke me up to that more than my first adult arrest. As a teen, getting caught for some crime usually meant getting shook down by the cops and smacked around before being chased home. This first gambling arrest, where my door had been smashed down really caught me unaware of what the real deal was. One detective took me into the bedroom and closed the door. I sat on the edge of the bed, watching him walk back and forth through the corners of my eyes, not listening to him but preparing to roll with the punch when he struck. Finally, without ever throwing a punch, he arrested me. I was so proud that I hadn't said a word and couldn't wait for the pats on the back and compliments for standing up when I got back to the club. Imagine my shock when the first words out of the attorney's mouth was, "You moron!" What? "You're a moron and you'll always be a moron! This detective said he talked himself blue in the face, trying to get you to come up with some money, but you refused." I hadn't heard a word the cop had said, instead wanting to avoid having my jaw wired. "You didn't have to get pinched at all."

Later, on a felonious assault case, where I was on the lam, friends reached out for the guy I hit when he had attacked me over a traffic argument. They offered him a thousand dollars (easily five or more times today's value) to drop the charges. His battle axe of a wife refused to let him take it. She only wanted to see me go to jail. Plan B:

We gave the judge five hundred dollars, half what we offered the victim, and he dropped the charges. That judge became targeted by the Knapp Commission and was drummed out of office. Seems I was nothing compared to what he'd accumulated in bribes.

Time to open an after hours club, or a poker game, or a full casino, our first stop would be to the local precinct to identify the location and make a deal for protection. If word came down from the Boro or City that a raid was coming, a call from the precinct would get there first and the raid would find nothing. As a matter of fact, the Gay Pride Parade has its roots in police corruption and a reaction to it. In those days it was illegal for two men to hold hands, kiss, etc. If Jack and Joe stole a kiss in someone's bar or restaurant the liquor license of the establishment could be lifted. Mob guys used that condition to open illegal after-hours clubs for homosexuals and lesbians. They had the juice with the cops and the muscle to protect their clients, who were often brutally victimized. One club like that, in Greenwich Village, was called the Stonewall. Every time a raid was to ensue, a call would come from the precinct. The only thing the sex squad ever found was a few guys from nearby Little Italy playing cards. That infuriated one police official. One night he launched a secret raid. All his frustration came out during the raid, and instead of just arresting everyone he had his men destroy the interior with axes: bar, walls, everything. That didn't sit well with the clientele or the neighbors of the club. For three days homosexuals, drag queens, transvestites, and lesbians rioted in the streets, throwing bricks at police cars and creating high profile mayhem. That three day disturbance became known as the "Stonewall Riots." It was the catalyst for the gay rights movement. The Gay Pride Parade each year celebrates the Stonewall Riots.

I could go on and on with anecdotes of how mob money bought privileges from law enforcement and politicians. This did not apply to the Feds for two reasons: 1) FBI Director J. Edgar Hoover was a homosexual being blackmailed by the mob with hidden photos taken in a Florida motel room, which made him deny the existence of organized crime (I am working on two separate biographies with relatives of Meyer Lansky and Vito Genovese, both of whom refer to the same Florida motel photos), and 2) there was a clear line between federal and state crimes, making it easy to dance on the state side where there was always someone to be bought). Handing a politician a bundle of money wrapped in brown paper and rubber bands made us feel like kings.

Those days are gone forever. Yes, I miss them. They were heady days and, in spite of the danger of losing my life or spending years in prison, of the stress of avoiding bullets and the law while trying to make a (dis)honest living, they were the best days of my life. But I stress to all young people contemplating a life of crime based on the past, THEY ARE GONE. There is no more neighborhood support for mobsters or widespread corruption at the street level. There's not even a sense of humor or a kick in the ass mentality in society today. One thing that breaks my heart is when I see sons or grandsons of my old pals going to prison for decades. I can almost see them sitting at my friends' knees, soaking up stories of our glory days, of the days when we were kings, without those war stories being qualified the way I've done today: that those days are history, just as the Wild West is. If we felt like kings at one time, we are kings in exile, left with little but friendship toward the few that survive...and memories. My advice to you young people who concern me so much: find a better way.

MOB BLOG #21:

Mob Wannabes

As someone who lived most of my life on the front lines of organized crime, trust me, guys, there's nothing left to wannabe. One of the things that really bother me is when I see the sons and grandsons of my friends going to prison. I know how it all began for them, listening to their elders relating "war stories" from the golden days of the mob. The stories were exciting, funny, and interesting, and the fact that it happened to Nonno, or Pop, or Dad made the youngsters say, "I want be like him." Their formerly innocent eyes would light up at tales of beatings, shootings, robberies, or court cases beat through bribery or chicanery. I know; I have bags full of those stories. The problem is that the older guys left out one essential part of each and every story: a preface that it was a very special time when these war stories occurred, and that it could never happen that way today.

Years ago, from the first waves of immigration, first from Ireland then later Italy and Eastern Europe, especially in big cities, there was minimum exposure for maximum profit. Crime was a way to get out of poverty with a small chance of going to prison, and, yes, a little bigger chance of winding up with lead poisoning, but, if you played by the rules and didn't get caught up in a political struggle, it was okay. Today, the paradigm has reversed itself. Now, it's maximum exposure for minimum profit. Sentences are especially high in Federal Courts that now judge cases that were never under federal jurisdiction. Conviction rates in those Districts are much higher than State convictions. For example, the Southern District of New York boasts a conviction rate like a body temperature, more than ninety-eight percent. Sentences today are meted out in decades not years, and instead of being eligible for parole at one-third and maxing out at two-thirds of that time, now it's a flat eighty-five percent.

To make the point better, let me give you some personal anecdotes. By far, the biggest asset and encouragement for young hoodlums years ago was that every area of law enforcement was open to bribery. At the social club where we hung out, Friday was Precinct Day. A black and white from the local precinct would pull up at the club, and a friend of mine would hand them a brown paper bag of money through the car window. Broad daylight. In return, we'd have inside information of warrants being issued so we could go on the lam, unless the cops were able to bury them so they never got found to be served. Remember, there were no computers. I was once released from jail pending charges, without bail having been posted. No one ever knew. Back to the cooperation of the authorities, if any of us wanted to open a crap or card game, or an after hours club, the precinct was the first call. If a raid was scheduled, we'd get a call to abandon the place before the cops arrived. Sweet, huh? Doesn't happen like that anymore.

On my first major pinch as a teen just beyond JD (*Juvenile Delinquent*) status, the cops were from the Boro Squad, a step up from the precinct guys we knew. One separated me from everyone in the house; brought me in the bedroom for a talk. As a JD, a talk meant being beaten around the head and shoulders by the officer. I braced myself to get hit, and totally ignored whatever the cop was saying. Oddly enough, I didn't get hit, but got dragged downtown and booked. Called the lawyer; couldn't wait for his praise about what a strong, standup kid I was; a few pats on the back at the club. Instead, when he arrived, his first words were, "You f _ _king moron!" Me? But, but... He continued, "This cop said he talked himself blue in the face, trying to get you to offer him money. He wanted to let you go." But, but... "You're an imbecile!" So went my glory.

Another time, I busted someone up over a car to car argument. I went on the lam while my friends tried to reach out for the guy who was hurt. They offered him a substantial amount of money to drop the charges. He was all for it, but his battle-axe wife wasn't. She insisted she wanted me to go to jail. What did we do? Gave the judge half the money we'd offered the other guy to drop the charges, which His Honor promptly did. Also bought my way out of a wild car chase involving a stolen car and three precincts chasing me. When they found out where I came from they saw dollar signs instead of an arrest. While they huddled, I hid money in my socks and underwear. The first thing they asked when they returned was how much money I had on me. I pulled my pockets inside out with the few hundred I had left in them. One snatched it without even counting then wrote a ticket instead of pulling me in. I waddled to the car, getting chafed from the major part of the money I started the night with.

We also had neighborhoods that protected us while we protected them. Clichés and stereotypes don't come from nothing. That the former has been applied to mob neighborhoods where residents could walk the streets safely at any hour of the day or night came from real relationships between its legitimate citizens and the local mob. I met an old Hispanic actor, Perry Lopez, a few years ago who told me that he had grown up in and around the Italian section of East Harlem during the Great Depression. He said he could still remember his mother waking him in the middle of the night and dragging him down to the local social club, where its members handed out part of whatever had "fallen off the truck" that day to local residents. He said that the gifts of food, clothing, and other items had kept his family going during those worst of times. On the other hand, I remember FBI Agents looking for me at my social club. I was a couple of doors away, playing pinochle in a luncheonette. The crowd watching the agents knew where I was, yet not one man, woman, or child would say a word. As soon as they left so did I...for Atlantic City until the problem could be straightened out.

Get it now? Today's a different era with conditions that don't encourage the kind of behavior we were able to get away with at that time. Sure, the war stories are great. The times were great. They were times of nightclubs, and restaurants, and beautiful girls; of junkets to a glamorous Las Vegas to see Sinatra, Martin, and Louis Prima live...all one hundred percent free. But those times are gone. There's nothing left to wannabe. Even if authorities are tempted to take a bribe, most are too afraid that you will rat them out. You young guys should enjoy the stories like you would stories of the old west...then go about life as if they both happened over a hundred years ago. For those of you out there who actually want to pursue the life, I love you guys. I love your spirit. Because there's a warm spot in my heart for young toughguys, I want to see you live your lives outside of prison walls, instead of inside. Do something else. Anything else. And for any of my old pals who might catch up with this blog, please guys give the young ones a chance. Tell them the stories because they are great. I love them myself. But make sure you let them know that our old glory days are gone...forever.

Good luck,

Sonny

P.S.

In keeping with the warning to wannabes about the best being a memory, here is a very personal memory of great days gone by. There was in the recent past a real mob culture that was rarely, if ever, seen by outsiders and little known today. Yes, there's the obvious dress, like in "Goodfellas" or "Casino" for the older generation and the Sergio Tacchini athletic suits and multiple oversized gold chains for the new wave of wannabes, or the Southern Italian fare that is served at the highly publicized restaurants of Mulberry Street or South Philly, and the songs of Sinatra that anyone who's ever turned on a radio or television knows. But there is a deeper culture, a very private inside one, that is more specific and goes to habits, foods, superstitions, and songs that have particular meaning to guys who have lived their lives on the edge – the last great generation of the mob, if you will. "Little Pal" is the most inside of all those songs. I don't know what the lyricist intended when he wrote it, or what Al Jolson thought when he popularized it early in the Twentieth Century, but Jimmy Roselli's version has been adopted by mob guys and adapted to their way of life, to the constant threat of leaving their loved ones, especially their children, for prison. Roselli's "Little Pal" is, in fact, the only real mob song.

My heart broke one night, when I sat alongside a dear friend as he sang "Little Pal" to his child, who was propped on his knee, as his own body was being ravaged by cancer. I sang it to my three year old the night before I left for prison the first time. "Little Pal" will always be special.

"LITTLE PAL"

Little Pal, if daddy goes away,

Promise you'll be good from day to day.

Do as mother says, and never sin.

Be the man your daddy might have been.

Your daddy didn't have an easy start,

So here's the wish that's dearest to my heart:

What I couldn't be, Little Pal,

I want you to be, Little Pal.

I want you to sing, to be happy and gay.

Be good to your mommy while your daddy's away.

Each night, how I pray, Little Pal,

That you'll turn out just right, my Little Pal.

And if some day, some day you should be,

On a new, a new daddy's knee,

Think about me, now and then, my Little Pal.

*   *   *   *

And so, till we meet again,

Heaven knows, knows where or when,

Think about me, now and then, Little Pal.

Pray for me, now and then, my Little Pal.

• "Little Pal" written by Al Jolson, B.G. De Sylva, Lew Brown and Ray Henderson

MOB BLOG #22:

Hollywood vs The Mob

Winners at Cannes are hits in Italy too

Published by mafia-news.com at 7:50 am under Movie

The mafia's allure

ROME — *This is the year of the mafia—at least at the box office.*

Two films on organized crime in Italy, each fact-based melodramas, took top prizes at the Cannes Film Festival in May and are drawing packed audiences here. The Italian movie industry was giddy over the double win.

"Gomorra," the film adaptation of a diary-like book by journalist Roberto Saviano that focuses on the Naples-based mob known as Camorra, took home Cannes' grand prize. "Il Divo," a film directed by Paolo Sorrentino, won the jury honor for its original portrayal and analysis of former Prime Minister Giulio Andreotti.

The 2008 article above illustrates one given: audiences respond very well to mob material. Of course, it helps if it is *good* mob material, not some of the garbage that passes for movies. That's a point discussed later. For now the question is: If audiences respond so well to mob material, why is it so hard to get mob projects made? The answer is the keyhole theory, that there is a huge audience out there for every genre, but to reach that audience projects must fight their way through a keyhole controlled by a bunch of executives who practice the religion of Groupthink, or Follow the Leader, or He's Smarter Than I Am So I'll Do Whatever He Does. Those execs who pray to the god of

Groupthink cower in their offices and desperately reach for salvation when mob or western projects come across their desks.

This religion is not new. When A-List director William A. Wellman wanted to do a mob movie he ran into a brick wall at Warner Brothers. "Not another mob movie," he was told by Jack Warner; there was nothing new in mob stories; audiences were tired of the mob; the writer was forty-two years old and had never done anything; yada, yada, yada. Wellman was insistent, and finally gave up his salary, with was huge for that time, for a back end deal. He attached Jimmy Cagney and Jean Harlow, and first time screenwriter's 1931 movie "Public Enemy" became legendary.

That is not an isolated case. Getting "Godfather" funded by Paramount was a long and bumpy ride for producers in spite of the fact that the novel was a huge best seller. If not for the pre-publicity from the publication the film would not have been made. It was just an offer Paramount couldn't refuse. Just recently, what is now a household word, "Sopranos," was turned down everywhere. David Chase has said that he was at the end of the road when he went to HBO; that everyone else had turned him down. I remember one of the stars of the show telling me at the very start, before a frame was shot, that he'd been cast in some show called "Sopranos," which was something about some mobsters and a priest. Who knew? Audiences. Who didn't know? Execs at all the network and cable stations that passed on the project.

I'm constantly contacted by someone or another who claims to have written a mob genre screenplay, and wants to get it made. First, on scripts in general, I gave a talk in front of screenwriters a few years ago, and my opening line was, "The most disappointing day of your life is the day you realize that quality doesn't mean anything." It's much, much worse when it comes to mob genre material.

Going back to the two Italian films that scored so well at Cannes, I realized a while ago that a true mob story might be much more salable than fiction. After all, the "Gotti" movie on HBO, starring Armand Assante, was an award winning success. I had been approached by family of former mob boss Joe Colombo to do a project. I jumped at the chance. I knew Joe, and marched with everyone at the FBI Building in New York, and attended the first Unity Day rally in Columbus Circle. Straight talk: there is no better true organized crime story in the latter part of the Twentieth Century than Joe's.

I hadn't written one word yet, when a friend who is a writer at a major magazine suggested I call a friend at Paramount, that he thought it was a hot property and shouldn't be shopped around. The conversation with the Paramount exec went something like this:

ME: *"Hi, I was told to call you by _____."*

EXEC: *"Oh, yes, _____. What can I do for you?"*

ME: *"I just got the rights to do a story on Joe Colombo."*

EXEC: *"Who's he?"*

ME: *"Did you ever hear of the Colombo Crime Family?"*

EXEC: *"Of course."* (with an incredulous tone)

ME: *"Do you think it was named after the yogurt?"*

Silence.

More silence.

ME: *"Hello?"*

EXEC: *"I don't think that's the kind of thing I want to do."*

Click.

When I'd finally written a screenplay to encompass the last fifteen turbulent months of Joe Colombo's active life, I sent it off to a producer friend who had done some big films. As a friend, he called me after having read it. His words to me were that it was another mob story, yada, yada, yada, but might appeal to him if...if...if it were done as a black comedy. I could only ask what part he thought was funny? The part where Joe got shot in the head?

Click.

That is only a couple of anecdotes from years of meetings with the top people in Hollywood; people who can green light projects. One precious response to my first novel, "Blood of Our Fathers," was from a network production company exec: "I didn't get a chance to read it, but I knew by the cover it was something I couldn't do." New Hollywood adage: *Never judge a book by its contents.*

Last year I had to fly to L.A. for a series of meetings for an interactive reality mob TV show. We met with producers in L.A. who had strong resumes of past and present reality shows. The meetings went great. Scheduled half-hour meetings turned into two hours or more. At one, someone there for a scheduled appointment was left sitting in the waiting area for nearly an hour. At the end of each, the producers would tell me that they were so fascinated by the material that they could talk to me for hours. I reminded them that audiences felt the same way. We left with my agent predicting we would have a bidding war for the show. They all passed.

Now, at this very moment, a reality TV producer from Hollywood is being kicked around by her inner circle compatriots at the networks and cable stations over a project she's done with yours truly. It developed when she ran into a mutual friend with the last name of Lansky, in L.A., at a dinner party. She confided that she wanted to do a reality mob show; he referred her to me. Young, smart, and confident, she flew to Florida and pitched her concept for a show to me. She wanted real retired mob guys for it, and asked if I could help. I picked up the phone, and within a couple of weeks had a reunion with pals from New York, Kansas City, Chicago, Boston, and Miami, all in L.A. All had prison records to validate them. All had retired for a number of years. *(Oh, they told you mob guys can't retire? Think of a ball team's injured list: inactive but still with the team. Same thing without the physical injury. Mental illness? Maybe).* Producer did a super job in putting together a four camera shoot then editing a fantastic four minute demo from nearly twelve hours of footage.

Time to sell.

Hot property. Big time reality TV production house with a number of shows on the air offered a firm deal. She passed because she'd never grown up in the streets and didn't think they offered her enough of a back end for us. I used to sell hijacked trucks full of merchandise for twenty percent *less* than the going hijack price, just to have my money under my pillow when I went to sleep. Old mob rule: A hundred percent of nothing is nothing. Anyway, buoyed by the great first response she got, she went off to her executive buddies at the networks and cable stations. Each and every one assured her that the show would be an audience favorite; that it was easy for it to create an audience buzz. Each passed. Audiences be damned. They were all worried about image, like no one outside of their little circles of gophers and other execs holds them in anything but the lowest esteem. They also worried about sponsors being attached to a mob project, like there were no sponsors for that "Growing up Gotti" abortion, or for those stations rerunning "Sopranos" episodes, or even "Mob Wives." Down but not out, my producer-partner, now nicknamed "Godmother," takes on the challenge of a new round of pitch meetings. Like David Chase we only need one. Like Clint Eastwood, we may have to take it to Italy, which, as you saw in the beginning of this article, loves mob stuff.

Now, a couple of proposals directly from the mouths of Hollywood geniuses.

First, a few years ago I was recommended to call a VP of a big name reality TV production company, who told my friend that he wanted to do a mob reality show. After introducing myself, the conversation went something like this:

 ME: *"I have a reality show that you might like."*

EXEC: *"We have our own idea of what we want."*

ME: *"Okay, what is it?"*

EXEC: *"We'd like you to find a mob guy on the run from the law, who we could follow around with a camera."*

ME: *"Okay. So you want me to become an accessory to a fugitive from justice, so I can get pinched when it's all over?"*

EXEC: *"Well, we can turn him in at the end."*

ME: *"So let me get this straight. First I become an accessory to a fugitive from justice then I become a rat, so I get killed when I go to prison,"* I said. *"Are all of you out of your f__in' minds out there?"*

Click.

Time passed, and a couple of years later I got an excited phone call from a producer aligned with another A-List reality production company. This time the call went like this:

PROD: *"I think we've got a deal. The company wants to do this show, and if you can put it together we'll get to shoot a demo on their dime."*

ME: *"Okay, what is it?"*

PROD: *"They want to put you and your guys together with a real crime scene cleanup crew. The catch phrase for the show would be, 'They used to commit the crimes; now they're cleaning them up."*

ME: *"If they want to humiliate us that badly, tell them to set up a camera in a room, and when we enter just hit us with baseball bats."* I went on to say that neither I nor any of my friends will give up our dignity for money; that I was sure there are guys out there who would, but not us. I ended by asking why anyone would tune in after the first show; just to see us clean up shit and blood and broken glass? Just for the catch phrase?

Click.

Both of those incidents are real and accurately reported.

Am I bitching and moaning? Some. The rest is a message to all my pals out there, even those I haven't met yet, who have a mob project that they believe is the best thing since tapered boxer shorts, that their road is not just uphill, but nearly straight up an oil slick wall with spikes at the top. All I can say, from the heart, is: "Good luck.

MOB SNAPSHOTS

Mob Snapshot #1:

Pretty Amberg

Think of the ugliest person you know...someone whose face would scare the life out of you if you met him on a dark street. Someone whose face would scare you into sobriety if you saw it while your alcohol level was elevated. Would you call him Pretty? Just like when a huge person is nicknamed Tiny, short and looks-challenged Louis Amberg was dubbed Pretty by those unfortunate to know him. When an inebriated in a speakeasy one night during Prohibition, Mayor Jimmy Walker saw Amberg, who had once been offered a job with the circus to be billed as a missing link, he instantly swore off booze.

Pointy-eared, beady-eyed, mole ridden and scarred Pretty Amberg was as mean as he was ugly. He was nasty to strangers, sometimes knocking plates off their tables as he walked through a restaurant, telling them to order different food. Everyone hated Pretty, who was known to leave his murder victims, estimated to surpass one hundred, in laundry bags mostly on Brownsville, Brooklyn streets.

Mobsters, trying to keep order in their new form of organized crime after having murdered dozens of "Moustache Petes" in the second "Night of the Vespers." Tough as nails Amberg was a loose cannon who threatened other criminals and killed connected gangsters without consulting higher ups. He did "work" for Murder Incorporated, but was not officially part of that group. He was given money from Abe "Kid Twist" Reles in a beef where he was obviously wrong because mediators Bugsy Siegel, Joe Adonis, and Albert Anastasia wanted to lull him into a place where he would trust them when they called. Unwittingly, he was tied to Dutch Schultz in a more profound way than he ever imagined. Once, when Schultz teasingly threatened to open a craps game directly across the street from Pretty's, the latter told Dutch to put a gun into his own mouth and see how many times he could fire it. He said that would be a better end than messing with him. It turned out that Pretty met his end on the same night that Lucky Luciano's men murdered Dutch Schultz at the Palace Chop House, in New Jersey, for insisting he would murder New York District Attorney Thomas Dewey despite orders from Lucky to drop the issue. Murder Incorporated members lured Pretty Amberg to a garage where, so fearful that he might survive their murder plot, they shot him, practically skinned him, chopped his limbs off, and burned him. Yes, everyone hated Pretty Amberg.

Mob Snapshot #2:

Night of the Vespers

From about 1880 to 1920, approximately four million Southern Italians migrated to the U.S. With them came a cultural phenomenon known as the Mafia or the Black Hand. While all immigrant groups had formed criminal gangs when they arrived to serve as a vehicle to lift them out of poverty, to the Italians, especially those from Sicily, it was a way of life. There had been a thousand years or more of their island, which lay seductively at the crossroads of the Mediterranean, being subjugated by foreign powers passing by. At various times Sicily was run by Spanish, French, Greeks, Spanish, even North African Moors. Most of the conquerors didn't even bother to learn to speak Sicilian, so there was no legal redress for the natives, so a sub-rosa government was formed, known today as the Mafia. As a government, they needed funds, and those "taxes" were gathered by kidnapping, extortion, and more.

That tradition came to America with those Southern Italians looking for "streets paved with gold." They did not find gold, but they did find some of the same conditions they had left, namely a government run by those who did not speak their language. For justice, they once again turned to Sicilian criminals who had made the voyage as well. Sicilian gangs were broken down into sub-groups from individual provinces and towns who fought bloody wars for local supremacy. In New York, the two main rivals were "Joe the Boss" Masseria, a low-class thug, and Salvatore Maranzano, who fashioned himself after an ancient Roman Caesar. Maranzano loved fine clothes, fine food, poetry, opera, and power. Those old style Sicilians, dubbed "Moustache Petes" because of their traditional handlebar moustaches, took umbrage easily, refused to deal with non-Sicilians, and kept heavy hands in the pockets of their underlings.

In 1283, Sicilians had driven out the Bourbon French at the ringing of the Easter Vesper bells. It was known as the "Night of the Sicilian Vespers." Seven centuries later, after a number of meetings of younger, Americanized gangsters who put profit above petty grievances and ethnic purity, like Lucky Luciano, Frank Costello, Vito Genovese, Bugsy Siegel, and Meyer Lansky, a second "Night of the Vespers" against "Moustache Petes" across the country was executed. From September 10̄11, 1931, more than sixty old timers across the country were assassinated. Today, some authorities dispute that the event happened because they do not have that many reported murders for those dates. What they miss is that many of their families were here illegally and, even if they were, as a cultural tradition they would not deal with police and report the crimes. I know of one old man, now deceased, who was shot on that night but survived. He begged to retire instead of being killed and was granted that request. Little Davey Betillo, who went to prison with Lucky Luciano for prostitution, said he was sent out of town to kill a Sicilian boss. A young man who looked much younger at the time, he shined shoes outside the boss's headquarters until the boss himself stepped up for a shine. Davey pulled a pistol out of his shine box and shot the man dead.

That bloody forty-eight hours ushered in a new, American version of organized crime, run by those who planned it, and has survived way beyond its time until its present demise.

Mob Snapshot #3:

There is No Mafia

One day a while ago, I logged in to my favorite organized crime news site. Okay, I'm still interested in crime. I don't commit them any more, but since I do write about it and am called to shows as an expert on the subject, I like to keep up. A lot of what I say and write is from first hand experience; the rest is common sense. For example, Bill O'Reilly had me on "The Factor" as an expert in, of all things, assassinations, when they were looking for Chandra Levy, and suspected Congressman Gary Condit of having gotten rid of the girl's body. In a pre-interview, O'Reilly asked if I thought Condit had really made her disappear. I said, "This guy couldn't get rid of a watch box without getting caught. How do you expect him to get rid of a 110 lb girl?" That was common sense. O'Reilly thought so too. He introduced me on the show by saying, "I know he couldn't get rid of a watch box without getting caught..." Stole my line.

Back to the aforementioned site I logged on to, the headline read, "Korean Mafia member arrested in Manila." KOREAN MAFIA?!! There is no such thing as a Korean Mafia, a Russian Mafia, or a Scandinavian Mafia. Yes, there are criminal groups in all those places, but outside of Sicily there is no Mafia. The Italians know that. Calabrians have *N'drangheta*, Neapolitans named their group *Camorra*, the latter of which at some point founded *Sacra Corona Unita* in Puglia. Let the Koreans, Russians, and Scandinavians get their own goddamn names. Why don't the Koreans have a Korean Yakuza? They're certainly closer to Tokyo than they are to Palermo.

Sicilians have worked for centuries to develop their Mafia, which is more than just a criminal fraternity. Mafiosi have entwined themselves in the business, politics, and general life of Sicily. They have run major legal international businesses, helped the Allied invasion in WWII, and been elected to important government posts. They are administrators of hospitals and have worked closely with the Vatican. Don't they have a right to exclusivity of their name, and not to have themselves used as an umbrella for worldwide groups made up of nothing but thugs? Would the media call all terrorists Al Qaeda or Skinheads? The Icelandic Al Qaeda? The Somalian Skinheads? Each of those groups gets to keep its own name, why not give the Mafia the same consideration?

While we're at it, surprise, surprise: there's no Cosa Nostra...or, at least, there shouldn't be. I am proudly old enough (*many of my friends never made it this far*) to remember a time before Joe Valachi. I also remember hearing the term *cosa nostra*, but it was with lower case letters, as in, "This thing of ours...this thing that has no name." Then came Valachi, an illiterate half-moron, who told the world that this generic phrase of confusion was a proper noun...and they believed him. Suddenly capital letters were thrown on it, and it became "La Cosa Nostra," and the American version of the Sicilian Mafia *(at least he gave it a different name...though writers call it, "La Cosa Nostra, the American Mafia.")*. The worst part is that not only did civilians get taken in by this stumbum, but so did mobsters themselves. Thirty years later, no less than John Gotti was recorded saying, *"This will be a Cosa Nostra till I die,"* or something like that. A *Cosa Nostra?* A thing of ours? That's almost as bad as the Jersey wiseguy who had his guys commandeer the jukebox in a diner he scheduled meetings at, and play the Godfather theme all the time he was there. Good grief! No wonder organized crime is fast becoming history, leaving only chaotic, violent crime in its wake.

On behalf of Sicilian Mafiosi, who I don't even know, stop committing copyright infringement and calling those criminal groups from Brazil, Uganda, or Romania "Mafia." Yo, crooks, get your own damned name.

Mob Snapshot #4:

A Moll Can Be More Than a Moll

Moll [*commare* in Italian] (n) – A gangster's girlfriend (*Merriam-Webster Dictionary*)

It's no secret that females have always been attracted to mobsters. Anyone who visits a nightclub or restaurant where mob guys hang out will see the hens flock around those criminal roosters. And why not? Mobsters usually have great cars and clothing, have disposable cash, have plenty of spare time to entertain in and out of the bedroom, and, most of all bring an aura of daring and violence that women find vicariously thrilling. For those who haven't been around the mob, take my word for it. As a young man, I hooked up with females who went with me because they mistook me for my boss, wives of legitimate guys whose husbands had bragged about their mobster pal, and two or three who'd ignored me till they saw me in a fight or getting pinched. Flash and money are big, but take second place to raw animal violence when it comes to those women who go with mobsters.

Oddly, Southern Italian females have taken it a step further, actually becoming mobsters themselves. I never thought I'd see the day, but there is solid documentation that Camorra, the Neapolitan Mafia, has many women running various families. A *madrina* (godmother) may even have a nickname, like *a' masculona* (tomboy), *la gattona* (fat she-cat), or *pupetta* (little doll). And they kill as well as order killings.

Why so prevalent within the Neapolitan Camorra and not the Sicilian Mafia? It goes to the inherent differences of the organizations. While the Sicilians have a long time organization that chooses men by birth or deed to become *Un uomo d'onore*, or "a man of honor," and join a Mafia Family, the *Camorra*, and in fact the Calabrese version, *N'drangheta*, form their membership entirely from within blood and extended families. That tradition of inducting sons and son-in-laws, cousins and nephews, and brothers and brother-in-laws also accounts for the much lower rate of *pentiti*, or turncoats who testify against *la famiglia* in court. It is a natural extension of that belief in trusting only family members that females whose husbands or sons have been murdered or imprisoned would step into their places. It is also natural that these women, having borne centuries of being regarded as second class citizens would bring an added measure of toughness and viciousness to the job. They kill as well as order killings.

To prove the point, see the article below. Thought I'd never live to see this one, but I guess if you live long enough you see everything. I thought Jackie Collins' novel, "Lucky," was ridiculous and laughed at Sopranos when they brought in a beautiful Mafia boss from Sicily. I admit now that they saw more than I did, being too close to mob life here. This story illustrates how right they were:

Mafia Donnas

04. 11. 09. - 18:00

Austrian Times

Ruthless Godmothers are taking over Cosa Nostra clans after a massive campaign by anti-Mafia cops put most male Dons in jail.

Police in Alcamo, Sicily, this week arrested a jailed Godather's wife and her top henchwoman who were running the gang even more viciously than her husband.

Boss's wife Anna Maria Accurso, 46, and her lieutenant Anna Greco, 49, ran a 1 million-a-month extortion racket until their arrest.

Police found dozens of guns, bombs and other weapons and also arrested nine other male members of the gang.

Palermo anti-Mafia police chief Teresa Principato said: "The number of women involved in the Cosa Nostra is increasing more and more and their role is very important.

"Today the women of Cosa Nostra are essential for running their protection businesses."

"They are even worse than the men. Not only are they more vicious, they stick together and don't waste their time stabbing each other in the back," added one officer.

If I had to make an educated guess, I would say that this Southern Italian trend among criminal groups will not make its way to America any time soon. Relax guys. Just don't introduce your molls to Lorena Bobbit.

Sonny Girard

Mob Snapshot #5:

A Kiss is Just a Kiss

I never kissed a man as a boy growing up...not even my father. It just wasn't something that was done, or something that was done in private. (*Good grief, no!*) Women kissed. They kissed each other, they kissed us kids, they just kissed, and it was okay...that is unless it was the elders, grandmas and other extended family oldsters whose kisses sent us running for towels and into hiding for the rest of the visit. Outside of family, we were more likely to get punches than smooches; fighting being a way of life in the poorest sections of Brooklyn. Generally, among more civilized adult males, greetings were limited to handshakes; a two handed shake showed true affection.

Then I changed my social status. I became a gangster in training (GIT). Suddenly, I found myself surrounded by men who kissed men on the cheek upon arriving and departing. Those who occasionally visited from Italy, or were recently-arrived residents from the other side, kissed on both cheeks. At first, it looked strange...very strange...especially since as a new kid on the block, none of those men I considered superiors, kissed me. I brushed my teeth, had smoothly shaved cheeks, and wore cologne, and still nobody in our crowd found me worthy of a peck on the cheek. I was still a newbie, and wondered what I had to do to step up to the kissing rung on the ladder. The kisses first came from other GITs, who copied our mentors. Then, of course, the kisses came from those we idolized, as we sort of proved ourselves worthy.

In time, the kiss became comedy for me. When things got legally hot for us a dictum was handed down by our executives (*we didn't know who actually issued it*). The new word was that our smooches made us stand our too much and made us too easy for law enforcement to identify. Up until then, we liked the attention outsiders gave us upon recognizing our kissing status.   Now, we had to shake hands like everyone else. Now, some guys got angry if you bent to kiss them on the cheek, almost as if you were painting a bullseye on their cheeks. As things cooled, we got another official message that it was okay to kiss again. I have to admit that caused a little confusion. Two of us would meet, shake hands, move toward a kiss then stop as our cranial computers tried to figure out what the latest rule was.

Little did we know the brilliance of our bosses allowing us to kiss once more in public. We were not privy to the master plan: the mob was now going to have everyone kiss. Look around you today. Guys with pen protectors in their shirt pockets and adhesive tape holding their eyeglasses together are man-hugging and kissing when they meet each other (Many look like they'd be less comfortable doing the same with a female). That was the brilliance of our mob bosses: kissing camouflage. So, the next time you see two men greet each other with a peck on the cheek, or if you are one of those participating in that kiss, remember you are following a style set for you by top mobsters of years gone by.

Mob Snapshot #6:

The Really Good Old Days

When we talk about organized crime or its mobsters, it's almost always in negative terms. That's understandable, but there's another side, good that has been done by mob guys *because* of the power attained through the darker side of their lives. I started thinking about this when I tried to do a favor for an old friend, who happened to be my barber for decades. When he thanked me, I told him that it was why another friend, an alleged highly placed mobster, had told me earlier that day that he wouldn't even talk to any guy in the life who was under fifty or sixty years old. It wasn't just that they couldn't be trusted, but, as he said, "They have no understanding about what the life is really about." I told him that it was about friends helping friends. No obligations; no owesies; just friends.

The incident made me think back to some of the things my old pals said...and did. I remember a guy I loved...smart, tough, and funny...Funzi Mosca. One day, when he reminisced about his early days, he told me that when he grew up, in his inner city neighborhood, someone in each family had to enter the mob to "put an umbrella" over family and friends. "In my family, it was me," he said. "Because of my position, my brother was able to build a great legitimate business and raise a family without ever looking over his shoulder or wondering when a knock on the door would come and he'd have to go to jail."

That was the way we were all brought up in the past. It was one of the things I loved. There came a day when I had to settle a gambling obligation my father had accumulated with a couple of bookmakers. The deal I made ended with a promise that if they allowed him to gamble again they would get nothing. It was the first time I was able to use influence for good that I'd won in battle. But, then, I had a great teacher. Our headquarters was in a poor neighborhood of Brooklyn that had gone from mostly Italian to primarily Puerto Rican. Every Thanksgiving, my guy would have a truck full of turkeys brought to the block. The doors would swing open and we would all hand out turkeys to the neighborhood residents, who had quickly surrounded us. No one in our neighborhood, poor or not, wasn't going to celebrate the holiday. Some of our guys actually ran into a burning building and rescued a family. They made the papers for their heroism, but they'd never thought of that when they were skipping around the flames to save a mother and her children. Toughguy is as toughguy does.

Having been brought up in that classroom, I tried to follow that for the rest of my life, even as my guy had passed on and we split up to regroup under different stars of the same flag. Once, I had a guy who owed me money, who I saw sitting on the steps of his house, head in hands. When I stopped the car and questioned him, he said the pressure of having no money since he lost his job had gotten to him and he'd smacked his wife and put his fist through a glass door. Even though he hadn't paid me a dime since he'd been laid off, after a lecture about hitting women, I drove him to the nearest pork store and had them fill two large bags with provisions for him to bring to his family. I also bought a wagon for him and put him into business in lower Manhattan, where he made more money than he had made on the job he'd lost. Unfortunately, bad habits being what they are, he had dealings with other mob guys, and at some point, caught in some crime or other, became a government witness against all the guys he dealt with...except me. There's also the "no good deed goes unpunished" side, where I was arrested for hurting someone who was shaking down a legitimate business friend and a jail sentence for becoming part of a RICO conspiracy when I defended a borrower from shylocks at a meeting that was bugged. Win some; lose some.

The most telling example of the better side of a life on the dark side was told to me by an actor in L.A., Perry Lopez. Perry grew up in an area that was turning from Italian Harlem to Spanish Harlem during the Depression. He told me that when he was a child, his mother would wake him up sometimes at night and drag him down to the local social club, where the local hoodlums would disperse the contents of trucks they'd surely hijacked to the neighborhood residents. It could be food, pillows, or anything the nimble thieves had gotten away with. He said to me, "Without them, I don't know how we would have gotten through that terrible time." Well said.

This article is not meant to glorify the old mob days. It's meant to show that mob life in the past was not all about blacks and whites, but various shades of grey. Those grey areas are missing from today's bastardized version of what traditional organized crime used to be. Somewhere the threads of crime and honor that were so intertwined became separated, and the latter was mistakenly discarded. It's why the mob has become a pariah to all. It's because there are no more of the "good" old days guys like me were lucky enough to share with others.

Sonny Girard

Mob Snapshot #7:

Mob Movies We Love: Across 110th Street

This 1972 film has special meaning for me because, in spite of some of its production cheesiness, it presents an accurate portrayal of underworld social change I lived through in New York at that time. In the movie, black gunmen rob a mob bank, kill a couple of mobsters (*including a young Burt Young in a non-speaking role*), and murder a couple of cops during their escape. Both the mob and detectives are after them.

Along the way, we discover an old school, rough-em-up, police captain on the take (*Anthony Quinn*) and a younger, more modernized and idealist lieutenant (*Yaphet Kotto*) who wants his job. That transition was an important one that was actually launched by the Knapp Commission that surrounded the testimony of Frank Serpico, later played by Al Pacino in "Serpico," but is not the one that struck me as closely (*though I did get arrested for bribery twice after cops pulled their money grubbing hands back after Knapp*).

During the previous years, blacks in areas like Harlem, Bed-Sty, or the South Bronx were underlings to traditional organized crime guys. What's more, they operated in fear of the mobsters. I had one black runner in Bed-Sty who told me that when someone was slow paying he'd threaten them with, "*Don't make me call the white man.*" I did a favor collecting a loan in a Harlem tenement by banging on the debtor's door with a .38 revolver. Other doors opened, but shut even more quickly. Pals and I commonly hung out in places like the Blue Book and Baby Grand, in Harlem, or Town Hill, in Brooklyn, and were treated like royalty.

But then things started to change, and Tony Franciosa as the local mob boss's inept son-in-law assigned to exact revenge on the black thieves accurately highlights the subtle change that had begun a couple of years before. Average blacks were beginning to feel empowered by vastly different movements like the Black Panthers and Martin Luther King. Little by little the welcome attitude became less welcome; we began to feel less comfortable in the old Harlem haunts. Fewer blacks wanted to work for us, preferring to find black criminal leaders of their own. When we staged a small fair in a Harlem park, a gang of youths challenged us to either pay them extortion money or close up. We had two choices: shoot it out with them or put a call in to a Black Muslim leader who we'd done legitimate business with before...we had arranged for an extremely large amount of whiting for them to buy for their holiday. Once those gentlemen arrived the gang fearfully and quietly dispersed. Black Muslims at that time were known for disciplinary violence that rivaled ours. We decided to wrap it up there, and never even considered another Harlem operation.

The film loads up enough murders, shootouts, and mayhem to entertain anyone who loves the genre. At the end, the local black crime leader, who had been subservient to white mobsters in the past and resented the brash young Franciosa, "cops a sneak" and has him murdered. To me it was symbolic of the change I felt and very personal. Because of that, "Across 110th Street" is a movie we love.

Mob Snapshot #8:

The Jewish Mobs

There's no way to talk about the mob and not talk about the Jewish mobs of the first half of the Twentieth Century. Like the Nineteenth Century Irish immigrants before them, some immigrant Jews fought their way out of the ghetto and poverty by turning to lives of crime. It's easy to forget the powerful Jewish mobsters because, like the previously mentioned Irish, Jews viewed crime as a vehicle to take them from poverty to affluence...and out. Most Jewish mobsters sent their sons on to become doctors, lawyers, and businessmen. Ian Schrager, for example, of Studio 54 fame, or infamy, and current luxury hotel owner, is the son of the late Max "The Jew" Schrager, Meyer Lansky's gambling czar in Williamsburg, Brooklyn. Max was a big numbers banker. Ian went to law school. While Italians were handing mobdom down from generation to generation, Jewish mobs disappeared, their descendents melding into the mainstream fabric of America.

Burton Turkus and Sid Feder's book, "Murder, Inc.," is a wonderful look at one of the most vicious bands of primarily Jewish gangsters ever. It relates, based on the testimony of Murder Incorporated member-turned-stoolpigeon, Abe "Kid Twist" Reles, a visceral account of personalities and events within the gang. Reles was, however, a pigeon who couldn't fly, and was found smashed on the ground below the hotel room (*See my "Rat Squad" slide show on www.SonnysMobCafe.com to view Reles' end*) where he was being protected by New York's <u>finest</u>? The book is also a colorful picture of an era long gone. Moreover, it clearly highlights the heyday of organized crime by illustrating its expansiveness during the era following Prohibition, when it could use its money and muscle to control production and distribution in the garment, baking, and fur industries, to name a few. The chapter on Lepke is priceless.

One of the great pleasures I had growing up was to sit and talk with the old timers, guys who had been around during the glory days of the mob. Generally, they all regarded Albert Anastasia as the most dangerous man they'd ever met. It was said that when Albert would squint at you through the smoke of the cigarette that dangled straight down from his lips your blood would run cold. It was also agreed that, pound for pound, the toughest guy they had ever met was Lepke. Louis Buchalter: "Lepke" to his friends. "The Judge" to most of the underworld.

Lepke was the guy who ran Murder Incorporated for Albert Anastasia. Not Meyer Lansky or Bugsy Siegel, who were connected to Lucky Luciano's family, which later became known as the Genovese Family. Anastasia's family later became known as the Gambino Family. And Lepke headed up a Jewish subgroup of that latter family that centered in Brownsville, Brooklyn, and whose members killed as easily as downing kosher hot dogs and potato knishes. It was ripe with deadly but colorful characters, like "Kid Twist" Reles, "Pittsburgh Phil" Strauss, and "Pretty" Amberg, whose signature was to leave the corpses of his victims in the streets of Brownsville in laundry bags. And, who did they answer to? Lepke.

The book is also interesting for things it is missing; information that may not have been known at the time of its writing (*1951*), but made its way through an oral running history of the mob that finally got to my ears. An exceptionally interesting chapter of the book relates the downfall of Waxey Gordon after a jail term for income tax evasion. Most interesting is how that felony conviction came about, with Lucky Luciano and Meyer Lansky sending the latter's brother, Jake, to the Feds with the damning evidence against Gordon in order to short circuit the escalating "War of the Jews." Rats? There's no little bit pregnant, but it was a hell of a lot more subtle than those mobsters rolling over today.

Mob Snapshot #9:

Where in the World is Jimmy Hoffa?

Saw one day that FBI Director, Robert Mueller promised to solve the Jimmy Hoffa mystery. My first reaction was, "Who, other than family, gives a flying f _ _ k? I'm more interested in someone squeezing into a scuba outfit and searching for Luca Brasi. Then I remembered how many people had been burned by the Hoffa disappearance, how much speculation there has been over the years, and how much money has been made by it. Over those same years, I've done a number of shows in which I was asked about the disappearance. Not having been a participant, I figured I'd recount some of those questions and some of what I've learned over the years...second hand, of course.

The first experience I had with the Hoffa thing was with a guy I had been introduced to by friends in the street then met again in prison. When I first met the older Jewish gentleman, who was the accountant for the Teamsters, he rode around in a chauffeured limo, and DECLARED three million dollars a year in earnings. Nice guy; down to earth; no gangster. When I met him again, in prison, he was a man who showed me more strength than I'd ever thought he had. He had been charged with a minor tax violation and sentenced to TWENTY YEARS to try to get him to roll over against Hoffa's successor, Frank Fitzsimmons and his guys. Sixty Minutes did a story about how the old man had been railroaded, but to no avail. The Government wanted to solve the Hoffa case, and didn't care who they buried to do it. A while later, this man's partner, Alan Dorfman, was murdered. Guess he wasn't as strong.

Some time later, I got calls for interviews because some nut job had sold Bob Guccione a story about Hoffa being buried under Giant Stadium. Did I think it was possible? My answer to them all was in the form of a simple question, and went pretty much like this:

"Let's say you killed a guy in Michigan. What would you do? Would you do a real version of 'Weekend at Bernie's' and drive around the country with him, or would you want to get clear of the body as soon as possible?"

Each host sort of stammered; said they never thought of it that way; and eventually settled on the latter.

"There's your answer," I'd say then chat about some other crime topic.

Later on, Hoffa's aide and sometimes driver admitted to the murder on his deathbed, to a lawyer he couldn't afford, for a book that would pay the lawyer and leave money for his family. Hmmm? Suspect situation for a confession? I'd admit to killing JFK, RFK, and MLK if I could leave money for my kids when I die. Okay, Marilyn Monroe too if they pay. Why am I so sure the driver is full of crap? Because I knew someone who recently passed away who used to drive the driver around long after Hoffa disappeared. No way, he said. The other guy had committed many crimes...he knew where the skeletons were...but Hoffa wasn't one of them. Had he driven Hoffa to the spot? Maybe. But he was not the shooter; did not leave a hot pistol WITH the cadaver (*and his fingerprints*) for others to dispose of. I read the account and found it laughable. Guys responsible are now all dead, a couple from natural causes, one shot in Little Italy.

What probably happened that day was that Hoffa was murdered then brought to a pre-dug grave as close to the murder scene as possible, dumped in with enough quicklime to dissolve titanium, and covered up. A few months later, plants were growing over him. A second choice would be crushed in a car, but that would mean letting another conspirator in on too important a hit. Weighted down with chicken wire and chains and dumped in Lake Michigan? Could be, but I like the quicklime better. It's closer, faster, and generally performed in an extremely secluded spot.

So, given a choice, I'd prefer losing a few pounds, slipping into a wetsuit, and searching for Luca Brasi...preferably in the Caribbean. Director Mueller, wanna fund an investigation?

Mob Snapshot #10:

The Last of the Real Men is Gone

One day I received the news that Anthony Spero had died. Spero was reputed to be a top executive of the Bonnano Family, one of New York's five organized crime families. He spent most of the last seven years of his life in super-max conditions in federal prison, in solitary confinement twenty-three hours a day, with no fresh air and no company. His conviction was based on circumstantial evidence, testimony of one lowlife looking for a deal, and the weight of the Federal Government. "The UNITED STATES OF AMERICA vs Anthony Spero." Try and beat that. He was treated no differently that Osama bin Laden would if he were captured and confined. Spero was 79 years old when he died; only 72 when he began his sub-human confinement.

When I heard the news, I called an old and dear friend, who had also known Spero. He said: *"The last of the real men is gone."*

Hopefully, he was wrong; that there are a few, admittedly very few, still around. For how long? Not too much longer, to be sure, since they are practically all have passed the half-century mark and most are approaching or are already in old age. That made me reflect on why that statement, if not entirely true, was close enough to true.

Environment makes tough guys. Spero was born just as the Great Depression (the old one) began. He grew up in a poor but tough neighborhood, where loyalty was a greater value than instant gratification; where that loyalty was bred by having to depend on others to survive; where friends were family; where biological family was closely intertwined with other biological families; where neighbors were family. Forget for the moment the physical threat of becoming a rat. How would a rat face those he knew from the neighborhood? How would his kids have felt at school, when the kids of others his father had sent to prison would have to see him every day? How would his wife have handled going to the local grocery or beauty parlor or church? Cousins. In-laws. Parents and grandparents, who, even if they were not mob connected, would not understand why their loved one had sunk so low. Spero was not unusual in being willing to suffer for someone else. He was unusual in that his inner strength and resolve would mark him as a leader of men...all the way till his last breath.

Things are different today. Inner cities no longer have ethnic white ghettos that spawned the strongest mob figures of the past. No more Meyer Lanskys or Bugs Morans or Albert Anastasias...or Anthony Speros. Today, wannabe gangsters grow up in mostly isolated conditions. They never need anyone else to survive so they have no deep seeded loyalty to anyone. They are part of a modern culture that is self-absorbed, self-indulgent, misogynistic, and superficial. They can be heartless; beat someone up, even kill them. They really believe they're toughguys. But, when the MTV and Face Book are taken from them, and they wonder who their girlfriends are having sex with, and they alone have to face hardened criminals who will take a shot at turning them into girls, they roll over and trade someone else's freedom for their own. A former partner of mine used to say that everyone is a toughguy as long as the shoe fits; it's when the laces get tight that you see who screams. Today, there's a cacophony coming from the mob. The difference between today's wannabes who talk the talk and yesterday's who really became and walked the walk, guys like Anthony Spero, is clear enough.

A mutual friend of Spero's and mine used to visit him in prison. He was obviously much closer than I was, as I only knew Spero peripherally, engaging in some conversation when I was at the Bath Avenue social club to spend time with a cousin through marriage who was extremely close to him. This celebrity friend was incensed over Spero's trial and conviction, which he still considers a railroad job by the federal government's misuse of power. He offered many times to interview and pay for new lawyers to appeal the conviction. Spero was always explain to him in a fatherly way to put it to rest, that there was no hope to win an appeal; that it would take to long in the system and that ultimately, as he put it, "They all get their paychecks from the same place." Instead of whining about his conditions, he would assure our mutual friend that he was fine; that it wasn't all that bad. How bad is bad? For the last of the real men, nothing could be that bad. I'm reminded of Gene Wilder in the film "Stir Crazy," when he's subjected to various punishments to get him to succumb to the warden's will over a sporting contest. When they open the dark, dank underground "hole" that they've kept him in, he squints at the sudden light then asks if they could leave him there some more. I will always think of that when I think of Spero; when I picture him in his less than fashionable outfits and his staid expression; when I see him in that Bath Beach social club, with it's nicotine-stained ceilings and felt-covered card tables; with its crew of toughguys and hanger-ons, bookmakers and thugs, old men playing pinochle and younger ones waiting for a pat on the head from Spero, "Paulie Zach," or "Jimmy Brown."

R.I.P. Anthony Spero

Sonny Girard

Mob Snapshot #11:

Frank "Funzouale" Tieri

For a period of time in the 1970s, you could not get Pellegrino water, Perrier, or Saratoga water in any Italian restaurant from Little Italy to Bensonhurst. The only *aqua minerale* available was Bella Donna, which tasted as if a dirty mop had been wrung out into its source. Jokes were made about its unpleasant taste, but there were also whispers; words of explanation of why it was the only accompaniment for otherwise good food: *"It belongs to Funzouale."*

Alphonse Frank "Funzouale" Tieri was the latest street boss of the Genovese Family, having been anointed after his predecessor "Tommy Ryan" Eboli had died of lead poisoning, not from paint but bullets. Funzouale was an older, quieter mob leader in the style of his good friend and boss of another crew, Carlo Gambino. His personal style, however, was different, as he wore custom clothing and could be seen regularly up and down Mulberry Street, sipping espresso at Café Napoli or schmoozing with those diamond and gold purveyors under his command at the jewelry center at 74 Bowery. He could also be seen strolling along Bensonhurt's Bay Parkway, stopping into Alley's or George Richland's men's shops, or on 65th Street in the original Sbarro's and across the street at Cangiano's Pork Store. Funzouale was well liked, well respected, and feared.

What made him feared was not a violent temper like Tommy Ryan (*when he was a fight manager, Ryan once punched out a referee when he thought his fighter got a bad decision*). What made Funzouale feared was his Machiavellian-like reputation. He had one of his captains murdered. Once that was accomplished, it dawned on him that he hadn't a clue where all the money and businesses this top earner had.

The only one who might be able to draw him a treasure map was an associate of his departed underling. Instead of working over the deceased captain's man, who claimed he didn't know where any of the treasure Funzouale sought was, the old man brought him closer into the fold, elevating him to a position as his occasional private chauffeur. One Gambino wiseguy who didn't understand what was going on, nearly went through the roof of his Bath Beach social club. The sometimes Genovese boss's chauffeur he said, was a rat, who threatened to go to the District Attorney when they were at a sitdown to settle a Gambino-Genovese beef over someone who had given him a bad check in his construction business. None of that seemed to matter to Funzouale, as it is unthinkable that a Gambino higher up didn't approach him with the story. A year or so later, Funzouale shocked everyone by dispensing goodfella status on his newfound buddy and sometimes driver. With that done, he told the newly made wiseguy that since they were now bound by a blood oath he should share the treasure map he had etched in his brain. Once the man did, Funzouale had him murdered. As the Gambino wiseguy had claimed, Funzouale's underling was never wiseguy material, but had served an important purpose for the boss of the Genovese Family. (*Later, it was claimed that Funzouale was merely a street boss and front man for the man pulling the strings, Benny Squints, who was immortalized by Jimmy Breslin in a number of satirical articles about a character he called "Un Occhio, or "One Eye"*)

Despite a long life of crime and reaching the heights of criminal power, Funzouale spent decades between an early arrest in 1924 for armed robbery, when he was twenty years old, and a RICO conviction (*the first ever under that statute*) and a sentence of ten years in prison in January, 1981. At that time, a bail hearing was held for Funzouale, who attended the proceedings in a wheelchair. The old man's lawyers argued for bail pending appeal based on the fact that their client was a sick man who had gone through a number of operations, including one for throat cancer. The government argued that it was all an act, that Tieri should be remanded immediately. While the judge, Thomas P. Griesa, looked like he could go either way, Funzouale asked if he could approach the bench and speak with the judge up close, since his voice was little more than a whisper since the operation on his throat. The judge agreed. When Funzouale got close enough, he dropped his pants to display a network of scars on his body. Judge Griesa was repulsed, but granted the convicted RICO offender bail. It turned out to be a wise and compassionate decision. Alphonse Frank Tieri, aka Funzouale, died two months later, on March 31, 1981, of natural causes in Mt. Sinai Hospital.

Mob Snapshot #12:

Albert Anastasia

Albert Anastasia was known as " Lord High Executioner of Murder Incorporated," because that group of mostly Jewish murderers from Brownsville, Brooklyn, guys like Pittsburgh Phil Strauss and Kid Twist Reles answered to Lepke Buchalter, who answered directly to him. When added to his own reputation as a cold killer, he was one of the most intimidating figures in organized crime at that time. Mobsters who'd racked up a number of notches on their own belts reported chills going through their bodies when they sat across a table from him for some dispute or other. A cigarette usually dangled almost vertically downward from his lips, making him squint icily; his huge hands appearing as though they could rip a man apart in seconds. A sudden move by Albert at the sitdown would have made them shit in their pants.

A telling anecdote about the kind of person Anastasia was is the case of Willie Sutton, a bank robber with no mob affiliation and a proclivity for escaping from prison. One day, while Sutton was on one of his self authorized furloughs from jail, a young haberdasher named Arnold Schuster spotted him and reported his whereabouts to police, who promptly arrested him. Sutton had been and continued to be a headliner in newspapers each time one of his adventures ended in his capture and incarceration. Schuster traded in on Sutton's fame and became a mini-celebrity in his own right, always ready, willing, and able to grant an interview to anyone who would listen to his crowing about how he had helped return Sutton to prison. Television was in its infancy, and of course a mobster of Anastasia's stature had one. When he saw Schuster talking about what he'd done on TV, he declared, "I hate squealers," and ordered the haberdasher murdered, which, of course, he was. Arnold Schuster, the upstanding citizen who'd done what he felt was his duty, was shot twice in the groin and once in each eye.

Umberto Anastasio, later known as Albert Anastasia, was born in 1902 in Calabria, Italy and moved to the U.S. when he was in his teens. By the time he was in his twenties he was well on his way to a fearsome reputation by murdering a longshoreman, which landed him in Sing Sing penitentiary. When his conviction was overturned and a new trial ordered, witnesses suddenly disappeared and no retrial was held. As a close associate of Lucky Luciano when they were both aligned with Giuseppe Masseria, he also became one of the founding members of the modern day criminal organization that was born at the 1931 gathering in Atlantic City. The meeting, which was hosted by Luciano, included mob figures from around the country, including Meyer Lansky, Frank Costello, and Al Capone.

In the new organized crime order of five families, Anastasia fell under the Family headed by the brothers Mangano. Both brothers disappeared some time afterward, making room for Anastasia to step into the top spot as boss. He was loyal to Luciano, who headed up what is now called the Genovese Family, and to Frank Costello, who substituted for Luciano when the latter went to prison. He respected them for their brains and sophistication, but hated Vito Genovese. When Genovese had Costello shot, Anastasia wanted to exact revenge for his pal, but Frank quickly threw in the towel and retired. Though Costello was no longer a rival, Genovese still felt insecure. Neither was Carlo Gambino, who wanted the same kind of opening at the top that Anastasia had created when the Mangano Brothers were killed. The opportunity arose when it became known that Anastasia had been selling memberships in his family; charging fifty thousand dollars a pop to bestow "dunsky" status, which was what "made guys" were commonly called in those days, on those who could afford it. It resulted in a Commission-sanctioned hit on Albert while he was getting a shave at the Park Sheraton Hotel's barber shop, on October 25, 1957.

Anastasia's long lasting legacy was that his successor, Carlo Gambino, closed the "books" to new members being admitted in order to clean house of the unfit wiseguys Albert had anointed for cash. Other than a small number of exceptions, that ban stayed in effect until Gambino's death in 1974.

Sonny Girard

Mob Snapshot #14:

(Remember, we don't do 13?)

In the Beginning

Morte Alla Francia, Italia Anela!

The year is 1282. The day, Sunday, March 30th. The sun is bright, the weather balmy on this glorious Sicilian spring day. Laurel trees bloom to fill the nearby hills with verdant color. Churchgoers parade along the dusty piazzas in their best dark wool suits and black dresses. Beautiful day for a wedding.

As the Vesper bells echo from one side of the island to the other, a young man and woman, hand in hand, make their way to the church to be joined in body for a lifetime and in spirit forever.

At the church, the young man, after a sneaked kiss, tears himself away from his beloved to go fetch the priest. He leaves her waiting amidst the reds, blues, and yellows of the garden flowers, a flower herself waiting to give her body and soul for the first time to the man she loves.

But the French are everywhere. The most recent invaders in a past and future line of foreigners that had and would occupy Sicily, their soldiers traipse and trample as if they truly own every bit of Sicilian ground they've occupied.

And its women.

Pierre Drouet, drunk and a sergeant in the occupying army, comes across the young bride-to-be as she waits for her future husband to bring the priest. She attracts him, and, her being Sicilian, he feels, makes her his for the taking.

A fondle.

A try for a kiss.

Drouet insists on having his way with the raven-haired beauty. He grabs her, trying to drag her to a more secluded spot where he can throw her white dress over her head and relieve his manhood between her naked thighs.

The girl, however, wants none of the drunken invader, and struggles to be released from his grasp. She falls, crushing her head on the wall of the church she is supposed to be married at.

She dies.

As a result of the brutalization, thousands of Sicilians shout the battle call, Morte Alla Francia, Italia Anela!...Death to the French is Italy's Cry! The acronym for their shout becomes the password for a secret organization dedicated to driving the French from their island: MAFIA!

Is that legend the beginning of the Mafia true? Probably not. It sounds great, and, but for the fact that at that time Sicilians did not consider themselves Italians (some still don't ☺), makes sense.

What is important is that the mob in America today had its roots in Sicily. Yes, there was a Neapolitan *Cammora* and Calabrian *N'drangheta*, and too recently to count a Pugliese *Sacra Corona Unita*, it was the Sicilian *Mafia* that had the greatest effect on the establishment and growth of American Organized Crime. To understand the latter now is to know what came before. Claire Sterling's "Octopus" (*Touchstone/Simon & Schuster, Pp. 46-53*) relates some of that history, including other theories on how the Sicilian organization know as the Mafia got its name.

Mob Snapshot #15:

"Sally the Shiek" Musacchio

Salvatore "Sally the Sheik" Musacchio operated in a neighborhood and era where everyone knew who the local wiseguys were, what their rank was, and what they did; who ran the *ziganette* game and who was the shooter. They would never think of relating that information to the authorities and afforded their mobsters the utmost respect. Every morning, the dapper "Sheik," in suit, shirt, and tie, who was a captain in the mob family of Joseph Profaci, would parade around one such area, the East New York section of Brooklyn, with two of his larger underlings as bodyguards. During that time he would make a daily stop at Joe the Barber's shop on Liberty Avenue for a shave. Later, he would enjoy a mid-day meal at Don Peppe restaurant, which he was said to have a piece of and which would later move its business to a location closer to the yet to be born John Gotti's sanctuary area of Ozone Park. For the time being, Sally the Sheik lorded over his area in East New York, giving solace and assistance to those who petitioned him and won, and threatening justice to those who broke the mob's rules.

One of those who fell under the Sheik's wing was a young Ralph Calletti. In truth, Ralph was the godson of Vito Genovese, a powerful figure in the family Lucky Luciano had built, and future successor to that group. Genovese eventually became the namesake of that mob family, replacing Luciano's and forever solidifying his position as its leader. Though in different families, Sally the Sheik and Vito Genovese were close friends. Because of that relationship, the Sheik took it upon himself to look after Vito's godson, Ralph. One evening, Ralph Calletti, who liked to gamble, got on the wrong side of some bookmakers he owed money to. Their discussion left him with a black eye. The next day, at the barber shop, the Sheik asked him about it. Calletti mumbled some lame excuse and ended by saying it was nothing. That day, Ralph got a call from his godfather, Vito Genovese, to meet him. Vito showed up with two future bosses of the Genovese Family, Thomas "Tommy Ryan" Eboli and Vincent "Chin" Gigante.   The result was that the bookmaker who had hit Vito's godson was taken out of a crap game in New Jersey run by another future boss, Jerry Catena. Ralph was given a baseball bat and told to go to work on the bookmaker, starting with the shins and knees so he fell to the floor where he was a better target. Ralph Calletti remembered two things about that incident: the sound of bones cracking and not to let Sally the Sheik find out anything he didn't want Vito to know.

Sally the Sheik was typical of his time, where wiseguys' world was so all encompassing that they didn't always keep track of things going on in the wider world. One incident that made Ralph laugh was when Sally looked out of the barber shop's window and spotted a car parked down the block with two people sitting in the front seat. Sure that they were some arm of law enforcement, he sent one of his bodyguards, Joey Ecco, to check them out. Joey returned from his mission to report that the two heads were in fact headrests, which had recently been installed in automobiles. Of course, Ralph and everyone else at Joe's Barber Shop laughed *after* Sally and his men had left.

Within the Profaci Family, Sally the Sheik's position was stronger than just a position earned through deeds. Profaci's brother-in-law, Joseph "The Fat Man" Maglioccio, was also the uncle-in-law of Sally's daughter. When Maglioccio was elevated to boss after Joe Profaci died of cancer, he dragged Sally the Sheik upstairs with him as underboss. Magliocci, as unfit a boss as could be imagined at the time, allowed Joe Bonnano to talk him into a plot to kill Carlo Gambino and Tommy Lucchese and consolidate the five families under them.   Maglioccio gave the assignment to another future boss, Joe Colombo, who, realizing the stupidity of the plot, informed Carlo Gambino.   Maglioccio was magnanimously allowed to step down instead of being killed. Sally the Sheik took over as acting boss. Both he and Maglioccio died of natural causes a short time later, leaving the top spot to Colombo.

Mob Snapshot #16:

Benny "The Sidge" LoCicero

Benny the Sidge was born into the mob. His father, Charlie the Sidge, was an important member of Joe Profaci's inner circle who taught his son to, according to the late Benny, "Kill hard and fast." Charlie was Joe Profaci's emissary and negotiator to the Gallo Brothers when they kidnapped some of the top executives from Profaci's inner circle, including his brother-in-law, "The Fat Man," Joseph Magliocco, during the early days of the internecine war between them. He was also successfully shot-gunned to death in the second attempt on his life, the first having hit him with a number of non-fatal bullets dozens of years earlier.

One thing Benny had picked up from his father was loyalty. There were few soldiers as loyal to bosses as he was. His exceptional guile and force of personality earned him money but that weapon was never turned on those above him, though he carried personal slights as if they were open wounds. When one of his former captains, Charlie "Moose" Panarella, would call in the middle of the night to meet him at a Coney Island diner, Benny would show up with guns ready to set blazing only to find the former was trying to pick up a waitress with a demonstration of his power. He'd have coffee, wait till he was dismissed by his superior, and grumble about it privately for a couple of decades, far beyond the time when Charlie Moose had been demoted to common soldier. And Moose was not the only one. Anyone who had ever won a sitdown with Benny became a lifetime enemy.

Besides being a Colombo Family "workhorse" (*figure it out on your own*), the strongest memories of Benny have to do with his heavy gambling, his used car salesman force of personality (*he actually worked as one while on parole*), and his hyper demeanor. That hyper movement and speech pattern used to get him in and out of bizarre situations at times. He could talk someone into holding a bagful of "diamonds" that were really glass and giving him thousands of dollars for the shot to profit from their sale when they weren't hot anymore.

Once, while going through the scratch sheet (*racing form*) in a neighborhood luncheonette to pick his daily bets, a regular customer approached him. The young man said he had been watching Benny and knew he was in the mob. He wanted to know what he had to do to become a member. Benny paid as much attention to the man as he would a fly that landed on his third race pick. Without looking up from his form, he told the man to come back with a black suit and shirt with a white tie...and a briefcase with twenty-five thousand dollars in cash. A few days later, the young man approached Benny again. This time he had his mobster costume on and carried a briefcase with the money he had been told he needed. No one could have been in more shock than Benny. He did, however, recover quickly enough to take the sucker downstairs to the luncheonette's cellar, conduct a mock mob initiation ceremony, relieve him of the briefcase, and send him on his way a happy man. Needless to say, Aqueduct relieved Benny of the money as quickly as he had taken it.

Benny was famous for his scams, fueled by desperation over gambling losses. Once he sold the departed Meyer Lansky's spot to a Jewish Miami businessman who was introduced by a union official. Benny's elaborate scam included turning an old man who maintained a friend's social club into "Don Carlo di Catania." He was even loaned flashy jewelry. The old man was ordered not to say a word, but to whisper what would appear to be answers into Benny's ear so he could answer. Benny stood by the bathroom door when Don Carlo took a leak for show, but in private berated him and warned him not to get let the phony character leak into his real life. After a few meetings, Benny took the new Meyer for some polyester suits and got tens of thousands of dollars to anoint him. As an afterward, the new Lansky went back to

Miami, gave someone in a bar a "Do you know who I am?" and got slapped around. Too timid to ask for a refund, he sent his wife. Benny told her to meet him by Port Authority at night. Dressed in a trench coat, hat with the brim pulled down, and sunglasses, he pulled her into a doorway and explained that the don was dead and now his life was in jeopardy. Scared to death, she immediately flew back to Florida...without the money...and never contacted Benny again.

But, if there is a classic Benny the Sidge story, that truly illustrates his eccentricity, it is one when I was in a motorcycle accident. I was lying on a gurney in the emergency room of Coney Island Hospital at night, in excruciating pain because my shoulder had been dislocated and I was laying on my left arm, when I spotted Benny hurrying through the door with his head in constant motion, looking for me. Dressed in a tan trench coat (*probably the same one he had worn when he frightened the wannabe Meyer's wife off*), with pajama bottoms sticking out under his pants, and house slippers, he rushed up to the gurney and announced that he'd just heard about the accident.

"How's your neck?" Benny asked.

"Fine."

"Lift your head," Benny said.

"Benny, leave me alone; I'm fine."

"No, lift your head. I want to see that your neck's not broken."

Slowly and painfully, I lifted my head just to shut him up. *"Satisfied?"*

Benny promptly slid open the front of his coat to reveal a pistol in his waistband. *"I know you wouldn't want to live if you were crippled,"* he said.

"Thanks, Benny," I muttered. *"You're a real pal."*

Benny the Sidge was disliked by more than liked, except for his family members, who he was devoted to and who returned his affection and loyalty. Many of those who disliked him really feared him more, as he was known to be quick on the trigger. Those who knew him better knew that his loyalty to mob order wouldn't allow him to move on anyone unless it was with an okay from his higher ups. One example of that was the fact that he privately confided that he believed Greg Scarpa was a longtime stoolpigeon, but would do nothing about it. He was loyal. He cried in the shower over things he'd done, but he'd stick a gun in his waistband and go wherever he was told. There are a lot more Benny the Sidge stories, but the names would have to be changed to protect the guilty.

Mob Snapshot #17:

Louis Capone

One of the greatest mistakes so-called "mob experts" make is confusing Meyer Lansky and Bugsy Siegel with the goings on of Lepke Buchalter and Gurrah Shapiro in their running of the Brownsville organization known as "Murder Incorporated." Lansky and Siegel were underlings of premier organized crime family boss, Lucky Luciano. The Sicilian Luciano and Neapolitan Costello were among the first to have working relationships with Jewish gangsters, and as a result wound up with major Jewish associates in their crew. Most of those Jews were part of the organization that answered to Lansky, and to a lesser degree, Siegel, who was less of a team player; guys like the Rosenbergs, Sam and Ralph "Beaky" (*Beaky was later accused of killing the black owner of Queens nightclub, Conrad's Cloud Room*) and Max "The Jew" Shrager, whose son Ian went on to co-own the infamous Studio 54, became a rat, then went on to own a chain of chic hotels that include the Delano in Miami Beach and the Mondrian in Los Angeles.

Across the river, in Brownsville, Brooklyn was the gang known as Murder Incorporated. It was run at the top by Albert Anastasia, his underling Louis "Lepke" Buchalter, who was a Manhattan mobster, and finally by Louis Capone, a wiseguy in Anastasia's family from the nearby neighborhood of Ocean Hill. Capone had an Italian pastry café in his area where youngsters Abe "Kid Twist" Reles and "Happy" Maione (*another myth is that Murder Incorporated was all Jewish*) hung out and received the tutelage of the Anastasia wiseguy. Capone encouraged the two, who were often at odds, to pull together the other young toughs they hung out with into an enforcement and earning arm of the Anastasia Crime Family. And Murder Incorporated was born.

The dapper and exquisitely groomed Capone's claim to fame was a close connection with the Purple Gang of Detroit, and was in fact involved with them in a shylock operation that blanketed a good part of the nation. Though they had the same last name, Louis Capone was not related to Scarface Al Capone, of Brooklyn and Chicago. Louis Capone's *pasticceria* was not a hub of criminal activity just because of his *cannolis* and *espresso*, but because his boss, Albert Anastasia, and other members of what was then the crime family of Vincent Mangano and his brother Philip frequented it.

Between Capone's nationwide network and his group of Murder Incorporated killers, he began to take contracts from other families and even other cities to bring money to the Mangano-Anastasia's coffers. When, in 1936, Lepke Buchalter had trouble with a trucker who was giving his top union operative, Max Rubin, a hard time, and was rumored to be talking to the authorities about mob control in garment center trucking, Lepke ordered him killed. The order went to Louis Capone, who in turn, made sure it was taken care of. When Kid Twist went bad and testified for prosecutor Burton Turkus about, among other things, the murder of trucker Joe Rosen, Lepke Buchalter, his hulking bodyguard, Mendy Weiss, and Louis Capone were convicted and sentenced to death.

On March 4, 1944, Louis Capone was electrocuted in the chair at Sing Sing prison, in Ossining, New York. Buchalter and Weiss followed him to that doom.

Mob Snapshot #18:

Mob Ties

To me a mob tie is a piece of silk with pictures of Lucky Luciano and Bugsy Siegel. On the other hand, to authorities from local to federal, it's an excuse to profile and persecute people in a way that they could not to any other group.

I read a story about the investigation of a New Jersey Waterfront Commissioner for recommending a young man for a position as a harbor cop, who, supposedly, had *mob ties*. The Commission itself was set up over a half century ago to protect the waterfront from the kind of organized crime influence as portrayed in the Marlon Brando classic, "On the Waterfront." The particular commissioner under investigation is a former New Jersey police officer. What raised eyebrows of Commission investigators when, upon being asked to name his supervisors at the club, the applicant named two *reputed* members of organized crime (*I don't know if those two were ever convicted of a crime, or themselves merely have unsightly mob ties, which would make the applicant another layer removed from the mob*). Before you ask, the applicant did not give false names or refuse to name his supervisors. Is this a case of "guilt by association"? It certainly didn't seem to matter when hiring a President of the United States, who associated with a confessed terrorist. The President got thousands of nukes. All the harbor cop could have gotten control over would have been a gun and maybe a Taser...and, of course, the obligatory bag of donuts when he's hiding from duty.

Another pal of mine licensed an historic landmark as a restaurant from whichever agency oversees these things in New York. He assumed the responsibilities for the location after a couple of notable failures. Over thirteen years or so he built a highly successful business that paid higher and higher rents with no problem. Then a Gambino rat threw the restaurateur's name into the mix as a family member. This friend, who has worked twenty-five hours a day for all those years, was given the boot from the location. Arrests over those years? None? Liquor license violations? None. Bounced checks? None. He lost his livelihood all because a real rat alleged that he was a mob member.

The question is, "*What would you like both of these men, not accused of any crime, to do?*" Are the authorities saying that those either *reputed* to be a member of or convicted of crimes related to organized crime should not go straight? Is working a business infiltration? Would the authorities prefer they drive men to crime instead of allowing them the simple American right to be innocent until proven guilty and given the right to a legitimate pursuit of happiness? Sure they would. Organized Crime brings funding and publicity to law enforcement agencies and prisons, which brings more funding. Let's face it, the mob is reeling... it's on its way out, soon to be nothing more than history. It's time to stop the bugaboo and concentrate on those who want to blow up our citizens, not be a harbor cop or work one's ass off in a restaurant.

Would the authorities behave the same way with any Muslim who attended a mosque or worked in the legitimate business of a terrorist, and deny him a job because of that association? At a time when America whines and wrings its hands how we treat those who chop our people's heads off, don't those who work for or are *reputed* to be part of organized crime deserve the same consideration? Catch someone in a crime, organized or not, do what you have to; drive people away from legitimate business and into a criminal lifestyle, be ashamed. Wear mob ties; don't speculate about them and ruin lives.

STORIES OF ME

STORIES OF ME:

FEDS vs STATE

Everyone knows that federal prosecutions score much higher than those in the State of New York or any of those states that had/have sizeable organized crime communities. For example, the prosecutors in the Southern District of New York boast a conviction percentage of organized crime figures of something like a normal body temperature. Their investigators, FBI agents, are better than their comparative state or city detectives, and their prosecutors are head and shoulders above their counterparts in the state; they have to be in order to work on organized crime, corporate fraud, or major narcotics networks successfully. State prosecutors and detectives are overwhelmed with rapists, street drug peddlers, spouse killers, etc. They just dull their talent with the sheer amount of low end crimes, and are not prepared for long, sophisticated multi-defendant trials. In the past, state justice workers from cops, to prosecutors, to judges have been known to be open to the occasional bribe. Every mob guy knows it. What most don't realize until they go through both penal systems is how different they can be too. This Brooklyn mobster learned it the hard way.

It started with the State Organized Crime Control Bureau, which infiltrated my gambling operation and became close with me over a number of years. The main undercover detective on my case ate in my house, played with my kids, and even offered to confirm my son when his godfather was late for church—and engaged in plenty of illegal activities that lined his pockets (*newspapers reported that he was allowed to keep his illegal profits in order to maintain his mob lifestyle*). Eventually, his actions led to my being spirited out of my home in the dead of a Friday night and brought to a secret location in a Manhattan office building where I was confronted with my employee and pal of three years wearing a detective's gold shield. Why bring me there instead of just arresting me? It was for the offer. There's always an offer to cooperate. Problem was, I wasn't buying, but was concerned that two dozen of my friends and associates who he'd met through me would be surprised by arrests that could also find guns, gambling records, etc. Since it was a Friday night and I had no other option, I threw a Hail Mary pass and said I needed the weekend to think about whether or not I would cooperate. The geniuses conferred then granted me seventy-two hours, with the understanding that I would be arrested if I decided not to play along and allow the undercover to keep working on the case. What a choice: sink or sink. Since I knew my wife had already called my lawyer, I sat back down and refused to leave. I told them that the undercover had to be formally arrested: booked, fingerprinted, mugshots taken; everything my lawyer could find when I told him I'd been grabbed for questioning about something the undercover was being charged with and let go.

Within hours, as the sun barely gave its first yawn, I met with my next guy upstairs and explained everything that had gone on, word for word. I offered to play along so we could take control, like the double agent stuff the CIA does. He nixed that immediately but told me to contact everyone who might have come in contact with the undercover; tell them the story and tell them to clean house before they were pinched...no gambling slips, money, or weapons around...which was exactly what I did, and they complied. The dozen and a half arrests were amazingly orderly for the police, who, I'm sure, wondered why. Bail was set and everyone was immediately released through waiting bondsmen. No one even had to skip a good meal outside. They were collecting money from bookmaking and shylock customers that day.

In the end, everyone walked on the case except the target of the investigation, me, and I only went to prison because of a motion snafu my lawyer made. He was a close friend and had saved my ass many times, so I knew it wasn't intentional; it was just a legal screw up. In fact, I was sort of happy to be sentenced to incarceration, which I knew dispelled any doubt anyone might have had that I somehow knew the undercover and intentionally introduced him around.

Then prison.

New York State prison regulations at the time mandated ten days of each month as "good time," which meant that if an inmate didn't get in trouble and have days taken away, he could only do a maximum of two-thirds of his time behind bars. When I got to reception at Dannemora, after a brief stay at Sing Sing, I asked the interviewer if I had worked at a real job on the outside, did he think I would have stayed out of prison.

"*I guess so,*" he said.

"*Well,*" I replied, "*if I didn't work outside for serious money, what makes you think I would want to mop your floors for thirty-five cents a day?*"

He was quick to answer, "*Because if you refuse to work, we can take away your good time.*"

I saw his point immediately, but got an opportunity to have it both ways when I went for the obligatory medical exam. Instead of giving me a thorough exam, the "doctor?" asked if I had any conditions. I told him I had chronic phlebitis instead of the truth, which was that I had had phlebitis once when a cold settled in a thigh vein. In reality, it was temporary, and it was during that period when I was bedridden that the undercover was able to worm his way in closer to me by doing some of my collections and chauffeuring me around when I could walk but not drive. Anyway, the prison doctor wrote exactly what I told him with a recommendation that any job I took had to be a sitting one. Halfway home. They would not be able to assign me to any job where I would have to stand on my feet.

When I got to my first home prison, I was interviewed for a job. The counselor said he saw on my file that I could not stand much and asked if I typed. Of course I said no (*I had taken typing in high school*). He asked how he could get me a sitting job with no typing? I replied that wasn't my problem, that it was his job, and that he should write on the file that I did not refuse to work. Mission accomplished.

After seven or eight months of taking sun, reading, or making phone calls to friends and family while the other inmates spent their days working at some prison labor, the counselor called me in one Friday. He said he had finally found suitable work for me: clerk in the prison hospital. For those inmates who weren't as opposed to "working for the man" as I, that was considered the best job one could hope for. Not this incorrigibly lazy guest of the state. I asked if there was any typing required. He said none. I was forced to go to Plan B. When my wife visited the next day, I asked her to do me a favor and visit me early every day for two weeks. I said that within that time the hospital staff would get so disgusted that the clerk was never there that they would send me back to unemployment status.

That following Monday, I reported to the hospital at the ungodly time of 8:30 a.m. The first thing I asked the head nurse was if there was any typing on the job. She answered, *"It's **all** typing."* Ha! She would be easy. For my first assignment, I was given a list of thirty-three inmate names and corresponding numbers and told to type three Rolodex cards for each entry.

"When will they be done?" the battleaxe of a head nurse asked.

"What's today, Monday," I mused out loud. *"Figure Thursday,"* I replied to her question.

Probably thinking I was just another smartass prisoner breaking balls, she shot me an impatient look then went about her business.

Wrong again.

I took one Rolodex card, spent a ridiculous amount of time lining it up in the IBM Selectric typewriter, sized it up for a few moments, then finally said, *"Nah,"* and pulled it out to start over again.

About a half-hour later, nurse came by again. *"How's it going?"* she asked.

I responded, *"Fine. I'll have them when I told you. Look, I have one done already."*

She huffed off, only to be replaced by a hack who escorted me out of the hospital and back to my unit.

When my wife showed up for our scheduled first visit, I told her the story. *"You don't have to visit every day,"* I told her. *"I thought it would take two weeks, not a half-hour. They're too easy."*

That's when I got booted out and sent to another institution...

...Where I found a counselor determined to get me to work. On my first encounter with him, he said that despite my documented medical condition, which he didn't know was phony, he wanted to take a chance and put me to work in the kitchen. Fully aware that I could lose my good time by refusing to work, I agreed, but asked for the exact spelling of his name. When he asked why, I responded, *"Because when my lawyer sues the institution, I don't want him to spell your name wrong."* He threw me out of his office...but he didn't stop trying to get me to work, calling me down to his office a couple or more times a week. One day he said he would have thought I would want the money for working.

"How much do they pay, thirty-five cents a day?" I said. *"How about I give you thirty-five cents a day to leave me alone?"*

Needless to say, I went home after a couple of years without ever giving the prison system that kept me from my loved ones even one hour of my labor.

Then, a couple of years after being released from State prison came a R.I.C.O. arrest by the Feds.

The United States of America vs. whoever is so powerful that the case is practically lost the moment the indictment, which the government admits is so easy they could "indict a ham sandwich," is handed down by a grand jury. One doesn't really have to be guilty to be smashed by the government legal machine. Add to that the complete ruthlessness of prosecutors trying to build a record they can turn into cash when they eventually go into private practice, and it's no wonder their conviction rate is the same as your normal body temperature. The Government will fight to have decent defense attorneys thrown off cases, will show photos of the insides of defendants' garment closets to raise jealousy from juries, and out and out lie, writing scripts for and coaching witnesses.

Rudy Giuliani once told an audience of law students at Fordham University that if he "thought" someone was guilty of a crime, nothing he did to put them in prison was off limits. In my case, that including coaching a witness I had never met to say he saw me meet every week with a captain in the Gambino Family...a person I had only met once or twice in my entire life, and coaching a witness during a lunch recess, and rifling through a defense attorney's papers during another break. The judge was made aware of all those indiscretions, but it had no effect on him. It's not hard to understand when you realize they all...FBI Agents, U.S. Attorneys, and Federal Judges...get their checks from the same place...they're a team; the prosecution team for The United States of America.

Of course, I was convicted.

Sitting in MCC, things took an unexpected turn for me, a now convicted R.I.C.O. offender, who had had my bail revoked upon conviction. The "danger to the community" argument the U.S. Attorney used to keep me in prison during the appeal process was that I'd associated with Anthony "Tony Gawk" Augello, someone who just happened to have been dead for three years at the time. The turn came in the form of my wife's stepfather, Biagio, a Sicilian who would dispel every stereotype of males from the island being manly, approaching my wife with stories of my having had an affair with a younger female and encouraging her to divorce me and move on with her life. Stuck behind bars, I called another relative, Paulie Zach, who was a well known Gambino wiseguy and asked him to order my rat father-in-law to stay away from my wife. Instead, Paulie told him that I had taken out a contract on his life, but that he had taken it away. Of course, that sent Biagio right back to wifey with the claim that I had tried to have him killed. Thanks, but no thanks, Paul.

I think I had more mobster close friends in MCC with me than were left out on the street. One was "Little Dom" Cataldo, someone I'd done business with and stayed friends with for about fifteen years. I said I wanted to pull the same kind of ploy I had pulled years earlier with the NY State detectives, the events of which he was well aware of, and say I needed some time in the street, even a few days, to think about cooperating. I'd take care of my rodent problem with Biagio myself then return a couple of days later. Dom laughed. He said the feds would never buy it, but that I was welcome to give it a try. That's where I found the first major difference between the state and the feds. The feds wouldn't even hear of any kind of play, even for a weekend, even for an hour, unless I gave them something concrete, which, of course, I couldn't. Dom laughed at me a second time when I had to admit he was right and that couldn't pull it off. Biagio got a pass, but faded into the background...some guys don't realize how lucky they really are. However, the damage had already been done and I was divorced halfway through my term.

The federal difference was apparent in prison too. Even before I got to a designated prison, I decided I would pull the same no work scam I had in state prison. Instead, the feds sent me for a thorough medical checkup and determined that there was nothing wrong with me beyond morally. The first job they assigned me was outside on a lawn crew. I immediately threw my prison uniforms in the trash and showed up for work in sweatpants. I claimed I had put the clothes the BOP (*Bureau of Prisons*) issued me in the washing machine and someone had stolen them. I was sent back and an appointment was made for me to get new uniforms. When I got them and reported for work, I slipped on the ice and had to be carried back to the infirmary. I was fired before I got to work an hour.

The problem, I later found out that in the federal system you earn your good time instead of getting it given to you by statute. By the time I understood the federal system, my shenanigans had cost me sixty days of good time; sixty days more I would have to do in prison before ultimately getting released. Now, I HAD to find a job. Through pals in prison, I was given "no show" jobs, like tutoring a student who was only interested in writing letters to his girlfriend. I'd correct his letters from Monday to Thursday (*Friday was my Trivial Pursuit day*) at three o'clock in the afternoon. In yet another institution, friends got me a gig where all I had to do was sign in and out of the prison's power plant each day. I actually spent more time in the plant than I had to because the hack there was a good guy who had a portable electric stove and let me cook the food my pals stole from the kitchen, which I brought back to the unit after sharing some with him.

I had put the brakes on my loss of time, but none of that got the sixty days back. Then serendipity struck. I heard one correction officer complain to another that he had been turned down for a job promotion because he wasn't able to do well on the essay part of the application. The BOP posts job openings, takes applications that include an essay part, then come back with a rating, the two best being "qualified" and "best qualified." I told the officer that if he applied again I would write the essay part, and if he got one of the top two grades, I would want a few days good time. After the first "best qualified" was returned, I became extremely popular among staff and actually got back all sixty days of the good time I'd lost.

A WORD ABOUT PRISONS:

Unfortunately, the lesson incarcerated inmates learn is that their crime was not the thing they were convicted of, but getting caught was. There is an endemic corruption among those who run prisons that ranges from inconsequential to criminal, and which teaches the aforementioned lesson to those they are in charge of in the name of the government.

The corruption in state facilities is many times at the lowest level: guards. They will do innocuous things like allowing inmates to exceed the food limit for a price to carrying in drugs for them. Since the inmate population is generally one convicted of crimes from turnstile jumping, to rape, to murder, the guards (*known to prisoners as hacks*) who can stand the population on a daily basis tends to identify with them at some point and commit more base crimes, like drugs. It's a case of "Tell me who you stay with and I'll tell you what you are." Those hacks also commit individual crimes like trying to shake down inmates' families for so called advantages or protection and sexual advances to female visitors with the same promises for their incarcerated loved ones. Those things diminish considerably at prisons built in areas considered the "assholes of the earth," where talented people leave and those who remain depend on the prisons for jobs that are otherwise unavailable. They tend to look down on prisoners, since without them they would be the bottom of the economic and social heap. State prison guards tend to be those who could not make it in the private sector.

Corruption in federal prisons is more noticeable at the top. Whole families make their careers in the Bureau of Prisons, having relatives who are wardens, assistant wardens, supervisors, etc. in other institutions. They do resemble mob families and feel the same sense of entitlement that mobsters with blood connections to executives in other crews do. Some wardens bill goods for their personal use to the institutions they run. Theft?

There is a prison system of "contracts," where inmates will buy goods or services from other inmates who can provide them, and pay in cigarettes or other commissary items or money sent to the contract from relatives. Contracts can cover anything from someone doing one's laundry or to kitchen workers who provide food. I usually found a kitchen contract for food delivered to my cell in every prison I was in.

That food was almost always whatever would be served in the mess hall that day, which allowed me to avoid the inconvenience of going to that institutional zoo. One contract delivered a bag of food each day when his overnight shift ended at about 6:30 a.m. If he gave me a bag of pork chops, for example, I would eat them all day, breakfast, lunch, and dinner. One morning he woke me and gave me a plastic bag filled with something I couldn't identify. The contents were white and green and had no discernable form. It turned out to be crabmeat and asparagus, something the warden had had delivered and billed to the prison, only to be brought over to his house for a Saturday night party he was about to have. My guy had stolen some of the food the warden was stealing from the government and brought it to me. I ate my entire contents of epicurean delight at that early hour.

Officials also play corrupt games. In one detention center, air space was measured from floor to ceiling in a three story rotunda and fraudulently passed off as inmate air space mandated by Washington. Not bad if the inmate was thirty feet tall. Another institution was required to submit a report that the air conditioning was working. The report had to be certified by an outside air condition specialist. Since the management didn't want to report it was out of order, it hired an air condition specialist from a nearby state prison to certify that it was working. Martha Stewart went to prison for lying to an FBI agent. What is lying to the B.O.P. worth?

Some of the other cover up-type corruption seems ridiculous, like painting grass green before inspections from Regional or Washington staff or herding non-working inmates from building to building out of sight of inspectors who can report that the institution is not overcrowded and efficiently run, with no inmates hanging around units in the daytime. That way, the institution can get paid for the larger number of inmates. These kinds of things may sound stupid, but it teaches those convicted of crimes that their real crimes were being caught.

The corruption that inmates see also goes all the way to the government itself. In 1985, a new sentencing act was to begin. That law included new guidelines for sentencing, the elimination of earned good time and replaced with a paltry fifteen percent mandatory good time, and the elimination of the Board of Parole with all current prisoners to be *given a date within their sentencing guidelines*. The first two were implemented immediately, but the government allowed a five year extension on the last. Consider that all it would take to comply with the new law would have been to check inmates' information on the computer and match it to a release date within their posted guidelines.

For those who don't understand parole guidelines, they are determined prior to sentencing and include prior convictions, seriousness of the offense, violence, and money involved among other aggravating and mitigating considerations. So, if, after knocking all this out on the computer according to predetermined slots, an inmate was determined to have guidelines that ranged from 36-48 months, he or she would have expected to be released within that time if they obeyed prison rules and stayed out of trouble inside. However, a judge might sentence that defendant to ten years. At the time, that meant the inmate would be eligible for parole at forty months with a maximum of eighty months. The Parole Department would then have all discretion as to when to release the inmate, up to the maximum of eighty months, or thirty-two months beyond his or her maximum guidelines.

What shutting down the Parole Department would mean would be turning the featherbedding parole officers and other bureaucratic staff out to pasture. Five years would give them time to lose many by attrition, which, in reality, was stealing money from taxpayers to pay off their pals. If that wasn't bad enough, at the end of the five years they asked for and were granted another five years to comply; more government funds stolen while they kept inmates in prison beyond their guideline dates at an additional cost to taxpayers. The new law was supposed to bring release into compliance with guidelines, which would put parole bureaucrats out of work and harm the B.O.P. by easing the overcrowding they require to demand more money for prisons and staff, which in turn is more power. It was fraud when it was done, and I tried at the time to interest newspapers and other media outlets in that story, the facts of which were easy enough to verify. None would touch it. I was out and out told by certain TV people that they didn't want to screw with the government at that level. I don't know if the parole board was ever completely shut down, but, after robbing ten years of money, does it really matter?

STORIES OF ME:

THE LAWYERS

Spending time "in the streets" necessarily means getting to know and spending time with lawyers. They are alternately loved and loathed; laughed at and embraced; and, at least in one case, killed.

Just to get the murdered attorney out of the way, he was one of my first, who dropped away from us to deal with some bigger paying drug dealers. Drugs have always been and remain bad news. I heard that the lawyer, Bob Weisswasser, had taken money from one of his drug clients for some kind of a deal that never happened and they believed it had died in his pocket. That was never verified, but, realistically, when you're dead you're dead. Does it really matter why? Bob played with fire by taking on dangerous clients, and got burned.

Joe "Cupie" Iovine was also there from the beginning. He was the lawyer sent by my pals when I took my first adult pinch; no kick in the ass and sent on the way or JD card. I was called at the club by detectives who had already broken down the door and were inside my house, had found bookmaking slips, and had my mother lying on the sofa with a cold compress on her head. The choice, I was told, was to get home quickly or they would pinch mom. When I stepped over the door I was immediately ordered into the bedroom by the lead detective. *Uh oh, more slaps on the head...maybe punches...and a couple of kicks for good measure.* I sat at the edge of the bed as he paced back and forth directly in front of me, chatting stuff I wasn't even listening to. Instead, I was doing what was instinctive: watching every move, every bit of body language that would give me a change to fall away from the blow and sustain minimum impact. After what seemed like an endless period of watching every minor movement of his hands, he led me back out into the living room, handcuffed me, and took me to central booking, where I refused to give up any information than my name. Sometime later, Cupie showed up. I couldn't wait for the praise I would get for standing tall and keeping my mouth shut.

"You're an idiot!" were the first words out of Cupie's mouth.

"What??"

"You're an idiot, and you'll always be an idiot! This cop said he talked himself blue in the face trying to get you to offer him some money, but you wouldn't."

"Money? All I wanted was not to get hit!"

"You didn't have to take this pinch at all. You're just an idiot."

Welcome to the big time.

Cupie also colored how I looked at lawyers for the rest of my life. One night, sitting at the bar, having a drink with him, he said, *"You know how you guys are always dreaming about making the big score?"*

"Okay," I said.

"You know what my dream is?"

"I haven't a clue."

"My dream is that one of you makes that big score, stashes the money in a safe place...then gets caught and calls me."

I was once told that there is only one lawyer joke; that everything else said about them is true. Cupie proved that.

Times changed and with them new lawyers. Two former Brooklyn Assistant District Attorneys went private and became the legal representatives for me and a number of my pals. Jay Zerin and Ira Cooper were as different as two people could be, yet remained partners for a number of years. Socially, Jay, who, incidentally, was Andrew Dice Clay's uncle, loved to hang out with us, day or night. Ira, on the other hand, spent his non-working hours at home with his family. That's why I have lots of Jay stories, and not too many about his partner.

One of the things that really made Jay feel good was to be treated like he was a street guy. *"Did you see the way that guy looked at me?"* he'd ask. *"Like he wasn't sure if I was an FBI agent or one of you guys."*

One night, Jay came with me to see comedian Jack Carter at the Royal Box nightclub at the Americana Hotel, in Manhattan. The maitre d', who I'd always staked extra to sit ringside, warned that Carter was abusing everyone at ringside, and that I'd be better off at another table. I gave him another fifty to go back and tell Carter that there would be a guy in a green suit (*I still remember that shiny green mohair*) sitting ringside with a very big guy who would hit him over the head with a chair if he said a word. Jay put on his hardest look when Carter got around to our table. Carter stared for a moment...then moved on. Jay talked about that event for months.

Another time, he had breakfast with me and two other friends at a Bensonhurst pancake house owned by Larry Pistone, a Gambino wiseguy who was the immediate superior to the other two, Eddie and Mario (*Jay used to call them Frank and Jesse. Mario was later killed and Eddie got 150 year sentence by the feds*). It was two or three a.m. when a young man and a hot looking blonde entered and took a table near the front. At the owner's private table at the rear, we joked about kidnapping the girl and who would get stuck separating the guy from her. Some time into their meal, the couple began arguing. Suddenly, the blonde bounced a fork off the table at her partner and stormed out of the restaurant. He followed and we followed him, ready to turn the jokes into a reality by defending her and probably beating the crap out of him if he laid a hand on her. Instead, we saw them pulling away from the curb in a Volkswagon bug. It had all been a scam to beat the check.

Since Jay's new lavender Coupe de Ville was parked right in front, we all piled in and began chasing the Bug along the underside of the elevated train tracks made famous in the movie "Saturday Night Fever." I don't remember if it was Mario or I who leaned out the window and took a shot at the speeding Volkswagon, but it wasn't long before we were both hanging out the window firing at the car.

"Faster!" we yelled.

Jay, caught up in the chase, stepped on the gas, then, waking from the dream to reality, slammed on the brakes, nearly throwing Mario and me out the windows. *"What am I doing?!"* Jay screamed. *"I'm a lawyer! I could lose my license!!"*

We might have lost the girl, but we had one of the biggest laughs, imagining Jay locked up with us in a bullpen. We really loved the guy.

In court, Jay and Ira were a dream team. They got me out of more jams than I could safely explain. What I can say is that during their years of representing me I was advised how to write a script and find the players to win a trial; had a weapon and gambling slips disappear from the property clerk's office; and walked out of jail on multiple felonies with no bail posted but court papers showing that it was (*there were no computers at that time; just paper*). They cried when I won a case and brooded the one time they couldn't save me. It may sound as if they were as criminal as I was, but everything they did required criminal cooperation from the justice system, which was in fact responsible for everything that followed. If hands weren't extended by authorities, no one could have stuffed money into them...and I would have nothing to write about today.

STORIES OF ME:

GAMBLING

I've never bought a lottery ticket. To me, government run gaming is no different than Fidel Castro or Hugo Chavez nationalizing a business, any business. My friends and I were harassed and arrested time after time, not because there was an immoral component to what we were doing, but because we were muscled out so the government could nationalize our business. If it were you, would you give your money to someone who did that to you? Like I said, I never bought a lottery ticket.

Bookmaking was the first of my "operational" unlawful endeavors. My boss told me I was too smart to be doing the various "scores" I was involved in, and to get into a steady business that would yield maximum profit for minimum risk. He put me on a half-sheet with a florist who was also a major horse and sports gambling banker, which meant I would get half of whatever profit we were left with from my clients at the end of each week. If my guys won, we'd apply our loss toward the following week's play, and so on. My first year was, I believe, 1964, but I can be off a year either way. I'd walk the main commercial street in the Brooklyn neighborhood I was working, pick up bets, and settle up there every Tuesday, since I got my weekly net figure on Monday.

As someone who didn't gamble, I hated the fact that my income was dependent on chance, but, as they say, it was a living...and a good living. I had my first taste of the better than good living gambling could provide that summer, when baseball season arrived. Though I booked more during football season, I had some heavy baseball bettors, who seemed to be more "chasers," doubling down on losses to try to bail out. They taught me an important lesson, one that in gambling, like life in general, always press when you're on a good streak and take it slow when things are going the other way. Life is, after all, ups and downs, good streaks and bad runs.

I remember that summer there was a three game weekday series between the powerful Detroit Tigers and the hapless last place Kansas City Athletics. Surprisingly, the A's beat the Tigers in the first game. That brought a torrent of money in the second day. Since I wanted to do all I could to help my income along, I didn't change anything from the day before: ate the same things, went to the same places, wore the same clothes, and refused to shower. Sure enough, my magic worked and Kansas City beat Detroit for the second night in a row. Odds were that Detroit had to win that last game in the series. The line moved up to ridiculous heights to discourage Detroit money, but the amounts quadrupled at least; one player of mine bet ten thousand dollars on the game. I wanted a shower badly, and I was averse to losing back what I'd already won, so I went to the banker and told him he could keep all the money for the rest of the week; that I would shut myself out, as I sometimes did, after the second game. Of course he made a beef about it, got me to a sitdown with our boss, and got me to hang in there with him for better or worse. Damn! No food other than what I'd had for the past couple of days, same clothes, and no shower. I will always have an affinity for Kansas City, as the A's beat back the Tigers for the third game in a row. By the next day, I tempted the bookmaking gods by eating what I felt like, changing my clothes, and showering. Fortunately, they liked me that week, and I continued the winning streak right through Sunday. Naturally, the bookmaker who had forced me to hang on wasn't exactly thrilled...though I'm sure he made a lot more on his total number of runners and clients than I did.

Gambling also taught me that we were only part of a network that included players, average working people adding to their income (*who didn't know an elevator operator who took numbers?*), and the authorities. Before setting up a card or crap game, the first stop was to the local precinct to inform them of the location and put them on the pad for a weekly pay. I've even had a correctional prison guard running bets for me once I'd moved to a position where I could have my own operation.

Another thing I accepted at the time, but didn't realize the importance of until years later, was the way our gambling businesses supported businesses and even communities. There were numerous amounts of numbers, horse, and sports bankers making tremendous amounts of money, controllers taking a piece of the business of those below him, and only God knows how many thousands of runners, including working people, throughout New York. All of them spent money on financing businesses, purchasing cars, clothes and jewelry for wives and girlfriends (*moms, sisters, and daughters too*), clothing and jewelry for themselves, shoe shines, restaurants, nightclubs, and just passing out huge tips for working stiffs. At the time, Broadway area men's clothing stores like Lou Magram, Leighton's, Phil Kronfield, etc. all flourished within a few blocks of each other. Around the corners were the Latin Quarter, the Metropole, and a number of unmemorable bars and nightclubs. Restaurants were too numerous to mention. Brooklyn and Queens had the same kinds of businesses, but to a smaller scale, as did Queens and the Bronx (*Staten Island was still known as "the country" until the Verrazzano Bridge was built, after which millions were poured into the borough for housing and businesses*). All the neighborhoods made money. Waiters and waitresses, salesmen for all kinds of goods and services, taxi drivers, and the owners of all kinds of small businesses in those areas where wiseguys hung around, all did well. I could go on and on, naming particular businesses. It was all good till…

OTB.

Off Track Betting was the beginning of various state governments' move to seriously muscle out citizen bookmakers for the sole purpose of taking over their businesses. The pitch to the public was that it was going to help education. The same claim came with every succeeding lottery scheme. Anyone reading this just has to ask how much of a surplus their local school has since their state began raking in gambling dollars? Short answer: they're in worse shape than ever. Not only has the money gone to support their own bloated bureaucracies (*numbers on the payroll = power*), but they've systematically drained vibrant neighborhoods of income. The money is sucked out, never to return. Where are the small individually owned businesses that used to keep those neighborhoods alive? Gone. Sure, you can blame banks, big corporations, chain stores, and malls for destroying neighborhoods, but state governments disarmed private citizens who might have been able to fight back and preserve their greater local prosperity.

Where is the neighborhood barber who had a steady clientele, like Jasper's, on Avenue U, in Brooklyn, where the largesse of bookmakers and gamblers helped to raise the resident barbers' families? Or, Alley's and George Richland men's clothing stores across the street from each other on Bay Parkway in Bensonhurst? Or Santarpia's fruits and vegetables on Avenue N? Gone, gone, gone. Add that to the financially strapped public schools to understand how much states have screwed their citizens through gambling. Think, and ask yourself how much better things might have been where you live if you or your neighbor were able to make that extra income, and how that money would have been distributed to those around you. Think of that when you are about to feed the bureaucratic government beast in the hope that you'll become rich overnight. Think.

I never bought a lottery ticket.

STORIES OF ME:

WRITING

The first time I thought about writing was after reading Mario Puzo's "Godfather." Though I thoroughly enjoyed Puzo's book, I realized it was an opera, sort of grand style and not representative of the gritty day to day organized crime life for the masses. It was a portrayal of a small number of elites and not the bulk of the guys who were on the street every day, hustling up a living or a few luxuries. It was a violent fairy tale.

The problem was, I couldn't write.

So, I decided to look for a ghostwriter.

I lived in Brooklyn but hung out in Manhattan at night, at some of the more upper class clubs, where the normally snobby patrons were reduced to groupies once they surmised I was part of the mob. One of those places was L'Etoile, where everyone sat at tables rather than at a bar, and conducted more civilized invited-to-the-table sex hunting. Lefraks hung out there, as did Mayor Lindsey. L'Etoile later became the Playboy Club, where I held court many evenings as a resident mobster. However, during the L'Etoile period I had tried for a time to get a ghostwriter, but with no success. One night at the club I met a female writer and pitched her on ghosting my novel. She told me to tape some of the anecdotes I said would make good reading then bring it to her and she'd see what she could do. I remember taking my son's tape recorder one Sunday morning, propped myself up with some pillows in bed, and beginning to tell a story about a past incident. I felt weirdly like Joe Valachi, and wiped out the tape.

That period ended when I went to prison on a three year sentence.

While I was at one institution, I signed up for college courses. The college actually took registrations and sent professors to that institution, unlike other prisons where they divert the federal grant money to their staffs who pose as professors. One of the courses I took was expository writing, where we had to write a short story every week using a different literary form. When the course was nearly over, the professor told me how talented he thought I was, and offered me an opportunity to enroll in the college at full scholarship once my prison time was done.

"That's very good," I answered. *"I'll just call my wife and tell her that when my time ends in prison I'll just be away at school for another few years."* Ridiculous. What I was too obtuse to realize at the time is something that recurred later on too; that there is an art and a craft to any artistic discipline, and that the art is innate and recognizable to others while the craft to make it viable takes a lot of work.

The idea of doing a novel kept gnawing at me after I left prison and returned to the streets. Finally, after a couple of years of freedom and more unsuccessful attempts to contract a ghostwriter, I decided to go to our local community college and take a writing course. *If you want something done right, do it yourself.* Unfortunately, doing things on my own didn't help. I wound up in a literature class reading Ibsen's "Doll House" instead of beginning my great American novel. To complete my first assignment, I wrote a tongue in cheek analysis about "nuts and squirrels."

Then I got arrested again.

I dropped out of my literature course unofficially, never notifying the college of my decision. Less than a year later I was defending myself in one of Rudy Giuliani's first big R.I.C.O. trials. One day, upon leaving the courthouse, I crossed paths with the professor of that course I had left.

"You were the one who did the nuts and squirrels report," he said. *"What happened to you?"*

I explained my situation, and how attending his class, any class, was the furthest thing from my mind. He shook my hand, wished me luck with my trial, and said, *"It was my honor to work, however briefly, with such a talented writer."*

I thought he had become one of the nutty squirrels, but later, much later, realized that it was the recognition of the art once again.

With the weight of the United States of America as my adversary, I was naturally convicted and sentenced to prison. While awaiting designation to a prison facility, I was offered a private deal that could keep me close enough to home to maintain family...natural family...ties. As I had done with another incident, I threw it out at other pals who were also incarcerated with me. As usual, I was told that I could do what I wanted, but that it wouldn't work. It didn't. Instead of being close to home, I was sent far enough to warrant a plane ride for potential visitors. I was assigned to a unit and put into a cell with another prisoner, an old guy from Philadelphia, who much later, years after being released, rolled over for the feds and helped bring down Philly's mob leadership. At that time, however, he was not a rat and was a pretty good cellmate. I settled in with two things: pinochle and reading. One day he asked, since I read so much, if I would like to read the manuscript of someone on our unit who had just sold a novel to a major publishing house.

Thank you, Lord.

One of the things I truly believe is that things that look terrible at the time they are happening often work out for the best. Based on that belief, I reasoned that I had been convicted, lost my deal to stay close to home, and put in this particular unit of this prison for one thing: to get my ghostwriter. After I had read the manuscript, I asked to meet the author. After being introduced, I pitched the man on becoming my ghostwriter.

"I'm from out west," he said. *"I don't know anything about the life*

you're talking about. Do you think you could write out one or two of the anecdotes you told me about?"

I said I could, and immediately got to work.

"This stuff looks pretty good," my potential ghostwriter said, after he had read the first two anecdotes I'd delivered. *"Do you think you could do some more, so I could get a better handle on that stuff?"*

After I'd delivered about ten thousand words of mob stories, he said, *"This stuff could make a very good novel, but what do you need me for?"*

"Because I can't write," I replied.

"You just did," he said, holding up the pages I'd given him.

"But you don't understand," I insisted. *"I don't know how to do underlying themes or secondary characters; all the stuff I know a novel needs."*

He handed me the papers, patted me on the shoulder, said, *"You'll learn,"* and walked away, leaving me clutching my ten thousand word investment.

A short time later, he came to my cell and explained that no one could tell my story like me. He said I had the ability to write...I had proven that...but that I had to be willing to work at it. He even introduced me to his literary agent on the phone. I remember writing a letter to the agent months later, in which I told him that I was trying to put everything together into a coherent storyline, but couldn't.

Then, one day, the entire story came to me; so complete that I could outline each chapter, from beginning to end. When I would get blocked on the story in sequence I was working on, I'd just jump to another chapter and work on it. That eventually became "Blood of Our Fathers."

If I missed the boat at all, it was in not keeping a diary of the process to turn out that first novel. I did a phone in radio interview with the ass

Curtis Sliwak and his wife when "Blood of Our Fathers" was first released in hardcover. I heard the lead in from the dipsy duo, in which they chatted about how easy it was for guys who went to jail to write books, and how they were tired of it.

When they finally got me on the air, I said, *"Before you guys talk about how easy it is in prison, I think you both should do a couple of years there."* Both stammered and stumbled for words before completing the interview completely tamed.

To begin, there was no typewriter in my cell and none on the unit. The only ones were IBM Selectrics in the Law Library. I therefore did my creative writing by hand, on a legal pad, all through each night (*I had managed to scam the system and not attend a prison job each day*). That meant my cellmate had to agree to sleep with the light on and never play his radio, which distracted me. I did approximately three to four thousand pages that way before ever attempting to type the manuscript. I would read some pages and marvel at how wonderful they were, then alternately decide everything I'd written was crap and should be thrown in the trash, and back and forth like that throughout the process.

When I did begin to type, I had to skip dinner and stay pressed against the outer door of the Law Library, more often than not in bitterly cold weather with a knit hat pulled down over my ears and gloves that didn't seem to warm my fingers, so that when the doors opened at six p.m. I would be the first one pushed through by the well fed group of more inmates than typewriters available that had built up behind me. Once inside, I found that all the typewriters had different removable Selectric font balls, so I had to steal one so that my pages had uniform print. I also had to steal paper, since they occasionally ran out, and hide it beneath a six foot high locker, where I also stashed stolen toilet paper (*yes, they'd run out of that too*). This was pre-computer age, so an edit on a page anywhere other than the end meant re-typing the entire manuscript so the pages lined up correctly. I typed approximately seven thousand pages during that period, for a total, when added to my handwritten ones, of about ten thousand.

I also learned a lot about what it took to appeal to a readership larger than one made up of big city people who loved mob material. I gave an early draft to another inmate, James Van Brun, who was a highly intelligent racist from Virginia, and who most recently was shot and died after killing a guard at the Holocaust Museum in Washington D.C. After he had read it, he went into a tirade I'd never thought he was capable of (*I had met him when we would reserve the music room occasionally to listen to Beethoven, Mozart, and other classical composers' work*). He cursed my characters; called them scum of the earth who he hoped all got cancer, and on, and on in that vein. I immediately realized that to appeal to a wide readership I had to make my protagonist, Mickey Boy Messina, the best and most honorable of the characters, someone who was forced or manipulated into the mob one way or another like Michael Corleone in "Godfather," someone who never killed anyone, and someone who went to prison for a crime he hadn't committed. Much of that was already in the manuscript, but I rewrote it to encompass all of it and to create an antagonist, Little Vinnie Calabra, who actually committed the crime he went away for and who was an ongoing threat. I firmly understood that I was not "writing for me" or Brooklyn-type readers alone, and that if I hoped to get published, I would have to communicate properly to readers all across the country. I had others read my manuscript, took in their negative comments (*their positive ones didn't mean any new work*), sifted through them to see which were viable and which didn't make sense to me, and rewrote, rewrote, rewrote. That process helped me work easily with my editor, Doug Grad, at Simon & Schuster later on, after I had sold that company my novel.

Once I had shown I could work well with an editor, that everything I wrote was not in stone and that I was willing to make changes, Simon & Schuster ordered two more books: "Sins of Our Sons, the sequel to "Blood of Our Fathers," and "Something About Her...," which was later changed to "Snake Eyes."

"Sins of Our Sons" was easy, as I'd already thought out a sequel. The entire manuscript I submitted took me between ninety and one-hundred-twenty days, and the edit took me no more than two weeks. Quite a change from the ten thousand pages it took me to complete "Blood of Our Fathers" to my liking. It was a piece of cake.

Then there was "Snake Eyes."

I began "Snake Eyes," which was originally entitled "Something About Her...," but was changed when my editor argued that the name was too soft, and that "Snake Eyes," which had been used before, was stronger and would attract more readers. I thought he was wrong, but gave him the benefit of the doubt since he was the professional, and changed it. I still believe it was a mistake, but it turned out not to matter.

The novel itself began with only a pattern. Novels have patterns that they use over and over. For example, the highly successful Harold Robbins pattern was to start with a guy growing up in mean conditions who rises to power in some ruthless, illegal, or unseemly way, then loses everything, only to rise like the Phoenix to greater heights as a better man with the help of a woman. Robert Ludlum's pattern in all his fantastic spy novels was to take a man, get him caught between two agencies, like KGB and CIA, that want him dead, get him beat up and shot up, only to emerge victorious with the help of a woman. Notice how they are sort of similar, especially at the end?

For "Something About Her...," I chose Ludlum's pattern, but expanded it so that I caught my protagonist, Neil DiChristo, between *three* agencies, GRU (*Russian Military Intelligence*), FBI, and the mob. I also put him in a cross between *two* women. Wonder which was more dangerous? You'll have to read the book to find out.

"Something About Her..." was a totally different writing experience for me. I created Neil, completed an in depth bio sheet for him, as I usually do with main characters, then threw him into a situation. I had a plan for what would happen, but at some point the characters came to life and demanded honesty, not my manipulation of them. They started behaving in ways that threw my story completely off track. They said things I didn't want them to say. I suddenly found myself in the role of reporter, following them around and recording what they did. Now, when I got blocked up, I was *really* blocked because I had no idea what they were going to do next or where the story would take me. Totally frustrating, to say the least. If I hadn't had the couple of hundred page investment at that point, I would have abandoned the project.

Then, suddenly, out of nowhere, my cast of characters would come to life, whistle, and I'd follow. After six to eight months "Something About Her…" was completed, and I, in a fit of hysteria, typed, "The end, the end, the end, the end…" all the way to the bottom of the page. Despite the pain, or maybe because of it, I believe "Something About Her…" ("Snake Eyes") is the best of my three published novels. I had planned to do a series of books about Neil, but due to a contract dispute with my publisher that never happened. They were shitheads who broke every promise, and I was still too filled with my street guy anger and hubris to settle amicably.

As a result of that experience, I put aside what was to be my *coup de grace*, a three generation mob saga, "Night of the Vespers." I began with no pattern, but a title, which was a real incident in the history of organized crime that took place in September of 1931, where the new order of mobsters like Lucky Luciano, Bugsy Siegel, Albert Anastasia, Vito Genovese, and a bunch of younger Americanized gangsters murdered a few dozen old "Moustache Petes" whose old country ways of vendetta interfered with earning the millions of dollars available. The patriarch of my fictional mob family murders his boss on that night, as his boss leaves a trysting session with his girlfriend, an up and coming opera singer. It was the most enjoyable of all my writing, as I was able to research the era in great detail, and felt as though I'd actually stepped into a time machine. I dug out baseball players and standings, political life, prices for everything from shaving cream to automobiles, and entertainment facts. I even listened to old Amos & Andy radio skits and incorporated them into the novel. For 175 completed manuscript pages, I accumulated more than 350 pages of typed research notes. When everything soured with my publisher, I tucked the papers away and hadn't revisited them since. However, now that research is much easier due to the Internet, I have gone over the pages again and will probably complete "Night of the Vespers" soon.

In the meantime, look for more new Sonny Girard books, including a novella in the editing stage, "Alternative Measures." You can purchase signed copies of all my books or let me know your thoughts at my website, www.SonnysMobCafe.com

© 2011 R.I.C.O. Entertainment, Inc. /www.SonnysMobCafe.com

Sonny Girard

STORIES OF ME:

CONFESSIONS

Ha, ha, fooled you. I don't do confessions. If I had wanted to, I could have avoided all those years in prison. Enjoy the rest of the book.

© 2011 R.I.C.O. Entertainment, Inc./www.SonnysMobCafe.com

Sonny Girard

STORIES OF ME:

PINOCHLE

One of the relatively innocent pleasures that is a mainstay in the lives of mob guys is pinochle. It's glue that binds guys together; it's addictive, infuriating, calming, and at the center of a few pinochle stories. I remember playing for twenty four hours straight and giving one of the guys around me money to pick up my date and take her to dinner on a Saturday night so I could play for another hour or two in the kitchen of the bar, the Cocoa Poodle, where we all hung out. Pinochle also reminds me of incidents with different mob characters:

Paulie "Zach" – Related to me through marriage, Paulie was a Gambino wiseguy who was one of the few I've come across who actually read books for pleasure. That gave us another level of friendship beyond our common criminality and relatives. He could be jovial and quick, but could also become irascible and violent, especially when playing pinochle. I would visit him in a Bensonhurst social club where he hung out with the likes of "Jimmy Brown" Faiella (*there were two Jimmy Browns who counted in Brooklyn at the time*), Anthony Spero, and another pal of mine, Frankie DeCicco, who was later infamously blown up in a car on 86th Street. When Paulie's name is mentioned, usually the first image that pops into my mind is walking into the club and seeing an ashtray he had swept off the pinochle table in a rage flying past my face.

Second comes cutting up money we'd made together, and lastly the fact that I went to prison partially, but not exclusively, because of him. When a situation was brought to me, I went to Paulie for union help to squashing the problem and give us both a payday. Probably because he was too diverted by trump cards, he never took care of the issue. Eventually, it festered into something that required me to engage in a physical solution...which, in part, I went to prison for. That didn't matter much because there were other responsibilities for it, including mine, and I really liked and respected him too much. On the other hand, when I finally came home, the Bensonhurst social club was one of my first stops. I could have sworn Paulie was sitting in the same seat and wearing the same clothes as the last time I had seen him, a couple of years before.

"Hickey" DeLorenzo – Hickey was Manhattan guy, and more than a little whacky. He was involved in the case where Maurice Sindona came to the U.S. with Vatican money to invest and got taken to the cleaners. The Vatican wound up fleeced for a lot of money and Sindona wound up dead, poisoned in an Italian prison cell. Hickey and the rest of the American mobsters in on the deal wound up with a lot of money.

Hickey was infamous among wiseguys for one of his antics. At the time he was being held in MCC, which is the federal detention facility in Lower Manhattan, the feds would allow inmates passes to visit their own dentists and return a few hours later. It gave the feds a way to save money and the inmates a breather for a little while; maybe a chance to play house with a wife or girlfriend. Hickey got a dental pass one day. He returned five years later. He forgot to tell them that the dentist he went to was in Argentina. Of course, after that dental furloughs were nixed for MCC inmates.

A major stunt pulled by The Hick was when he had run into a personal problem with The Chin. People who had problems with Gigante were few, as the number of those who survived was infinitely small. One day, on alert, and returning to his digs, Hickey spotted a couple of suspicious looking guys. He hurriedly ran inside and went to the window, only to see them making their way toward his house. In Hickey's mind, the only rational thing to do was start shooting. Unfortunately, or maybe fortunately, they were not Chin's hit men, but FBI Agents. Once their surrender message got through to him, Hickey behaved as any off-center-minded person would. He walked out of the house with his hands in the air. One little difference was that he was totally naked and rambling about being attacked by space creatures. He was able to skate with little more than a parole violation after extensive psychological tests.

I never could figure out how much of Hickey's nuttiness was an act and how much was contrived. He swore that his father who had disappeared in Florida was eaten by alligators. Maybe, after he was thrown in with them? In prison, Hickey had just about everyone who didn't know him, inmate and guard, that he was insane. He bugged out one guard by eating a "mouse" that he had constructed out of a pear half and some cigarette ashes that the guard, a Deep South country boy who could barely speak English, wouldn't come near him.

I played pinochle in prison with Hickey for a short time then refused to play with him again. In our daily afternoon game, I had a partner from the Jersey crew and Hickey had an old man, Sal, who used a cane to navigate even a small walking space. One day he played a card that infuriated his partner, Hickey. Suddenly, Hick stands up, reaches across the table, and slaps Sal in the face. That was it. I threw down my cards, called "*game over,*" and left. For the rest of the time we spent together in the same facility, Hickey would ask me to play pinochle and I would refuse. All I would say was, "*You slapped that old man.*" He'd argue his case again, but I wouldn't play. I loved the the game, but couldn't sit by and watch him slap his partners when he'd lose.

Hickey took it on the lam to California when he came out of prison, with Chin still not pleased with him, but returned when he was told to forget it and let bygones be bygones. He was murdered when he came back to New York.

Paul Vario – Paul was the character Paulie was based on in "Goodfellas," and was a real trip. He was sick of heart and sick of body. His heart was broken because he had treated Henry Hill like a son, and his son had betrayed him. Why he liked Hill is somewhat of a mystery, as most street guys thought him a total scumbag and used the term, "You respect a dog for his master," often when talking about him.

Maybe it was the fact that Paulie's youngest son, Lenny, died in a fire, and Henry became a plug for the hole in the old man's heart.

I played pinochle with Paulie in three different prisons. The first was in MCC-NY. Our game consisted of Paul partnered with Philly "Rusty" Rastelli and me partnered with one of the unnamed guys from Jersey, close with Anthony "Tumac" Accetera, who hadn't ratted his guys out yet, or Jimmy Nap, or Jimmy Burke. The reason my Jersey partner will go unnamed is because I couldn't stand him and don't want to memorialize him in print. But I needed a partner and he was in our "network" of relationships and available. Hey, any port in a storm. Pinochle's pinochle.

Anyway, Rusty, who was the boss of the Bonnano crew, pulled rank over Paulie, who was only a skipper with the Luccheses. Rank, in the street, runs vertically with those of lower rank, but horizontally across family lines. In other words, a boss of one crew outranks a captain of another, and relations between those of similar rank of one group are more closely aligned with those of the same rank in another; bosses will generally give other bosses priority over their own underlings, as will underbosses with other underbosses over captains, captains with other captains over made guys, and made guys with other made guys over associates. It works that way due to self interest and protection of position. Disillusioning and disappointing to me at first, though understandable and accepted as "just the way things are."

Back to pinochle. Because of his rank, Rusty used to rip Paulie a new ass over cards he played, ESPECIALLY if they were losing. I don't want to demean Paul by repeating Rusty's expletives, but they were pretty rough. Time, however, changed things, as Paulie was shipped to another facility. When I got there, I stopped by the game room, where Paulie, a skipper, was the top ranking guy who was partnered with a made guy from Connecticut. When the latter played a card Paulie didn't like, he'd rant at him using the EXACT SAME WORDS as Rusty had beat him up with. At the end of the day, in either place, none of it meant a thing. The ties that bound from being part of the same subculture, aside from personality clashes and differences, were stronger than with anyone else in the institutions. As the only one of our MCC game still alive, I wonder if those guys are playing three handed wherever they are, and if all rank ended there?

Two, three, four, or partners, pinochle is as much a part of mob life as a Frank Sinatra or Jimmy Roselli recording. I don't think I've played since I retired from the life. Miss it too.

Sonny Girard

STORIES OF ME:

THE MILITARY

My family has a mixed record of military service. We've had our share of heroes. My father won a number of medals in the WWII's European Campaign, including a Bronze Star and a Purple Heart earned in the Battle of the Bulge. My brother was Air Force Special Forces in Vietnam. Two of my uncles fought WWII in the South Pacific...on our side, of course. We also had an uncle who enlisted at sixteen years old, then took a crap in his pants in boot camp and cried till my grandfather picked him up. Don't think the army wanted anything to do with him after that.

We also had one who was not so militarily inclined. When WWII rolled around, my dad's oldest brother found it much too inconvenient to participate in. He had a job and a fiancée, and never believed uniforms showed him off to his best advantage. Though war had no place in his plans at the time, the U.S. Government didn't understand and sent him a draft notice. He could have shot off a toe, but hated pain and didn't want to ruin what were admirable mambo steps. He also could have claimed to be homosexual, but that was vetoed by his fiancée, who, of course, became my aunt. Instead, he had a plan. He went out to eat with my future aunt, then, after a large meal, swallowed poison. She screamed that he was trying to commit suicide, an ambulance was called, and the poison was successfully pumped from where it lay, on top of the food that had been packed into his stomach. Naturally, the "suicide" attempt precluded him from being killed, and the military rejected him.

That was the end of the story for about thirty-five years. At the later time, his marriage was on the rocks, and he and Auntie went to a

235

psychiatrist for counseling. One day, he showed up for his appointment looking glum. Doc asked him what was going on. He replied that his wife wanted a permanent split, and he had "nothing to live for." While he may have forgotten his "suicide" attempt of decades earlier, his record didn't. The doctor called in an assistant, who helped him help Unc into a straight jacket, and shipped him off to Kings County Hospital's psyche ward. That was when my cousin contacted me, asking if there was anything I could do to help him. After I laughed my ass off, knowing the infamous story of his WWII deferment, I called my criminal attorney, Jay Zerin, who incidentally was uncle to someone who would later be called Dice Clay. Jay filed a writ of habeas corpus and sprung him from the padded room forthwith.

Then there's me...

I got a draft notice during the Vietnam War. It was inconvenient for me because I was doing financially well with a bookmaking and shylock business among other things, but was not about to swallow something with a skull and crossbones on the package after a lobster fra diavolo dinner. First, with my luck it would have seeped through the claw meat and killed me. Second, I knew Unc's history. And, third, I wasn't that opposed to shooting guns...even overseas. My street boss at the time told me to forget about it; that they would never take me. I told him that defied logic; that if the situation were reversed I would ship my ass off to Vietnam immediately, and put me as close to the enemy as I could to make sure I got shot. He laughed and said they don't think like us.

The first problem I ran into was that the notice demanded I keep an appointment at Whitehall Street, in Manhattan, at seven or seven-thirty...in the morning! I was out every night and didn't get to bed until the a.m. hours. When I was due to report, my father tried to wake me up. In a daze, I told him I'd rescheduled and went back to sleep. Then I became paranoid. Were MPs going to drag me out of the bar at night? Raid the barber shop I went to each day? Disrupt a pinochle game to send me to the brig? All I got was another notice.

Not taking any chances, I spent the night at an after-hours club and drove straight to Whitehall Street while the rising sun burned my bloodshot eyes even with sunglasses. Since I arrived from a night out, I hadn't changed to All-American garb. I wore a black pin-striped suit, white on white lock-collar shirt, and white silk tie. I carried my grey sharkskin topcoat and grey fedora. I wore sunglasses. I was totally inconspicuous.

Inside, I found long lines. Hadn't they given me an appointment? I was given a form to fill out by a guy in a Navy uniform who stood about three feet taller than me. When I looked it over, I saw that there were two lines for criminal convictions. Though I'd had no convictions at that time, I'd had a number of arrests. I asked if I should list them. When Sailor Giant said yes, I asked for more forms. Zip to psychiatrist number one, without even removing so much as my cufflinks for a physical.

There were three of them; three psychs, one after the other, so remembering which is which is impossible, since at this stage of my life I'm still trying to remember whether the macaroni in the fridge is from yesterday or last week. What I do remember are parts. The form asked for the names of people who could be reached in case of emergency, which at that time was death from Viet Cong or friendly fire. I listed my boss, his brother, his dad, and everyone there was room for up the "family" chain. Since we were getting arrested regularly at the time, and making the newspapers most of them, Psychiatrist #1 recognized them.

"Is these the famous Mafia guys?" Doc asked.

"C'mon, Doc, you know there's no such thing."

"Well," he corrected himself, *"the gang?"*

"No gang; just a bunch of friends who hang out together."

One of my examiners (can't remember if it was one or two) asked me if I wanted to go into the service. I asked if I could ask him a question off the record. When he agreed, I was able to find out about something that truly interested me:

"I hear you can make a lot of money in the army. Is that true?"

I think it was that doctor who took out a big stamp worthy of what was used on the TV show "Dragnet," and stamped the outside of my manila folder "MORAL WAIVER."

I remember #3, since it was the only woman in the bunch. By the time I got to her, I practically needed toothpicks to keep my eyes open. I plopped down in a chair in front of her desk, with my topcoat folded on my lap and my fedora on top of it. I waited for what seemed like hours as she went through the notes in the folder.

When she finally spoke, she asked, *"How long are you going to go on like this?"*

"Go on like what, lady?" I shot back.

"Look at you," she said. *"You don't work and you're well dressed."*

If you don't believe anyone could ask something so stupid, just think how it registered with me. *"You would rather see me work my ass off and dress like a slob?"* I asked. *"Are you nuts?"*

"I have no classification for you," she responded, obviously wanting me out of her sight as quickly as possible. *"Wait here,"* she said, *"and I'll get you a subway token to go home with."*

"Please, give the token to someone who needs it," I said. *"Can I leave now?"*

I don't remember if she said yes or merely threw an ashtray at me, but I was done, finished as far as Uncle Sam was concerned. He'd deal with me later in other ways.

© 2011 R.I.C.O. Entertainment, Inc.

ASK SONNY

Real Q & A from readers of SonnysMobCafe.com:

ASK SONNY

NAME: Steve C.

SUBJECT: Just Comments

MESSAGE:

It's been awhile since I reached out to ya Sonny. Man, the website has improved and, I must say, I enjoyed some of you writings. The one about Bugsy was interesting. I didn't know you knew Stassi. I have read some pretty good articles on that guy. Old school to say the least. Lastly, your article about Jr. Gotti is dead on. These Black Panther scumbags are allowed to get away with whatever they want but the government clearly had a vendetta against Jr. Keep up the site, Sonny. I was wrong about who I thought you were. I will quit guessing but glad to see you didn't let Team America break you. You just had the insight to see what LCN was becoming. Take it easy.

Nice to hear from you again. I have a photo of Buffalo Bill performing his show in a Brooklyn parking lot at the turn of the Twentieth Century. The Wild West was fading as it modernized, and Bill was bringing that recent history to people who didn't really understand it before. I believe that's what I do now, just not in a parking lot. If you read my novels, especially Blood of Our Fathers, you will understand, through fiction, how the mob is deteriorating from the inside, not from outside pressure of law enforcement. You can read free preview pages on my website and purchase autographed copies there too.

Sonny

NAME: Camille B.

SUBJECT: Mafia

MESSAGE:

       Who actually runs the Genovese Family?

Thank you for your question. Keep in mind that if I did have that information, I certainly wouldn't disclose it.

If you go through all my blogs/articles, you will see that no living people are mentioned. All my books, which have preview pages on the website and can be purchased as well, are fictionalized. As a general statement, all crews in New York are in some measure of disarray, with certain top tier guys running the show.

Sonny

NAME: Vinny M.

SUBJECT: Chris Paciello

MESSAGE:

> I warned people about Chris Paciello many times, but they did not listen. He is not even fuckin' Italian; that is not his real name! I forgot his real name, but he is Albanian or Hungarian or some shit. I am going to take a trip to NYC when the weather lightens up. I wanna see Mickey D. and Joe Crumb before they die. Great memories with those guys at the Feast over the years.
>
> Best, Vinny

I too have great memories of the Feast days. While I met both guys, it was Joe Carlo who I was closest with. If you know those two, I'm sure you'll remember him because it was with him that I met them a number of times. In fact, I had a stand one year that was put away for me when I was coming out of doing state time. I won't go into the whole story, but I wound up chopping the stand up with an axe at the end of the Feast so I wouldn't be tempted to do it again the next year.

Paciello is no different than any of those in the Rat Squad. Usually, someone had a bad feeling about them before, but were blinded by an opportunity to make money. Greed is a killer.

You'll enjoy reading my books, especially Blood of Our Fathers, much of which is set in Little Italy. There are about twenty free preview pages of each book on the website.

Sonny

NAME: George B.

SUBJECT: Tommy D.

MESSAGE:

>I found your comments about the junkie rat
>Henry Hill very interesting. In "Good Fellas,"
>Tommy DiSimone was whacked out when he
>went to the ceremony to supposedly receive
>his button. Is that the way it happened? I
>have found little info about Tommy D. Was he
>really the sick maniac cowboy as painted by
>Scorsese?

I didn't know Tommy well, though I did meet him and friends of mind did business with him. I am really not too impressed with so called "maniacs," who, like DiSimone, Carlo Lombardo, etc., usually wind up dead. To me there are only three possible contributing factors: a) a thorough lack of personal discipline, b) a desire to build a reputation, and c) fear. I think the latter motivates most of them. A real toughguy will break your ass and send you on your way to do whatever you're brave enough to do. The coward will kill you because he's afraid of what you'll do if he gives you a beating and leaves you alive. Not every offense

is a killing offense.

You'll see a couple of murders committed by and done to a couple of these guys disguised as fiction in my novels, especially Blood of Our Fathers.

Sonny

NAME: Giovanni M.

SUBJECT: Sonny, it's Giovanni

MESSAGE:

> Long time my friend. Love to talk with you again. I had a few ideas for a screenplay. Please contact me.

Yes, long time. Hope all is well. Screenplays don't seem to be worth much now unless there is money to shoot them or a star attached. The business is so screwy that I don't even try to get any scripts done anymore. More relaxing this way :)

Sonny

NAME: Joshua T.

SUBJECT: Noticed

MESSAGE:

How do you get noticed? I'm turning 20 next month and I'm not getting any younger. I have always wanted to know how to get noticed in the right way. Let's face it, it would be stupid to go up and ask a wiseguy, "Hey let me in will ya?" so I want to know how do you get noticed, and if there are no families around how do you start an organized crime racket and what exploits would be the smartest to begin on. And how would this "mini family" find good loyal recruits who won't snitch on the spot when things get too hot?

Of course, for legal reasons these are to be all hypothetical "what if" questions.

Thank you for your interest. It might be easier to resurrect the Roman Empire. At least there are costumes to buy. A friend from the Newark, New Jersey, crew once told me that there would come a time when some guys would be talking on a street

corner when another man approached. They would say, "Shhh, don't talk. Here comes a stand up guy." That time is now. So much for recruitment. Enjoy my blogs, free preview pages of my novels, and everything else on the website. They are a glimpse into the recent past. If you want to purchase any of my novels, and experience more of that time, you can get signed copies from the website or download them on Kindle.

Sonny

NAME: Priest P.

SUBJECT: A Question

MESSAGE:

Why is it that hollywood and tv can glorify gangsters, but the real people who live the life can't speak for themselves? (that is of course once that person tries to become legit)For example Cullotta was allowed to play himself in Casino, and he was a rat, Henry Hill got paid for being a rat, the Weasel got paid for his book n he was a rat and etc. So what do you think about that?

Thank you for your interest and understanding of the topic. Hollywood is fascinated with the mob, but only wants stories from those who will portray mobsters only in a terrible light. As in all lives, there are some bad and some good. The result is that they take lies from rats like Henry Hill. When Hill was bouncing around Brooklyn and Queens, street guys had a saying about him, "You respect a dog for its master." That was because they all thought he was a garbage pail, but Paulie Vario had an umbrella over him. He paid Paulie back by ratting that Paulie got him a no show job to get him into a halfway house. Paulie was convicted of that and died in prison. No good deed goes unpunished. You don't see either of those things in "Goodfellas" or in his book. He told Pileggi a bs story, and Nick, who I know, bought it because he was an outsider looking in. I did a Geraldo show where he brought Hill in via satellite. I ripped him a new ass and showed him to be a phony and a liar on TV. I was never called back by Geraldo, yet he's had Hill on a dozen or more times over the years.

I have had a lot of meetings in Hollywood and New York for both screenplays I've written and a TV mob reality show called "Mob Talk Live." I did a demo for a show called "Home Made," which you can view on the "Moving Targets" page of my website. Even with Adam Sandler's manager as a partner, we couldn't sell it. He was told privately that they were afraid to deal with us. The best I could get through have been my novels. You can read free preview pages on the website and buy them in autographed editions from the site or on Kindle. You can also read fifty to sixty articles I've written, which will all be posted on the site soon. Though they are fiction, they are based on compilations of real people and events.

Sonny

NAME: Larry Mazza

SUBJECT: Contact

MESSAGE:

Tommy Dades and I are writing a book. Maybe we can talk.

Don't know who Tommy Dades is. Your name sounds familiar, but Mazza is a common name. Where are you from?

Sonny

- *I later found out that Larry Mazza had rolled over and that Tommy Dades is a retired cop. I refused to bother with either one of them.*

NAME: Giovanni M.

SUBJECT: Your "Rat Squad" Section

MESSAGE:

I'd like to see you post some of their death photos after they got clipped. (the ones who didn't have the chance to flip).

Thank you for your interest and comment. Unfortunately, the only way rats die today is in bed. When I ask pals of mine to name one person in the Witness Protection Program who has been taken care of, they can't name one. Even those who testified, like Henry Hill, Sammy the Bull, and Michael Franzese, who are NOT in the program, walk freely and do TV shows. That only encourages more wannabe wiseguys to betray their pals. In the old days, it was different. If you pay attention to the website photos, you'll see

those of Kid Twist Reles, one alive and another one of his body after it was tossed out of a hotel window. You'll get a real understanding of why these things happen by reading Blood of Our Fathers or, especially, Snake Eyes. Although they contain fictional characters, the why and way things happen are 100% authentic.

Sonny

NAME: D. Layne C.

SUBJECT: Hello

MESSAGE:

I am trying to locate "old" Friends that use to run clubs in Manhattan back in the late 1970's into the early 80's. One of the bars was called the Mardi Gras on Broadway and the other one was on a side street off Broadway called Annie's also the Golden Key in the Bronx I think....I believe some of their names were Pauly and I remember meeting a Sal and Vinny. Those days were the good ole days.

I moved away from the area 25 years ago...and I am now back living back in NYC. Wow, has it changed.

Thanks for your interest. Boy, you brought back some memories. I remember a couple of people, one got murdered, who hung out at the Mardi Gras. I also had an after-hours club downtown that used to draw clientele from those clubs. I went to prison the first time in the late 70s, came out and did a turnaround with the Feds. While I keep in touch with whichever of my old pals is alive, even in jail, that West Side area isn't one I spent much time in. If you know any of the guys from the West Side crew, down in the Village, they really had most of their guys there. Check out the free preview pages of my three novels and my articles (blogs), both newer and archived. You'll find a lot of interesting things, especially New York locations.

Sonny

NAME: Linda S.

SUBJECT: General info; curiosity.

MESSAGE:

        I was surfing web, stumbled into site by

accident. Being Italian-American, born-raised in N.J. and always have had a fascination with organized crime. I was also a big fan of the SOPRANOS, as it took place in my old neighborhood and State. I have a bizarre respect for the "Mob", they seemed to always have a sense of respect and honor to themselves. So, I am hoping to enjoy this website. Be well, Be safe.

Thank you for your interest. Not too many people understand that there are a lot of shades of grey in life, not just black and whites. Yes, collectively, we did a lot of bad things, but we also did good for others. For example, I ran into an actor in L.A. who came from East Harlem. He said that during the Depression, his mother would wake him up at night and drag him down to the local mob social club, where the guys would give neighbors things they probably stole: food, clothing, etc. He said if not for them, his family could never have gotten through the time. Part of having power was also the ability to keep an umbrella over others; to protect them and help them do well in life. Hope you enjoy the material on the site, including the articles and free preview pages of my novels. God Bless.

Sonny

NAME: Shane

SUBJECT: Irish-American Gangsters

MESSAGE:

Would you know if the West side gang (Westies) in Manhattan are defunct after Bosko left them, because I haven\'t heard anything since a long time.

Like you, I haven't heard anything much about the Westies or anyone else in that area. Was friends with an Italian guy, Vinnie Pacifico, who was a part of that crew, but he's since passed away. Fat Roy DeMeo, who was a dear friend of mine closely involved with those guys is also dead. What that means is my direct lines are pretty much gone. While I'm sure there are still crooks floating around the neighborhood, the organized nature of the Westies seems long gone, just the way the Italian crews are in many areas. Just the numbers of the Italian mob keeps it from being as vaporized as the Westies.

Sonny

NAME: Stewy

SUBJECT: Little Italy

MESSAGE:

Greetings from Australia. I have read many books on the mob and am intrigued in the lifestyle. I have visited Little Italy many times. Is there still much mob activity in the cafes/restaurants in Little Italy these days? Do you think with RICO the days of the mafia are over?

Thanks for the response. Love your site

Thanks for the interest. The mob in New York is on the run. By that, I mean that the old-style gatherings in clubs and restaurants are no more. It's now two or three at dinner in out of the way places for discussions and Little Italy for pure pleasure. While RICO is certainly a factor once the Feds have made a case, it is not a primary factor in the dissolution of the mob here. The primary factor is the upward mobility of the Italian-American community. There are no more tough ghettos that turn out top mobsters and prizefighters. Those neighborhoods ingrained loyalty as much as

toughness. It is really the autumn of the mob's years. If there were loyal people I could trust, I would probably still be a part of that life. RICO didn't make me change my life; the changes in the participants did. You can get a very clear picture of exactly how the mob is disintegrating from within by reading my first novel Blood of Our Fathers, and to a somewhat lesser degree in Snake Eyes. While they are fiction, many real events, and the authentic processes of the slide are presented for the reader to see. Keep in mind you have some pretty good guys from Italy operating in your country right now.

Sonny

NAME: Jes

SUBJECT: Frankie Saggio

In his book, he said he freelanced for all 5 families. Isn't it up to him to pick what family he wants to work for? How can a family step in and say "He belongs to us"? Does this type of thing really happen in organized crime? Did he portray himself to be bigger than he really was, or was he really as big of an earner as he says he was? Also,

I love the song that you have playing on this section. Good song.

Anyone who is worth anything will have a claim put in my one or more crews. Then it is up to him to decide where he wants to commit his loyalty. Does it make sense that someone did "work" for all five crews and no one wanted him? Exaggeration and lies are what sells books. I refused to do an autobiography for Simon & Schuster. I told them that a) I would have to lie and b) that a story needs a beginning, middle, and end, and by the time I reached a true end I'd be dead and couldn't write. In a word, all these books are filled with "bullshit."

Sonny

NAME: Ryan

SUBJECT: Past Family Connections

MESSAGE:

Hi Sonny,

My family lore has it that my great-grandfather was a bootlegger who ran some gambling operations in my hometown back in the 20s and

30s, was nearly whacked and exiled to Miami. I didn't believe much of it, thinking that these were tall tales. But a few years ago I was doing some research, skimming through some transcripts of the Kefauver Commission and I was shocked at what I saw. The story I was always gives was that my great grandfather, Little Frank Defilipo, had run card and craps games from the old family farm in my hometown of South Plainfield, NJ. I'd heard it from my grandmother's numerous cousins (Frank's nieces and nephews), many of whom are still alive and in town in their 80s and 90s, and some other old timers. My father told me what he was told by other, even older timers. Like I said, I thought it was BS. Until, I found a piece of testimony (forget from who specifically) that said the Joe Adonis crew ran regular craps games in South Plainfield. I mean I had seen some of the old stills used as essentially garden ornaments now, and read a letter he wrote about his escape from Cuba after the revolution, but this really opened my eyes.

I was wondering if there was anything you could tell me about operations ran by Adonis in New Jersey? Being trained in college as a historian (albeit amateur), I think this can help me put some things together about Grandpa Frank. Frank seemed like an interesting exciting guy: WWI vet, big game hunter and angler, and owner of multiple businesses. In fact, he built most of our (tiny) downtown.

Whatever info you can give me would be great, but if you do not have any that's cool too. I enjoy your website and insights into OC. Thanks

Unfortunately, that's a bit before my time, and the people who might have known him are dead. Since he was in Lucky's crew (Joe Adonis was in that crew, which became the Genovese Family), guys like Joe Rogers, who ran Havana for Lucky et al, or Jimmy Blue Eyes, would have been the guys to ask fifteen years ago. Joe Adonis' son may or may not still be alive, as the last time I saw him was more than twenty years ago. I doubt his father would have confided too much in him anyway. Have you tried finding an arrest record for him? Did you have relatives in Brooklyn? There's a De Filipo who I believe is still alive. Good luck with that search.

Sonny

NAME: Jes

SUBJECT: Joey the Hitman

MESSAGE:

In the book, "Joey the Hitman," he talks about a lot of hits that he claims to have committed.   Do you think that the book is authentic?   Also, who is the real Joey Black?   I heard that he hired people to kill him so his family could collect the insurance policy.   Do you think this really happened?

I, and others in the street, never believed Joey the Hitman was authentic when it was published, and still don't.   So many little details of how these things are handled rang false that we laughed that anyone would believe it.   After polling, we decided it was Jimmy Breslin, author of "The Gang That Couldn't Shoot Straight," using the Hitman gimmick, since he would have been laughed at had he used his own name.

If you take the time to read "Blood of Our Fathers," especially, you will understand how these matters are handled leading up to the acts.

Sonny

NAME: Jes

SUBJECT: Angelo Bruno

MESSAGE:

Sonny, I've been a big fan of your website. I've been getting a lot of responses from you through email also. My family is from South Philly. Fred Aldrich was killed in a car accident right down the street from my house. He was John Stanfa's bodyguard. He was driving the car when he was attacked on the Schuykill Expressway and Stanfa's son was shot in the face in retaliation for the Michael Changlinni hit. Just thought I would tell you that story. My question is: do you think that the Genovese Family did participated in Bruno's hit, and do you think that Tony Capaneggro actually pulled the trigger himself? Also, who do you think sanctioned the hit on Tony Bananas, was it to keep him quiet about the genovesetake over of the bookmaking operation, or was it because the hit actually wasn't sanctioned?

First, Tony Bananas was killed because of a money situation as it related to Bruno's betrayal and death. When his body was found there were bills sticking out of his ass. Who ordered it? To be honest, I don't

remember the discussions I had with my dear departed friend, Joe Marz, who was privvy to what was going on with that crew. Names like Joe Bananas had no face to me, so it didn't stick.

I don't think the attempt to kill Stanfa that hit his son in the face had one single reason. Sure, there are vengeance issues, but at the heart of it was a power struggle. The Ciangalini story is an especially sad one; two brothers on either side of the conflict; one dead and one crippled. Their father was a friend of mine, and I can't begin to even comprehend the pain he went through upon hearing that while in prison.

Sonny

NAME: Lance

SUBJECT: Restaurant

MESSAGE:

    Hey,
    I was wondering if the "Home Made" restaurant is in operation, and if so, where?

Actually, Lance, the restaurant was supposed to be opened in a small town in Iowa. It was part of the TV show proposal. However, since the show hasn't been

picked up, neither has the restaurant. Thanks for the interest. Hope there's a good Italian restaurant near you.

NOTE: The HomeMade presentation we made for a TV reality show can be viewed on the Moving Targets page of www.SonnysMobCafe.com

Sonny

NAME: Grandfather

SUBJECT: Change of Life

MESSAGE:

Disabled, broke, doing the best I can do to see that the needs of my family are met and forever falling short. How would one get in contact with the family to see if they could lean a helping hand?

Sorry, Grandfather, don't know where you are, but crew members around the country are just scrambling to stay alive and out of jail. Hope things turn around for you.

Sonny

NAME: Joey C.

SUBJECT: Loss of Environment

MESSAGE:

> I too come from an Italian neighborhood that is pretty much gone. Most people around me now are Italian by name only. How do you cope when everything and everyone around you seems to be foreign when really it's you?

As the number of friends I had dwindles, the few remaining seem to bitch and moan about how bad things are today. What I tell them is to be grateful that we have wonderful memories of a time gone by. I ask what memories this generation will have of their younger days in thirty or forty or fifty years from now? We may be saddened by the loss of what we once had, but young people will be saddened by what they never experienced.

On the more positive side, I never give up trying to instill tradition into my grandchildren (they're more receptive than our own kids, who are always rebellious and want to establish their own independent identities). I argued with one of my granddaughters who didn't want to eat fish on Christmas Eve, but now that she's in college understands it was more about

passing on a cultural root than eating baccala. I took three of them to a gelato cafe here that has an accordion player one "Italian Night" a week. They all loved it, including the oldest, who was fifteen. When they get into my car they listen to Lou Monte, Louis Prima, and Jimmy Rosselli. Their favorite is Mambo Italiano, by Rosemary Clooney. They are all small things, but I see the difference in them as they grow. They know who they are and where they come from.

You will probably enjoy my article on the demise of New York's Little Italy, either on my website www.SonnysMobCafe.com or on MySpace. Also, all my novels are filled with experiences, sights, and smells you will find familiar and trigger those fond memories I mentioned before.

Sonny

NAME: Tracey M.

SUBJECT: What if?

MESSAGE:

    Dear Sonny,

Hypothetically speaking, I am a made man and find out my wife has been having an affair with another married man NOT associated with the mob. What would be a typical outcome for all parties involved, the married man, the wife and yours truly?

Hypothetically speaking, being "made" doesn't necessarily mean you are equipped to handle that kind of problem. You might be a big earner who was "made" so your crew wouldn't lose your financial power to others, or like the one who had never fired a gun before the induction, shot into a tubful of water, and caught the ricocheted bullet in his body. On the other hand, if you're an old time-type guy, all those involved may have disappeared by now.

Sonny

To contact Sonny Girard with comments or questions, go to the Grill Sonny page on <u>www.SonnysMobCafe.com</u>

REVIEWS &

COMMENTS

ON

BOOKS WE LOVE

(Includes Sample Chapters)

REVIEW & COMMENTS:

OCTOPUS

by

Claire Sterling

Morte Alla Francia, Italia Anela?

The year is 1282. The day, Sunday, March 30th. The sun is bright; the weather balmy on this glorious Sicilian spring day. Laurel trees bloom to fill the nearby hills with verdant color. Churchgoers parade along the dusty piazzas in their best dark wool suits and black dresses.

Beautiful day for a wedding.

As the Vesper bells echo from one side of the island to the other, a young couple, hand in hand, make their way to the church to be joined in body for a lifetime and in spirit forever.

At the church, the young man, after a sneaked kiss, tears himself away from his beloved to go fetch the priest. He leaves her waiting amidst the reds, blues, and yellows of the garden flowers, a flower herself, waiting to give herself for the first time to the man she loves.

But the French are everywhere. The most recent invaders, in a past and future line of foreigners that had and would occupy Sicily, their soldiers traipse and trample as if they truly own every bit of Sicilian ground.

And its women.

Pierre Drouet, drunk and a sergeant in the occupying army, comes across the young bride-to-be as she waits for her future husband to bring the priest. She attracts him, and, her being Sicilian, he feels, makes her his for the taking.

A touch.

A fondle.

A try for a kiss.

Drouet insists on having his way with the raven-haired beauty. He grabs her, trying to drag her to a more secluded spot where he can throw her white dress over her head and relieve his manhood between her naked thighs.

The girl, however, wants none of the drunken invader, and struggles to be released from his grasp. She falls, crushing her head on the wall of the church she is supposed to be married at.

She dies.

As a result of that brutalization, thousands of Sicilians shout the battle call, Morte Alla Francia, Italia Anela!...Death to the French is Italy's cry.

The acronym for their shout becomes the password for a secret organization dedicated to driving the French from their island – Mafia!

Is that legend of the beginning of the Sicilian Mafia true?

Who knows?

It sounds great, and, but for the fact that at that time Sicilians did not consider themselves Italians, but only Sicilians, makes sense.

What is important is that the mob in America today had its roots in Sicily, and Sicily had a Mafia, whether it called it that or not, for centuries. Historians point to the fact that the term was first published in the mid-19th Century, so that must be when the organization started. Common sense will tell you that if Sicily was at the mercy of foreigners for centuries, and Sicilians could not get justice from those invaders, they must have had a sub-rosa, loosely knit form of government, that, locally, provided justice for the natives. And, as any government, the local "uomini di onore"...men of honor...needed funds to function. Their taxes came from shakedowns, kidnappings, and other rackets, a thread of criminality that would intertwine with another thread representing a code of respect and honor. Those two threads, braided together for centuries traveled to far away lands where their fellow Sicilians encountered the same experience they had in the old country for centuries. They did not speak the languages of their new homes, could not get justice from the ruling institutions, and turned to the only government that, for all its faults, had ever helped them: Mafia!

It was only when the Sicilian immigrants began to meld with the population of their adopted countries that the threads of honor and respect began to separate, leaving a choice of which to follow. Unfortunately, they chose crime.

* * * *

To understand what is now is to understand what came before. Claire Sterling's "Octopus" (Touchstone/Simon & Schuster Pp.46-53) relates some of that history, including other theories of how the Sicilian organization known as Mafia got its name, in its first chapter, "The View From Palermo."

Beyond that opening, Sterling's book is a wonderful and informative read, building through history how the Sicilians developed a business of international narcotics trafficking, whose tentacles reached across the globe...like an "Octopus."

OCTOPUS

Claire Sterling

Touchstone/Simon & Schuster 1990

ISBN: 0-671-73402-4

CHAPTER ONE: The View From Palermo (Pp.46-52):

The history of Sicily is awful. Every kind of invader since the mythical Cyclops has been lured to its nine thousand square miles of choice real estate. The island lay in the middle of their Mediterranean sea lanes, and the Mediterranean was the center of their universe. The Phoenicians took it, followed by the Greeks, Romans, Vandals, Ostrogoths, Byzantines, Arabs, Normans, Germans, Aragonese, Spaniards, and Bourbons. Some were more enlightened than others, but they were all incorrigible colonialists. Sicilian wheat fed their armies, Sicilian slaves grew their wheat, Sicilian land in vast tracts enriched them. Sicily abounded in secret sects under foreign occupation; avengers or plain bandits or both, reflecting popular hatred and rage. They are often called "Mafia," but they were only its precursors.

The word itself has been traced to nationalists in the thirteenth-century Sicilian Vespers uprising; to Freemasons in a Sicilian fishing village in 1799; to a witch in the Inquisition nicknamed "Catarina la

Licatisa nometa ancor Maffia," meaning one with audacity, power madness, and arrogance.

Some say "Mafia" comes from the archaic French *maufer*, god of evil. Others attribute it to the Arabic *mihfal*, assembly of many people (plus *mahyas* for braggadocio). It is more often said to stand for "Mazzini Autorizza Furti, Incendi, Avvelenamenti"; Giuseppe Mazzini, nineteenth-century leader of the Risorgimento that freed and unified Italy, is held to have "authorized robberies, arson, and poisoning" in Sicily to fight the Bourbon monarchy. He did have a secret band working for him there, which could be relevant.

Historians generally agree that the authentic Mafia got its start with Mazzini's flamboyant ally Giuseppe garibaldi. It was Garibaldi who drove out the last of the Bourbon kings and united Sicily to the new Italian state. Sicilians flocked to join him in an explosion of joyous excitement when his Red Shirts landed in Palermo in 1860, about two thousand *picciotti* were spoken of as *squadri della mafia*.

They were dazzled by Garibaldi's promises of dignity and social justice. Sicily was prostrate after two millennia of foreign rule – humiliated, eaten with corruption, destitute – but the young Italian nation failed to redeem it. The promises were broken, the Sicilians forgotten. In the absence of a state, the *picciotti* banded together and took over.

There is no document stating that this band was the Mafia. Nevertheless, an official dispatch dated 1865 cites it by name for the first time as a virulent, criminal secret society. A now-celebrated play in

Sicilian dialect, *I Mafiusi della Vicaria*, had just appeared in 1863. This comedy of prison life in Palermo described a *consorteria mafiusi*: a "society," complete with initiation rites and a hierarchical structure, of Mafiosi who commanded special respect inside the jail, imposed their own rules, exacted payoffs, daunted prison guards, and smuggled in clothing, food, and arms.

The hierarchical structure was lost to sight for the next 120 years, but the *consorteria* flourished. The crime rate in Sicily shot up so wildly that a state of siege was formally declared in 1893. By then, the Mafia had already grown so useful to the rich and mighty that it could never be dislodged. Feudal barons relied on it to keep unruly peasants in line. The Catholic Church counted on its protection for the enormous land holdings. Candidates for office would kiss the hand of a Capo-Mafia in public squares. A future prime minister used the slogan "Vote for X, a friend of the friends" – the classic Mafia label. Not a single Sicilian politician was elected to the Italian Parliament without the Mafia's stamp of approval from 1860 to 1924. Not too many are even now.

The poor turned to the Mafia because they had nobody else. There was no state apart from tax collectors, where they were concerned. The church, omnipotent in a solidly Catholic country, was in league with the barons and the establishment in Rome. The Mafia, though in league with all three, took pride in administering a degree of even-handed justice. This was a necessary ingredient of power; and power was once thought to be more intoxicating than money for a Mafia don. A simple citizen with none but honorary titles, he could command respect bordering on reverence, dispense wisdom and patronage, mediate disputes, choose public servants (including police chiefs and judges), elect lawmakers, and shape governments. Some peasants, therefore, got satisfaction from their *capo-cosca* (head of the clan); others received a blast from the *lupara*, the island's traditional sawed-off shotgun. It was rough, but it was justice of a kind.

From this confused and tormented scene, the Mafioso in Robin Hood's image emerged. He was manly and flagrantly contemptuous of the law, defending himself with bravura, and could even appear to be generous and wise, depending on who was looking. Foreign visitors thought him dashing, and romantic poets praised him. He was the essence of "beauty, grandeur, perfection, excellence," wrote the most celebrated of these last, Giuseppe Pitre.

Men of Honor love to quote Pitre. Probably no single man has done more to glorify a fraternity of murderous villains than this turn-of-the-century authority on Sicilian folklore. "The Mafioso is not a thief, not a blackguard...The Mafioso is simply a valorous man with no flies on his nose," he wrote. "Mafia is the force of the individual, intolerance toward the arrogance of others...Mafia unites the idea of beauty with superiority and valor in the best sense of the word, and something more: awareness of being a man, sureness of soul...audacity but never arrogance, never haughtiness."

There has never been such a Mafioso. Pitre was drawing on "distant and scented childhood memories," we are told tactfully by a former curator of the Pitre Museum in Palermo. "He did not invent facts but lived inside fantasy," explains this knowledgeable source. "He was not a historian, not a professional." No indeed.

* * * *

The two faces of the Mafia could best be seen in a contemporary of Pitre's named Vito Cascio Ferro: Don Vito to a deferential public, Sicily's first grand *capo di tutti capi.*

Don Vito was born in Palermo in 1862 and grew up illiterate, which was no handicap. Never again would the Mafia produce a man so widely admired. Describing him in *The Italians*, the late Luigi Barzini, Jr., wrote:

"Don Vito brought the organization to its highest perfection without undue recourse to violence...The Mafia leader who scatters corpses all over the island in order to achieve his goal is considered as inept as the statesman who has to wage aggressive wars. Don Vito ruled and inspired fear mainly by the use of his great qualities and natural ascendancy."

In point of fact, Don Vito was accused in his lifetime of twenty homicides, five burglaries, thirty-seven cases of extortion, a sensational kidnapping, and fifty-three other crimes of physical violence. One of his murder charges included cutting up the victim and stuffing the pieces into a barrel. He was formally indicted on such charges sixty-nine times, and acquitted sixty-nine times.

It was Don Vito who fathered the American Mafia. Fleeing to the United States in 1901 to escape arrest, he was the first Mafioso *di rispetto* (Man of Respect) to set foot on American shores. New York's Lower East Side teemed with Sicilian immigrants then, hardworking peasants slaving in sweatshops to survive. Sheltering among them, and preying mercilessly among them, were scores of Mafia fugitives from the first government crackdown in Sicily in 1893. The press called them the Black Hand.

By the turn of the century, the Black Hand was operating in St. Louis, Detroit, Chicago, Kansas City, New Orleans, New Jersey, and New York. The press and public were convinced that it was an extension of the Sicilian Mafia, stealthily overrunning America (in 1901!). Petrosino disagreed. To him, the group was no more than a natural product of the Sicilian émigré environment: a loose association of calloused criminals, cruel and rapacious, but disorganized. Then Don Vito Cascio Ferro showed up, and he changed his mind.

Petrosino came across Don Vito in 1903, when a dismembered head with genitals stuffed into its mouth was found in a barrel on New York's Eleventh Avenue. The victim was a Sicilian immigrant who had worked for Black Hand higher-ups. Petrosino was persuaded by the evidence that Don Vito was responsible.

Sicily's future overlord, a superlative organizer, had quickly gained ascendancy over the Black Hand. He personally had helped many of the members slip over from Sicily to the United States. Now he taught them discipline and established regular ties with Sicily to the United States – the Mafia's first Palermo-New York circuit. In the process, Don Vito perfected the most serviceable and durable of Mafia methods for making money: *'u pizzu. Fari vagnari 'u pizzu* means wetting a small bird's beak, a Mafia euphemism for buying protection by means of a monthly payoff.

The *pizzu*, first devised in New York in 1903, was exceedingly crude at the start. The Black Hand favored bleeding victims white, but Don Vito did not (or not quite). "You've got to skim the cream off the milk without breaking the bottle," he advised. "Don't ruin people with absurd demands for money. Offer your protection instead. Help them prosper in business and they'll not only be happy to pay the *pizzu* but they'll kiss your hands in gratitude."

Some did kiss Don Vito's hands. Unschooled though he was, he could calculate the limits of their financial tolerance to a nicety. By 1904, the Black Hand had become as coldly methodical as the Internal Revenue Bureau. Its demands for the *pizzu* arrived punctually, omitting no Sicilian immigrant with an income to tax – shopkeepers, peddlers, bricklayers, longshoremen – the sums fixed by sliding scale.

Don Vito took the system back to Sicily that same year. He might have ended his days in America if not for the Man in the Barrel murder case, a national sensation. Once on his tail, Lieutenant Joe Petrosino would not let go. Don Vito was forced to skip town, hide out in New Orleans for a while, and finally head home. He carried a photograph of Joe Petrosino in his pocket – an assassin's mark – when he sailed for Italy in 1904. There he became the island's reigning prince: a tall, distinguished gentleman with a "Mephistofelian beard" and "Mafiuso bearing" (read a police report), whose hand would be kissed by mayors and local dignitaries when he toured "his" towns. All Sicily was in his pocket when Petrosino showed up in Palermo five years later.

The visit was an insufferable affront. The Black Hand was under Don Vito's personal protection, and Petrosino's mission was to destroy it. He was going to track down its members' Italian criminal records, get them deported from the United States, and break up the whole Sicilian-American Mafia partnership. But Petrosino was shot and killed in Palermo's Piazza Marina before he could even begin.

The folklore tale is that Don Vito Cascio Ferro left a parliamentary deputy's table, drove to the Piazza Marina in his carriage, fired, and returned to finish his dinner. In fact, leaders of the Black Hand had met in New Orleans to discuss the problem, and dispatched two emissaries to meet with Don Vito in Sicily. The three of them shot Petrosino twice in the back of the head and once in the face.

Long afterward, Don Vito claimed personal credit for the murder. "Petrosino was a courageous adversary who did not deserve an ignoble death at the hands of a common *sicario* [killer]," he declared. It was the eve of World War II, and Sicily's peerless *capo di tutti capi* was dying in prison. Mussolini, dictator of fascist Italy, had put him there.

* * * *

Mussolini had decided, on his first tour of Sicily in 1924, that the Mafia would have to go. The mayor and *Capo-Mafia* of Piana dei Greci, Don Ciccio Coccia, was showing him around, and remarked of his large police escort: "Excellency, you're with me, and you have nothing to worry about. Why do you need so many cops?" Il Duce instantly understood the Mafia in Sicily. This was its kingdom, and he its guest – not at all his style. He was unlikely in any case to put up for long with this alternative power to his own. Within a month, Don Ciccio was in jail, and Mussolini's war on the Mafia had begun.

His Iron Prefect, Cesare Mori, set out to uproot the Mafia "as a surgeon penetrates the flesh with fire and steel, until he cauterizes the pus sacks of the bubonic plague." Thousands were flung into prison and tortured, guilty or innocent, their property seized and their families ruined. Where evidence was lacking, they were framed.

Sicily had fifteen mass trials between 1927 and 1929. An enormous cage, fifty yards long, was erected to hold 154 defendants in the first trial. "Fascist justice must be rapid and decisive. If the trial does not go faster, the liquidation of the Mafia will not be done until the year 2000," telegraphed Mussolini. Fascist justice triumphed; all but 6 were convicted. "The Mafia is dead, a new Sicily is born," affirmed the *New York Times.* "Mussolini has strangled the monster in its native lair," commented the *Times* of London. And the monster did retreat. Officially, the Mafia's kill rate on the island dropped from *ten a day* to three a week. Even unofficially, the rate fell by about three-quarters.

But the monster had not been beaten. The Mafia reappeared as if by magic when Mussolini fell at the end of World War II. Men of Honor, stout antifascists all, went straight from prison to public office. Their new *capo di tutti capi*, Don Calogero Vizzini, was installed as mayor of Villalba, his hometown; "Long live the Mafia! Long live Don Calo!" shouted friends in the crowd attending the ceremony.

Tall, heavy, and sturdy, jacket slung over his shoulder, and traditional Mafia *coppola* (beret) tilted over his eyes, Don Calo would hold daily audience at a café in the piazza as if the Duce's long reign had never happened. Describing his days, Barzini wrote:

"From the shadows along the walls and narrow sidestreets, people would come out and line up to see him – peasants, old women in black, young Mafiosi.

His magnanimous and protective manner, the respectful greetings of passersby, the humbleness of those approaching him, the smiles of gratitude when he addressed them, all recalled an ancient scene: a prince holding court in the open air."

Meanwhile, hundreds of his subjects had regrouped across the ocean. Eluding Mussolini's Iron Prefect during the 1920s, they had fled to America just in time for Prohibition and a fortune in bootleg booze. Several became famous fathers of Mafia Families: Joe Profaci from Villabate, Carlo Gambino from Palermo, Gaetano Lucchese (alias Tommy "Three-Finger" Brown) from Palermo, Joe Bonanno from Castellammare del Golfo. An especially large contingent had set forth from Castellammare, whose native sons would one day inaugurate the Sicilian-American heroin trade. So well did they fare that a replica of the Statue of Liberty stands in the town's main square, in homage to their adopted land.

- *Octopus is available on Amazon.com, Alibris.com & Half.com*

Review & Comments:

GANGBUSTERS

Chapter Nine: Night of the Locust (Pp. 253-280)

By Ernest Volkman

The characters in this chapter's true story illustrate as much as any how the mob has decimated itself from the inside out. While most blame law enforcement technology, stool pigeons, and laws like RICO, it is the total breakdown of common sense and honor that allows those others to take their toll.

I was intimately familiar with at least three of the major players in this drama. One, "Little Al" D'Arco, who became a boss, was in prison with me. I knew him superficially, but, in prison, even superficially is the same as in depth, since everyone lives together in a fishbowl environment and organized crime guys form their own clique, regardless of city or family of origin. There is an old prisoner's saying that "...there are no secrets in jail." Given the forced observation, this guy who handled the prison garbage seemed an unlikely candidate to be the boss of an entire family. In truth, if one didn't know the politics of how guys get made, money overcoming deeds, they would never guess he was even a "dunsky."(Bet you haven't heard that one before) D'Arco was a nice enough guy, but, then again, nice guys, especially bosses, finish last. My first reaction when I learned that he had been made boss was, "No way!" With that exclamation in my mind, the events that followed, with Little Al rolling over on his guys, came as no surprise to me.

Another of the guys, Bruno Facciola who was murdered, was someone I knew much better. I had had some dealings with him, and found him to be more honorable than many of the rest of the crew he was a made member of. Though the word put out for the public was that he was murdered because of fear that he was going to roll over that scenario always seemed extremely unlikely to me. Again, Bruno was an extremely honorable guy and a good soldier who believed in, rightly or wrongly, the mob system. Additionally, he was dying of cancer and had little to gain from testifying against anyone. What sticks in my mind is an unconfirmed version that some of us in the street were privy to, that Bruno was killed by a black group that he'd had a recent confrontation with, a confrontation I was aware of before his death. If memory serves me right, one of Bruno's brothers killed a black guy then went on the lam. Bruno was stopped in Canarsie, at the Foster Avenue Market, by a group of black toughs who told, not asked him to give up where his brother was or suffer the consequences himself. Bruno basically told them to go f__k themselves. He was murdered shortly thereafter.

The buzz in the street was said that after Bruno was killed, cars drove by his house and black power flags were thrown from them onto his lawn. In the early days, if that were the case his mob family would have gone to war. In the 1990s that didn't make any sense to a declining mob. By taking credit for the murder at the highest level, maybe no more than two executives, and circulating the fable among everyone else below them, they saved money, face, and lives. When I hear turncoats for the government tell how Bruno was murdered by his own crew, I generally believe he bought the family propaganda. When I hear Gaspipe take credit, it sounds more credible, but, then, rats lie. Why lie about murder? Again, not to show his poor performance as boss? I've known guys who went around giving hints that they'd eliminated someone I knew for a fact they hadn't, and others who confessed to murders they hadn't committed when copping pleas to a couple of others…in for a penny, in for a dime…and, it closed out cases for the Feds. Was Gaspipe's confession to this murder part of making a plea deal? Who knows? I do know he hasn't explained why he would murder someone who had less than six months to live. Is what I heard about Bruno's murder and the blacks really the way it went down? Who knows? I wasn't there. But it certainly wouldn't surprise me if it did.

Is that situation unique, where the mob has been reduced to more bark than bite? Absolutely not. I had seen it first hand a couple of times going back to the late 1970s. In one, a numbers banker friend of mine, Shanty, operated in the Washington Heights section of Manhattan. After years of having a field day with gambling operations, after hours clubs, and legitimate business in the area he was approached by "Marielita" Cuban mobsters who demanded partnership. He reported the shakedown attempt to his superiors who were located on Mulberry Street, in Little Italy. In the past, guns would have been brought out of safekeeping and handed out to family members to protect the northern territory. Instead, he was told there was nothing much to be done, since it was not close enough for them to lookout for him constantly, and that he should make a deal with the Cubans. Another guy, from another crew, who was on vacation, spotted a former mobster who had testified then skipped town. He called back east and reported the sighting, asking what he should do; did they want him to "do some work?" The answer: "Mind your business. Make believe you never saw him."

This brings us to the third member of the group in this chapter, the one I knew most intimately: Richard Pagliarulo (I can't bring myself to call him "Richie the Wig"). When we were young men we were partners. We were friends. When I was on the lam I hid at his parents' house. His family was like my family.

He was never very bright.

The biggest problem Richie had was that he was always trying to live up to an uncle who had been a mob star. From early on, when all of us in that age group were trying to gain reputations of our own, he was more driven and intense. He lived for the compliment or the pat on the head. When his uncle died at too early an age from cancer, it drove Richie into a tizzy, knowing that the promises he had been given by his uncle would never be honored by the family's heirs. His actions became rebellious and he eventually wound up getting made by another family: the Lucchese Family.

Though we more or less hadn't kept close touch over the Lucchese years, I was aware of what was going on with him and how he had become; for example, going drunk into a pal's restaurant and slamming a pistol on the table over some contrived argument. I realized that while most of us who had been young together had outgrown the need to prove ourselves, he hadn't...if not to others, then certainly to himself. He *also needed to prove his loyalty to his superiors, since he felt rejected by his last. But loyalty and blindness are two different things. He mixed them up and wound up killing dozens of people on orders. Most mob guys, after having justified the first few assignments in a short time, would have realized that their boss was out of control, and might have stopped the bloodbath by ridding the world of him. As I said earlier, Richie, rest his soul, was never very bright. Correcting the judge who was sentencing him that he had murdered forty-nine men instead of, as the judge had said, forty-eight proves that more than anything I can say. Richie kept in touch with me from prison, where he died a few years ago. Despite everything that happened, I will always remember him as my friend.*

All in all, these guys in this chapter illustrate the inner decay of the mob: ineptitude – one mobster, Peter Chiodo, actually turns witness to get a slice of pizza; loss of strength—another one, Little Al D'Arco, turned himself in without even being arrested or indicted; misplaced loyalty—crazy killing by two family leaders, Amuso and Casso, so irrationally afraid of prison time that, in a self-fulfilling prophesy, they actually turned their closest allies against them. RICO and the FBI only take advantage of these organized criminals' flaws.

* * * *

As for "Gangbusters," the major portion is the history of the Lucchese Crime Family from the time that "Three Finger Brown," Lucchese's street name, was running his rackets on the streets of East Harlem to the whole "Gaspipe" Casso affair that the book is supposed to be about. If you aren't intimately aware of the Lucchese Family saga then it's an interesting read. If, on the other hand, if you are as well versed in mob history as I am, which is very few, then it's old news and you spend almost two thirds of the book asking yourself, "When is the story I bought the book for going to start?" The last part of the book actually does a very good job in relating the turmoil from the late 80s to the early 90s that brought that mob family down. Volksman's a good writer, and brings a story factually based on the transcripts of the case. "Gangbusters" is definitely worth a read, and is a must for any follower of organized crime history and current events. The past explains the present and will do so for the future.

GANGBUSTERS

Chapter Nine: Night of the Locust (Pp. 253-280)

By Ernest Volkman

Faber & Faber, 1998

ISBN: 0-571-19942-9

CHAPTER NINE: Night of the Locust (Pp.253-280):

"Mother is the best bet and don't let Satan draw you in too fast."

LAST WORDS OF DUTCH SCHULTZ

Corrado (Dino) Marino could not have been more clear: the meeting was *important*, so don't be late. Gas doesn't like people who are late to important meetings. Frank Arnold hastened to reassure the emissary from Gas Pipe Casso that he understood the message. He'd be there, right on time.

On the appointed day, Arnold stood outside his home at the precise moment and was picked up by Marino and driven to the meeting site, an unused warehouse on Staten Island. He was nervous, for any meeting with a man of Casso's reputation was not an appointment to be regarded lightly. But he felt no fear. For one thing, he trusted Marino, an old friend. More important, Marino had used the word "sitdown," which would have signified some kind of problem that had to be ironed out. And, as far as Arnold knew, there was no problem. As the new Lucchese man in the Painters Union, succeeding the murdered James Bishop, Arnold had things running smoothly. The money from the labor extortion operation was flowing regularly upward to Casso, the organization's chief executive in charge of the racket. To be sure, the union's international was breathing down his neck and federal investigators were sniffing around, but so far they apparently hadn't found anything of consequence.

Perhaps, Arnold speculated, Casso had bigger and better things in mind for him. Or perhaps he simply wanted to establish face-to-face contact with his man in the union. Whatever the reason, Arnold felt honored that the new underboss of the Lucchese Family would take the risk of emerging from his hideout to meet with him.

But Casso was nowhere to be seen in the warehouse. Instead, Arnold encountered Peter Chiodo and Richard Pagliarulo, the Lucchese Family's most infamous enforcers.

"What's the problem?" Arnold asked, feeling the sickening tremors of fear. He looked at Marino, who simply stared at him impassively.

"*This* is your fucking problem," said Pagliarulo, jamming a sawed-off shotgun into Arnold's throat.

"Gas is sure you're gonna flip, Frank, so that's the way it is," Chiodo said, almost apologetically.

"Are you fucking crazy?" said Arnold, his knees shaking uncontrollably. "What the fuck am I gonna flip about? I'm not in any trouble; I got no indictments. Gas knows I love him."

"Gas had a dream," Chiodo explained. "In the dream, you ratted him out."

"*A dream? A fucking dream?*" Arnold was shrieking in wild fear as he fell to his knees.

His bowels gave way.

Chiodo wrinkled his nose. "I hate when they do that," he said. He signaled to Pagliarulo, and they both began walking away in disgust.

"Get the fuck out of here," Chiodo commanded over his shoulder to Arnold, who gathered his oiled self and on rubbery legs somehow managed to run for his life.

The wings of death had whispered very close to Frank Arnold, and were it not for the squeamishness of the executioners, what remained of him would have become a pile of ashes or dismembered parts scattered in garbage cans all over New York City. But he would be one of the few lucky ones in a bloody slaughter that had begun, among the bloodiest in the history of organized crime. It was also among the more senseless.

The slaughter was ordered by Vic Amuso and Gas Pipe Casso from exile. Seized by a murderous rage over the events that had forced them to flee to their rat holes, the two mobsters saw killing as the solution to all their legal problems and the essential object lesson for anyone in their organization who might be wavering. With a praetorian guard of killers, led by Pagliarulo and Chiodo, the Lucchese Family's boss and underboss set about to eliminate all threats – defined as anyone who had even the potential to cause problems. Like Hitler and his diehard band of Nazis in their Berlin bunker, they constructed for themselves a mad world in which paranoia became reality and the vaguest suspicion was sufficient for a death sentence.

In the process, they would destroy their world.

Bruno Facciola was among the first to discover that, in the new regime, even thirty years of unswerving loyalty to the organization was no immunity against death. From the days when he served as an apprentice to Paul Vario in Brooklyn crap games, through his years as an enforcer and his later career as one of the Lucchese Family's best fences, Facciola was a model Mafioso who prided himself on his reputation as a standup guy, the kind of mobster who actually spat into the faces of cops who tried to get him to talk. He had served several prison terms uncomplainingly, and in 1990, he was facing his latest legal trouble, an indictment for fencing stolen jewels. Out on bail while awaiting trial, he got a call one night to attend a "very important meeting" with Gas Pipe Casso. After dressing in his Sunday best suit, he drove off. Six days later, residents of a Queens neighborhood some distance from Facciola's home called police to complain of a foul odor coming from a parked car. In the trunk, cops found the broken body of Facciola, shot and stabbed so many times that the medical examiner found it difficult to arrive at a precise number of fatal wounds.

The style and method of Facciola's disposal instantly suggested a Mafia rubout, the savagery traditionally used to signify that the victim was a traitor. But since Facciola wasn't an informant, police were puzzled. They were equally puzzled by the subsequent murder of Michael Salerno, a leading Lucchese Family loan shark active in the Garment Center. Salerno was not facing any legal trouble and had the reputation of a loyal family soldier with consistent record: whenever approached by a police detective or FBI agent, he invariably opened the conversation by saying, "Go fuck yourself." Yet when the medical examiner investigated his body, also retrieved from a car trunk, he discovered that Salerno's throat had been slashed from ear to ear, the traditional Mafia signal that the victim had been executed because he was talking to authorities.

As far as the police were concerned, the only consistent pattern established thus far was that two solidly loyal Lucchese Family mobsters had been murdered. It could be safely inferred that the murders had been ordered by the family's leadership, but why murder two men whose loyalty was unquestioned? The same enigma arose in the case of a third murder, that of Patrick Testa, a premier auto thief who worked in the Lucchese Family's Brooklyn faction. Testa was not only fanatically loyal, but he was also known to be slavishly devoted to Gas Pipe Casso (he stole the black Jeep Cherokee that his superior used to flee New York). He had served a prison sentence for auto theft, refusing to utter even a word to cops. But somebody walked into the Brooklyn chop shop where Testa hung out and pumped nine bullets into him.

Two more murders were also mysterious. Larry Taylor and Al

Visconti were low level Lucchese street hoods who liked to consider themselves classic Mafia tough guys openly defiant of cops. They were both found shot to death. The only discernible connection with the previous murders lay in the fact that they were both very close friends of Bruno Facciola, a previous victim, and had openly vowed vengeance against whoever had carried out his slaying (although, like the police, they hadn't been able to figure out any reason for it, much less any suspects).

Peter Chiodo, the Amuso-Casso regime's chief executioner, knew why these murders were occurring. He knew that Michael Salerno had died because Casso had a *feeling* he might try to take over the organization while his boss was in exile. Additionally, Casso said, he was *probably* going to become an informant. Facciola died because Amuso and Casso had a *hunch* he would become an informant. Testa died because Casso deduced he knew too much about his flight into hiding and *maybe* would consider becoming an informant. And Taylor and Visconti died because, Casso decreed, their search to avenge their friend's slaying *might* eventually result in their learning of Casso's execution order, creating possible witnesses.

Like a tiny candle lighted in a dark room, these flimsy justifications for murder lit the first flickering rays of doubt in the mind of Chiodo. No one prided himself more on unquestioning loyalty to the organization, but even Chiodo began to wonder if Amuso and Casso were in the grips of some insane paranoia. As the veteran of several dozen murders, Chiodo had no qualms about killing witnesses, informants, and Mafia miscreants who stole money from the organization or defied the orders of family leadership. But this was different; men were being killed on what seemed to be the faintest whispers of suspicion.

This first crisis of faith, however faint, also made Chiodo begin to consider his own place in the scheme of things. As he was among the first to realize, if his bosses ordered men killed on merely the vaguest of suspicion, what about himself? Would they order his death if they woke up one morning and decided that their unquestionably loyal hit man might become an informant some day? Or that he knew too much?

Sooner than he could have anticipated, Chiodo was forced to consider the matter further when he committed an error – the kind of error his bosses had come to not forgive.

Of all the men for whom Amuso and Casso felt a deadly animus, Joseph Martinelli may have been one of the few who deserved it. A contractor who had functioned as a Lucchese Family associate for several years, Martinelli paid $100,000 a year to the family for the privilege of participating in the construction rackets. But coincident with the fall of Tony Ducks Corallo and his three chief executives, Martinelli stopped paying. The new Lucchese generation, in the person of Christopher Funari, Jr., son of the imprisoned Lucchese mobster, demanded that Martinelli resume paying. When Martinelli stalled, Funari consulted his father on what he should do. Beat him up, the elder Funari advised. Martinelli subsequently received a severe battering.

But that still wasn't enough to get the money flowing again, and the problem was brought to Casso for resolution. "Kill this cocksucker," he ordered Chiodo, who detailed two dimwitted street hoods to do the deed. They botched two attempts before any shots were fired (Martinelli was unaware of them), and an exasperated Chiodo decided to take matters into his own hands.

"Fuck it, I'll do it myself," Chiodo announced, then set about to lure Martinelli into his grasp. He approached Martinelli and, under the guise of peacemaker attempting to resolve a problem, told him that he had arranged a sitdown between him and Casso. Martinelli, eager to avoid another beating, agreed to the meeting, which he was told would take place at a deserted shorefront area on Staten Island.

The next day, Chiodo picked up Martinelli and drove him to the meeting site while Pagliarulo trailed at some distance behind the car as backup. As they reached a swampy area, Chiodo pulled out a .45-caliber pistol, pointed it at Martinelli's head, and pulled the trigger. Nothing happened. As the color drained from Martinelli's face, Chiodo pulled the trigger again.

And again, nothing happened.

"Look how real they make these toy guns nowadays," Chiodo said, laughing. "Scared you, huh?"

It sure did, and while Martinelli shook in fear, Chiodo pulled up to a roadside pay phone, telling him he was calling to "double-check security arrangements." He returned a few minutes later to announce that the meeting was off; Casso had detected law enforcement surveillance in the area. Chiodo drove Martinelli home. His intended victim seemed to have trouble breathing.

Later, Chiodo met with Pagliarulo to check out the gun. To his chagrin, Chiodo discovered he had failed to properly seat the clip. "Listen," he pleaded with Pagliarulo, "whatever you do, don't tell Gas about this. You know the way he is."

Telling Gas is precisely what the ambitious Pagliarulo did. As he probably calculated, the news sent Casso into a towering rage while igniting his paranoia. In the process, Chiodo became in Casso's mind the very personification of treason, the kind of rotten apple that had to be destroyed before he infected the entire barrel. In Casso's calculation, the sequence of events involving Chiodo assumed very sinister connotations. Chiodo had allowed Frank Arnold to live, and although Arnold's later indictment and imprisonment made the question of his execution academic, the fact was that Chiodo had violated a direct order. Following that, he had begun to openly question the decision to murder other people. Then came the Martinelli incident; was it possible he had deliberately fouled up that assignment? Perhaps that botch should be judged in the context of another Chiodo action that disturbed Casso, his guilty plea in the windows case. Could it be that Chiodo had made a secret deal with the authorities and was deliberately messing up murder assignments?

In a mind like Casso's, the conclusion was inevitable. So was Chiodo's fate: Casso ordered Pagliarulo to arrange for the execution of Peter Chiodo. Shortly afterward, Chiodo one morning pulled his Cadillac into a Staten Island gas station to check why the car's engine seemed to be knocking. He had opened the hood and was peering inside when a car with three men screeched to a halt near him. Two men jumped out and began firing, one shot chipping a piece of cement near Chiodo's foot.

Pulling out his gun, Chiodo fired back as he scurried into the mechanic bays. While the gun battle raged on, he was hit by seven bullets. Finally, weak from loss of blood, Chiodo collapsed. As his consciousness ebbed away, he heard the sound of an approaching police siren and one of the shooters say, "Let's get the fuck out of here; we've been here too long. He's dead, anyway."

But Chiodo wasn't dead. Astounded doctors later found that of the seven bullets that struck him – five of which passed clean through his body – none struck a vital organ. Chiodo's 547 pounds of blubber somehow had absorbed the kind of firepower that would have killed any other man.

While Chiodo recuperated in a hospital, Richard Pagliarulo was practically beside himself with rage. Now confronted with the difficult task of telling Casso that his important murder assignment failed, he vented his frustration to Dino Marino. "Jesus H. Christ," Pagliarulo fumed. "I told them to aim for the head. They must've seen a western."

He would have loved to get a second crack at Chiodo, but his target was out of reach. Under twenty-four-hour guard by federal marshals, Chiodo was recuperating behind an impenetrable security screen. His brief periods of consciousness were occupied by a steady parade of police detectives and FBI agents, who assumed that Chiodo was now ready to talk about events in the Lucchese Family. But ever the Mafia loyalist, Chiodo made it clear even seven bullets in his body were not sufficient to make him violate his oath of *omerta*. He was willing to talk only to the extent of anything he might know about the rat holes in which Amuso and Casso were located, but nothing else. His interrogators finally gave up, telling prosecutor Charles Rose there was no point in trying to convert a man that even an attempted assassination had failed to move.

Rose was not willing to give up yet, for Chiodo was a glittering prize – if he could be convinced to switch sides. A few nights later, Rose appeared at Chiodo's hospital room carrying a king-size pizza. He began a deceptively casual conversation and the two men chatted awhile about various inconsequential matters. Chiodo, occasionally wincing in pain from his wounds as he lay virtually immobile in a posture that enabled him to move only his head, began warming to the prosecutor. When Rose felt he had established a rapport, he got around to the more interesting subject of Chiodo's shooting.

"You know, Mr. Rose," Chiodo said through a thicket of intravenous tubes, "it's really strange when somebody tries to kill you. You can feel the breeze a bullet makes when it goes past your ear."

"I've never had the experience, thank God," Rose said. "Which raises the question, Peter: do you have any idea why somebody would want to kill you? Just thinking aloud, I wonder if Gas Pipe Casso perhaps may have felt angry at you for some reason and dispatched a few of his friends to kill you. You wouldn't have any idea why Mr. Casso was so ticked off, do you?"

"I don't know anything about that kind of shit," Chiodo said grimly, but Rose noticed that his attention had begun to focus on the large box resting in the prosecutor's lap. Rose slowly opened it, letting the aroma of the warm pizza waft around the room.

"I hope you don't mind," Rose said, detaching a slice. "I haven't had any supper, and I'm hungry as hell."

"No problem, Mr. Rose," Chiodo said. Rose saw that Chiodo had become nearly bug-eyed as the smells of the pizza penetrated the breathing apparatus in his nostrils; he was actually drooling while he watched Rose start to devour a slice. Apparently, the seven bullets had failed to put a dent in his gargantuan appetite.

"Jeez, I could go for a slice," said Chiodo, unable to resist any longer.

"Oh, I don't think the doctors would like that," Rose said, taking another bite from his slice. "How could I justify it? Federal prosecutor feeds forbidden food to gravely wounded Mafioso! My God, I'd be in terrible trouble."

"Listen," said Chiodo, almost whining like a dog for its dinner, "what the fucking doctors don't know won't hurt them. So we'll eat a little pizza, and, you know, talk."

The process began. Drawing a chair close to Chiodo's bedside, Rose detached a slice and slowly moved it toward his mouth. All the while, he conducted a dialogue with him; how fast the pizza slice was advanced depended on the extent and quality of Chiodo's end of the conversation. Occasionally, Rose would withdraw a slice when Chiodo appeared not to be fully cooperative.

Finally, Chiodo had devoured most of the pizza in the box. In the process, he became a witness for the federal government. His transformation came about in large part when he was persuaded by Rose's argument: since his superiors had tried to kill him without sufficient cause, Chiodo was no longer bound by his oath of *omerta*. It was a simple matter of contract law, Rose told him, a case where one side had broken a solemn contract. As Rose argued, the Mafia initiation ceremony was in effect an unwritten contract sealed by blood oath; while Chiodo had vowed to adhere to certain rules, the other side, among other things, guaranteed that he would not be executed without the Mafia version of due process. Where was the due process in his case? Was there a sitdown to discuss any grievances Amuso and Casso might have held against him? Was Chiodo permitted to present his side of events?

The result was a deal: Chiodo would plead guilty to one count of racketeering in the windows case in satisfaction of all charges (including the murders which he had either carried out personally or was involved in some way), and receive a sentence of twenty years in prison. In return, Chiodo would provide Rose and the FBI with everything he knew about the Lucchese Family. Given his role in that organization, Chiodo's revelations promised to be nothing short of sensational.

Something along the line of that very thought occurred to Amuso and Casso. Assuming that a wounded (and understandably angry) Chiodo might decide to defect to the other side, they tried to devise some way that would deflect him from that course. The method they chose, however, succeeded only in convincing their former hit man that he was doing the right thing in joining "Mr. Rose's team," as he liked to call the new organization to which he now pledged allegiance.

First, Casso dispatched two hoods to the office of Chiodo's lawyer, who was given a message for his client: "Tell him his wife is next." Then Mrs. Chiodo arrived to visit her husband in the hospital and told him she had begun receiving threatening phone calls. She was whisked into the Witness Protection Program.

That left Amuso and Casso with little leverage, and they then decided on an act that was to rock the Mafia to its foundations: Richard Pagliarulo was instructed to murder Chiodo's sister as a means of terrorizing him into silence. Pagliarulo assigned the job to three submorons from the most recent class of Lucchese recruits, Dino Basciano and the brothers Michael and Robert Spinelli. They stalked Mrs. Patricia Cappozalo for a month, and ambushed her early one morning outside her house as she returned home after dropping off her children at school. She was severely wounded, but survived.

No single act would so discredit the American Mafia as the

shooting of a Brooklyn homemaker. For many years of its existence, the Mafia had an ironclad rule barring the involvement of "civilians" (ordinary citizens) in any of its organizational disputes. There was, of course, a sound political reason for this dictum: involving citizens in shooting wars was an almost certain way of arousing public wrath against organized crime. A subsidiary rule mandated that the non-Mafia relatives of Mafiosi be kept out of any disputes on the sensible grounds that involving them would only set off dynastic struggles in which entire families might be consumed.

Casso's decision to begin killing innocent relatives of Chiodo – his sister had no connection whatsoever with organized crime and knew nothing of her brother's criminal life – set off a public outcry against the Mafia. It got even louder when Casso made his next move, ordering the murder of Chiodo's uncle, Frank Signorino. The body of Signorino was found stuffed into plastic bags in a car trunk. He had died simply because he was the only Chiodo relative available; he had refused to join the exodus of other relatives into the Witness Protection Program.

Among the more alarmed at this turn of events was the Lucchese Family's on-site boss, Little Al D'Arco. A veteran mobster who had spent most of his sixty-five years in the organization, D'Arco was perfectly aware that killing Chiodo's relatives was a colossally stupid act. It not only threatened to harden Chiodo's resolve to destroy the organization (which it did), but it also represented a public relations disaster of the first order. The rest of the Mafia began to regard the Lucchese organization as outcasts, and the newspapers were filled every day with accounts of the Mafia "animals" loose on the streets.

D'Arco became further unsettled when, in secret meetings with Amuso and Casso, he heard even more elaborate plans for wholesale murder. In one meeting with Casso, he was shown a list of forty-nine people Gas Pipe had picked to be murdered. With a start, D'Arco realized that half the names on the list were members of the Lucchese Family. Asked why so many people were targeted for elimination, Casso replied that they were "creeps." In another meeting, Casso insisted that the government would never be able to prove his and Amuso's guilt in the windows case. At some point, he said, the government would be forced to drop the case against them, and then they would return to New York. "When I come home," Casso vowed, "I'm going to have a party and invite all the creeps I want to kill. Then I'll kill them all." At still another meeting, this time with Amuso, D'Arco was ordered to contact the Philadelphia Mafia to recruit bombing experts for the purpose of another attempt to kill John Gotti. When D'Arco raised the possibility of retaliation by the Gambino Family after Gotti's murder, Amuso replied, "Don't worry about it; the robe knows about it."

"The robe" was Amuso's nickname for Vincent Gigante, boss of the Genovese Family, which suggested that Amuso and Gigante were still intent on killing Gotti, for reasons which seemed unclear. D'Arco took his sweet time contacting the Philadelphia Mafia, by which point the murder plot was academic: Gotti was ensnared in a RICO case that ultimately would send him to prison for life without parole. In any event, D'Arco had made up his mind that he would derail the plan to kill Gotti, somehow. The idea struck him as particularly stupid; considering the disrupted state of the Mafia at that point, the last thing the organization needed was another high-level murder – just the thing to stir up some real chaos.

For the first time in Al D'Arco's criminal career, thanks to his promotion as stand-in boss of the Lucchese Family for such purposes as dealing with the heads of other families and attending Commission meetings, he had a panoramic view of the Mafia's upper level. He was not impressed by what he saw. In a general atmosphere of disintegration, the high command was as unruly as an unsupervised kindergarten class, with hardly a real criminal brain in evidence. D'Arco's own Mafia family was a mess, but it was a paragon of stability compared to what was going on in the other families. The Gambino Family, disrupted by Gotti's legal troubles, was degenerating into warring factions, a chaos largely caused by Gotti's insistence that his arrogant and stupid son, John Gotti, Jr., take command of the family.

Widely despised throughout the family as an untalented punk with insufficient experience in running a criminal enterprise, the younger Gotti informed anyone questioning his leadership abilities that he would tell his father, who would arrange for their murder. The Bonnano Family, still barred from Commission membership, was preoccupied with dominating the heroin trade, while the Genovese Family was attempting to conduct business via a shaky communications line to a boss in a psychiatric hospital. As for the Colombo Family, it was busily self-destructing in a bitter internal struggle between rival factions that had already consumed a dozen lives.

In such an atmosphere, business negotiations at the upper level tended to be tense. One scheduled sitdown between the Gambino and Lucchese organizations on the division of spoils from a Bronx construction racket assumed the dimensions of a meeting between rival colonels of a South American military junta. D'Arco, the representative of the Lucchese Family, was concerned that the representative of the Gambino Family, Sammy the Bull Gravano, intended to use the sitdown as an excuse to gun down D'Arco and any other Lucchese man he could get his hands on. Not an unreasonable suspicion, considering Gravano's well-deserved reputation for disposing of business rivals (he would eventually murder nineteen of them). D'Arco armed seven Lucchese hoods with Uzi submachine guns and spotted them around the meeting site, unaware that an equally suspicious Gravano – believing that D'Arco would use the site to dispose of *him* – had spotted his own gunmen around the area.

D'Arco tried his best to keep things on an even keel while collecting enough money to keep Amuso and Casso satisfied during their regular rendezvous, when the chief topic of conversation was how much cash he had brought with him. The amounts usually ranged in the hundreds of thousands of dollars, but, as D'Arco perceived, both Amuso and Casso were beginning to regard him with suspicion. D'Arco had tried to keep track of all the various sources of cash payments by writing notes on little pieces of paper, but the sheer volume and complexity soon confused him, and he was having difficulty getting a firm grip of exactly how much was coming in.

"You sure this is what we're supposed to get?" Amuso or Casso would ask with increasing frequency. D'Arco sensed the question meant he was in deepening political trouble, confirmed when he was summoned to a meeting and told he was being demoted. From now on, on-site operations of the family would be run by a four man committee consisting of himself, Salvatore Avellino, the boss of the Long Island garbage racket; Frank Lastorino, the notorious hit man; and Anthony (Bowat) Barratta, a capo in the family's Bronx section.

D'Arco suspected that his demotion was merely a prelude to more drastic action Amuso and Casso had in store for him. He was on a heightened state of alert when, shortly afterward, he attended a meeting with four fellow-Lucchese mobsters at a midtown Manhattan hotel. He noticed that one of the men had a suspicious bulge under his shirt that had disappeared when he returned from a trip to the bathroom. Immediately, another mobster said he had to go to the bathroom, a scenario that suggested to D'Arco a classic Mafia hit operation – one man planting a gun in the bathroom, to be retrieved by a second man who would do the actual shooting.

Whether this was in fact the plan has never been determined. The important fact is that D'Arco thought it was. He excused himself to step outside the room for a moment, and, before anyone quite realized what was happening, he raced down the stairs. On the street, he jumped into his car and headed for his apartment in Greenwich Village. "We'll go – now!" he announced to his wife of thirty-eight years. Leaving a meal she was about to put on the table, they drove around for a while, finally ending up in the small city of New Rochelle, a few miles north of New York City. D'Arco walked into the FBI field office and announced his intention to defect. Agents, hardly able to believe what had dropped into their laps, immediately took him up on the offer. Within an hour, D'Arco and his entire family had been enrolled in the Witness Protection Program.

After agreeing to a plea deal in exchange for his cooperation, D'Arco got right down to work. In his first debriefing, he concentrated on two topics of immediate interest: his knowledge of anyone marked for murder in the ongoing Amuso-Casso murder spree, and any clues he might have to where the two Mafia leaders could be found.

In terms of imminent murder victims, D'Arco rang an alarm bell: he remembered Casso telling him just a short while before that the priority target was Aniello Migliore. At one time Tony Ducks Corallo's second in command, Migliore had been convicted in a 1987 racketeering case, but the conviction was overturned on appeal. While the government was considering whether to retry the case, Migliore was freed. Migliore had no intention of returning to the Mafia's upper echelon; sickened by the insanity that seemed to have gripped the organization, he passed the word that he intended to retire from organized crime and concentrate on his highly profitable tile business.

But Amuso and Casso didn't believe a word of it. As D'Arco learned, they regarded Migliore as a major threat, the man who undoubtedly would rally the diehard forces loyal to Tony Ducks Corallo, eliminate Casso and Amuso, then take over the organization as boss. D'Arco carefully asked Casso what proof they had of this scenario, and was alarmed to hear Casso tell him they didn't have any proof, just a "feeling." It was enough to set in motion a plan by Amuso and Casso to eliminate what they considered a looming threat.

D'Arco's revelation brought three FBI agents to Migliore's door. "Mr. Migliore," one of the agents said formally, "we are morally bound to tell you that we have incontrovertible evidence that Anthony Casso and Vittorio Amuso have planned your death."

Migliore demonstrated no reaction, although he became agitated when the agents decided to use the opportunity to mention the possibility that he consider the wisdom of seeking federal government protection – in exchange for his cooperation. "I wasn't raised that way," Migliore replied stiffly. "I've lived all my life with dignity and honor, and

I'll die that way too."

The agents rolled their eyes at this recitation of Mafiaspeak, shrugged, and left. A few nights later, Migliore was sitting in the glassed atrium of a Long Island restaurant when two shotgun blasts from a passing car shattered the atrium in a shower of glass. Migliore was hit by glass and pellets in the head, neck, and chest, but the wounds were slight. It was a close call that moved Migliore to play an interesting gambit to convey to Amuso and Casso that he was serious about his retirement plans. He gave an unprecedented interview to *Newsday*, the Long Island daily, in which he revealed the FBI visit to his home and his refusal to even consider cooperating.

"They must think I was born yesterday," he was quoted as saying, "coming to the house in the middle of the night, telling me they want to save my life, and all I have to do is tell 'em everything I know. C'mon!" Having established the point he would remain impervious to all blandishments from the other side, Migliore then addressed the question of any ambitions he might harbor to take over the Lucchese Family. He laughed that off, and when asked abut the rumors that Salvatore Avellino would become the boss of the family, replied, "He's welcome to the title – and the forty years [in jail] that goes with it." Amuso and Casso gradually became aware of the Migliore interview, and, while they weren't entirely convinced, it was sufficient to induce at least a temporary delay in their plan to eliminate him. (Like Chiodo and D'Arco, Migliore's devotion to Mafia protocol precluded an obvious solution: kill Amuso and Casso.)

There was a larger meaning to Migliore's gambit. Aside from the fact that Mafia leaders do not give newspaper interviews, his comments underscored a new fatalism that was beginning to infect the Mafia's upper echelon. Migliore was not the only senior Mafioso who had come to believe that any leadership position was a certain guarantee of jail, an extraordinary transformation from only a few years before when a position in the hierarchy was a virtual guarantee of untouchability. The fact that Migliore, a figure of immense prestige and respect within the

Mafia, had decided he wanted no part of it spoke volumes about the effect that relentless law enforcement pressure had exacted on la Cosa Nostra.

On a more prosaic level, the attempted murder of Migliore proved D'Arco right, and his debriefers now sought from him anything he might know about where they could find Amuso and Casso. D'Arco was more than willing to help, because he shared the general alarm about these two psychopaths. FBI and police teams, amounting to more than a hundred agents and police detectives, were busy looking into every corner of the underworld, thus far without success. D'Arco now pointed them in the right direction.

While on the lam, D'Arco related, Amuso and Caso maintained contact with their organization by means of a highly secure communication system. D'Arco and others were summoned to meetings via prearranged calls on pay phones, during which the meeting site was announced, usually the parking lots of various shopping malls or deserted areas. The same meeting site was never used twice. To coordinate this system, D'Arco said, Amuso and Casso would need a "callbox," one trusted member of the organization they would notify to set the meeting system in motion. There were a number of possibilities for that job, although D'Arco suspected that it was Frank Lastorino, the hit man who was very close to Casso.

The FBI and police hunters began to concentrate their attention on Lastorino, but before they could establish a link between him and the fugitives, quite unexpectedly Vic Amuso fell into their hands. It began with an anonymous phone call one afternoon to the FBI: Amuso could be found the next day around noon in a small suburban shopping mall in Scranton, Pennsylvania. The call electrified no one; two weeks before, the Amuso and Casso flight had been dramatized on the "America's Most Wanted" television show. While the FBI was pleased that two of its most wanted were displayed for the show's several million viewers, any one of whom might have some information, the flip side was that it inspired many fruitless calls that had to be checked out.

At the time the anonymous call arrived at the FBI, the Bureau had already run down hundreds of false tips phoned in by viewers, so the call was regarded as probably another dead end. Two of the most junior agents in the Bureau's Scranton field office – one had been on the job less than a year, the other less than six months – were dispatched to the shopping center to check it out. Accompanied by a posse of local police, they staked out the area and waited. Some forty minutes went by with no sight of Amuso, and the agents were about to give up when they noticed a man strolling into a store. They double-checked the photos of Amuso they had been given: there was no doubt. The man was suddenly surrounded by gun-wielding cops and the two FBI agents.

"Vittorio Amuso?" one agent asked, and when the stunned man didn't reply, added, "FBI. You're under arrest for unlawful flight to avoid prosecution."

Amuso made no attempt to deny who he was. "Fuck," he said as he was handcuffed.

There was a small celebration in Charles Rose's office on the news of Amuso's capture. When it ended, Rose and his partner Gregory O'Connell immediately set to work preparing a case against him. The still-pending charges that had led to Amuso's flight – his involvement in the windows scheme – were now embellished with an entire law library's worth of felonies as D'Arco and Chiodo piled on their recollections. Peter Savino, the chief prosecution witness in the original windows trial, was also enlisted to add whatever he knew firsthand of Amuso's involvement.

Within weeks, the two prosecutors had a fifty-four-count RICO indictment alleging crimes from racketeering to murder. A grand jury unhesitatingly approved it, setting the stage for the first skirmish in the spring of 1992 with Amuso's lawyer, Gerald L. Shargel, a highly regarded defense attorney with a long roster of prominent Mafia clients. At a bail hearing, Shargel fought vigorously to get his client released on million-dollar bail, but Rose had a strong counterargument: since Amuso was demonstrably a flight risk, he should be remanded to jail without bail.

Shargel lost that argument, as he probably expected he would; it is almost unheard of for a federal judge to grant bail to any defendant who is a flight risk, as Amuso uncontestably was. But Shargel didn't give up, and was back in court that December, arguing that Amuso should be released temporarily on what he called a "Christmas furlough." To buttress his argument, he packed the courtroom with Amuso's relatives, some of whom occasionally dabbed their eyes in sorrow at the thought that their beloved relative would be behind bars at Christmas. These relatives, Shargel told Judge Raymond Dearie (the original windows case judge now assigned the Amuso case) were pledging a total of $4 million in bond to guarantee Amuso's return to prison.

Rose found this move fascinating. A conversation with his new star witness, Little Al D'Arco, had provided some insight into what was really going on. The anonymous phone call that had led to Amuso's capture, D'Arco noted, was very interesting. Consider, he said, the circumstances: only someone with intimate knowledge of Amuso's movements could have made that call. The likely suspect was Casso, who had apparently decided to become boss by betraying his close friend and business partner. There already existed some evidence for this thesis: as Rose was aware, Amuso was increasingly suspicious that Casso had given him up. From his prison cell, he sent a note to Casso referring to "black Sunday," and demanding that he find the culprit who had dropped a dime on him. Casso had replied coolly, saying he would try. Casso's distinctly unenthusiastic answer hardened Amuso's suspicion about his underboss. The Amuso request for a Christmas furlough was in fact a bid to obtain the time necessary to kill Casso, along with anybody else he thought might be too closely allied with his underboss.

Rose argued that the request for furlough was a subterfuge for Amuso to kill his enemies – even assuming he would return. Amuso had no concern about jeopardizing the homes and businesses his relatives put up for his bond. "The only reason Mr. Amuso is even in this court in the first place," Rose said, "is because an FBI manhunt tracked him down. There is absolutely zero prospect that Mr. Amuso will return to this courtroom in the event that his motion for furlough is granted."

"I quite agree," Dearie said. "Motion denied. The defendant remains remanded."

Amuso shot Rose a malevolent look as he was led back to jail, and little imagination was required to understand what was going through that homicidal mind. Rose would come to expect that look as the pretrial process ground on during the next several months, a look he hoped the jury would see during the actual trial. In his years of dealing with some of the more deadly Mafiosi on the planet, Rose had never seen anyone who could project quite the sense of evil that Amuso could.

Rose was convinced that he had a sufficiently strong case to put Amuso away for good, but O'Connell worried it might not be strong enough. "We need more tape," he fretted. True, Rose conceded; ideally they would have liked the kind of tapes that had destroyed John Gotti – clear, unequivocal recordings of the defendant's own voice incriminating himself. They had a few tapes, mainly from the windows case and several culled from other cases, but nothing like the dramatic recordings of Gotti boasting of ordering murders.

Rose sought to reassure his fellow prosecutor. "We've got a secret weapon in this case," he said. "You know what the name of that secret weapon is? Alphonse D'Arco."

O'Connell was skeptical, for an objective look at the battlefield and how the opposing forces were arrayed revealed that the prosecution had several handicaps. Shargel was well aware of them, as the smugly confident look on his face demonstrated when the trial finally opened in the spring of 1992 – no slam-dunk tapes, and a roster of criminals turned prosecution witnesses, all of them vulnerable to cross-examination, when their odious pasts would be dragged before the jury.

Shargel's early confidence was rattled when Rose pulled a surprise move: his opening remarks took the form of a Mafia initiation rite, complete with the burning of a picture of a saint. Shargel noted the jury's rapt attention, which meant that Rose had won the first round – jurors had been swept into the world of the Mafia, precisely where the defense did not want them to be. Shargel attempted to minimize the damage as the case went on and was more than holding his own when Rose brought out what he insisted to O'Connell was the prosecution's secret weapon, Little Al D'Arco.

Unlike Chiodo and Savino, who testified with the unmistakable air of well-rehearsed prosecution witnesses playing out their required roles to win at least partial leniency for their crimes, D'Arco approached his inaugural appearance as government witness as the opportunity to conduct a seminar on organized crime. Relaxed and now expansive, he came across as every family's black-sheep uncle, the skeleton in the closet now trying to reenter the good graces of his blood relations. D'Arco was taken through his criminal career – street hood, heroin trafficker, racketeer, acting family boss – by the booming voice of O'Connell. In conversational tones, D'Arco elaborated on his criminal career, along the way educating jurors in the real world of the Mafia. More significantly, he discussed at great length his firsthand knowledge of Amuso's own criminal career, including every act alleged in the indictment.

The climactic moment came when O'Connell summarized D'Arco's life in crime and asked him, "Mr. D'Arco, was it all worth it?"

"No," D'Arco replied without hesitation, then launched into an extraordinary soliloquy about life in the Mafia. It was a cry from the heart, the anguished words of a man who was now confronting a nightmare: his life had been a total waste. "I'm sixty-five years old," he concluded. "What has it gotten me? Nothing, absolutely nothing. Yes, I have my wife and I have my son. But I was the one who got my son into the Mafia. And what did I accomplish by doing that? My son is a drug dealer! No, I've got nothing to show for it. What a waste of my life."

O'Connell was about to go on, but he felt Rose tugging at his sleeve. "Stop now," Rose whispered. "You can't do any better." O'Connell glanced toward the jury; deeply affected by D'Arco's heart-wrenching testimony, the jurors were sitting there in rapt silence. The courtroom had become hushed.

"I told you," a smiling Rose whispered to O'Connell, who nodded in understanding. D'Arco had reached the jury on an intensely personal level, which meant they found him credible. And that in turn meant that they were prepared to convict Vic Amuso.

Aware of the danger, Shargel went after D'Arco, but the witness proved surprisingly nimble, parrying the defense lawyer's best shots. To Shargel's distress, he noticed several jurors actually smiling at the witness as D'Arco established eye contact with them, chatting away as though he were at a family dinner, discussing the vagaries of his profession. Frustrated, Shargel began to get disoriented and finally made the mistake of asking, "Do you consider yourself a rat?"

Like a home run hitter given a fast ball right down the middle of the plate, D'Arco pounced. Pointing a finger at Amuso, he adopted an outraged tone: "I'll tell you what a rat is. There's nothing worse than trying to kill someone because they think he's a rat when they're really not!" Rose and O'Connell smiled contentedly as they noticed fascinated jurors staring openmouthed at the exchange.

Although Rose was confident the prosecution had won, a worried O'Connell paced as the jury retired for its verdict. Only seven hours later, word came that a verdict had been reached. "Trust me, Greg," Rose told him. "Only seven hours for fifty-four counts? You can bet the house they found the son of a bitch guilty."

Rose was right: the jury convicted on all fifty-four counts. Amuso, chewing on a mint, showed no emotion, but he gave Rose a long, lingering look of pure hate as he was led away. Four months later, during a sentencing hearing, he gave Rose another malevolent stare as

Dearie threw the book at him: life in prison without parole. As he left the courtroom and into a crowd of reporters gathered outside, Rose was confronted by an angry Barbara Amuso, the convicted boss's wife.

"There's been an injustice done!" she screamed as reporters scribbled in their notebooks. "You should hide your head in shame! You intimidate women and children!"

"The only women and children I think about," Rose snapped back at her, "are the wives and children of the men your husband had killed."

"Pretty good," O'Connell said as he watched accounts of Rose's confrontation with Mrs. Amuso on the evening TV news that night.

"Well, it was a genuine reaction," Rose said. Shoes off, feet up on his desk, he was celebrating the courtroom victory with O'Connell by sipping a soda.

"Well, one animal to go," O'Connell said.

As yes, the animal,, Rose sighed, instantly understanding that "animal" could only mean Gas Pipe Casso, who had now achieved his dream of becoming boss of the Lucchese Family. "I wonder if our friends in the constabulary are any closer to locating America's leading psychopath."

As if on cue, a grim-looking delegation from the FBI visited Rose the next day. But instead of the happy news Rose hoped they would bring, they had a distinctly disturbing piece of information. Casso had decided to kill the one man whose elimination, he was convinced, would end all his trouibles. That man's name was Charles Rose.

"Was it something I said?" Rose joked, but nobody laughed. Rose was told that Casso's decision to murder the federal prosecutor was not idle Mafia gossip; the FBI had solid evidence that not only had Casso ordered Rose's assassination, but planning for it was already well under way.

The key piece of evidence was a fairly high-ranking member of the Lucchese Family – to be called Mr. X here – who had approached the FBI and offered to provide information about a Casso plan he considered so insane that the only way to stop it was to let the FBI know. Mr. X's reasoning process came into sharper focus when he agreed to a meeting with Rose.

"What, is he fucking crazy?" Mr. X asked, somewhat rhetorically, referring to Casso. "Forget about it. The FBI will shoot us down in the street like dogs. Forget about arrests; they'll just hunt us down and you know what happens to us next."

"Not quite," Rose said. "Suppose you tell me."

X fixed him with a stare that suggested he wasn't quite sure if Rose was putting him on. "Oh, c'mon, don't tell me you don't know about the death squad," he said.

Rose decided to play the return volley cautiously. "Tell me how you learned about the squad."

Mr. X snorted. "What, are you putting me on? You fucking well know the FBI has a secret assassination squad. Anybody shoots one of their guys or a federal prosecutor, they get whacked. Clean. The bodies disappear. Nobody's the wiser. That's it. Fucking Casso, he gets a federal prosecutor whacked, and what'll happen? Right: the FBI assassination squad gets busy, and they whack every fucking wiseguy they find. End of me. End of la Cosa Nostra."

"Very interesting," Rose said noncommittally, aware now that Mr. X was concerned not about the murder of a federal prosecutor named Charles Rose, but about the presumed consequences to him and his fellow Mafiosi.

"So, obviously, you don't want that to happen, correct?" Rose asked.

"Fucking right I don't," X replied. "You think I want the squad to blow me away some night just because Gas has a hard-on for you?"

Rose did nothing to disabuse Mr. X of his strange notion about a secret FBI assassination squad, all the better to keep him at work providing a pipeline into the murder plot. As X subsequently reported, Casso had become obsessed with the notion that Rose was the source of all the damage the Lucchese organization had undergone. As usual, homicide was the solution: killing Rose would bring an end to the relentless assault against his organization. And, Casso concluded, the murder of so well-known a federal prosecutor would also serve to terrorize the entire federal law enforcement establishment and cause it to withdraw its talons from the Mafia.

Besides, Casso told X, Rose deserved to die for other reasons. For one thing, Rose was a "traitor to his people," by which Casso meant he had betrayed the Italian people by his pursuit of criminals predominantly of Italian descent. Puzzled, Mr. X asked Casso how Rose possibly could be guilty of that charge, in view of the fact he wasn't Italian. Actually, Casso replied, Rose was Italian and had Anglicized his name from his real one, "Rosetti." Casso did not explain how he had come by this interesting conclusion, except to say that Rose spoke Italian. (In fact, Rose was his real name; he was the son of a Welsh father and an Italian mother; he picked up the language from her.)

As Mr. X learned, Casso had delegated the task of murdering Rose to one of his protégés, George (Georgie Neck) Zappola, a somewhat dim-witted street soldier. But, however deficient mentally, Zappola had enough sense to stall Casso by insisting that a detailed reconnaissance would have to be carried out before the murder could take place. For weeks on end, while Casso pressed him to carry out the killing, Zappola, aided by several other mobsters, conducted an extensive espionage mission to determine where Rose worked and lived, along with his daily patterns.

FBI taps on several pay phones in the Manhattan neighborhood where Rose lived detected mobsters delivering cryptic reports on the location of his apartment, the layout of the lobby in his apartment building, and traffic patterns on the street. Combined with what the FBI was learning from Mr. X, the taps provided conclusive proof: Charles Rose was being stalked in preparation for his murder.

"Well, just even the score, that's all I ask," Rose said in an uncharacteristic descent into fatalism when an FBI delegation arrived in his office to deliver the news of Zappola's operation.

"*Nobody*, least of all Gas Pipe Casso," one of the agents assured him, "is going to shoot you." The agents threw a twenty-four-hour security blanket around Rose, who liked to joke he now felt like a Mafia boss with a bodyguard. But the heightened security was also inconvenient: it cramped Rose's busy bachelor lifestyle (mainly involving his weakness for tall blond models) and crowded his apartment, already populated by two cats, a retired bomb-sniffing dog that Customs agents had begged him to adopt, and an abandoned pet rabbit Rose had found shivering and hungry in Central Park one day.

Within the Eastern District offices, there was an air of disbelief at the sight of its most noted prosecutor walking around inside a phalanx of FBI bodyguards. After all, Rose had been in much more dangerous situations – nose to nose with mobsters during the pursuit of Gus Farace, transported by armored car to the heart of Sicilian Mafia territory while investigating heroin trafficking, and prowling around the narcotics underworlds in Burma and Thailand. Indeed, Rose had a reputation for fearlessness to the point of recklessness. Why, then, was the FBI now so concerned over the threat from one Mafia nutcase?

Because Gas Pipe Casso was different. He was the worst example of an ominous new trend in American organized crime, the rise of violent, unpredictable men who killed with an insane disregard for consequences. No one could have imagined a time in the history of the Mafia when it would actually take on the entire law enforcement establishment by attempting to kill a federal prosecutor simply because he was doing his job. A far cry from the day in 1960 when Gaetano Lucchese and three of his street hoods, sitting in a restaurant, were interrupted by a raiding party of several detectives investigating a shooting case that appeared to be Mafia-related.

"Good evening, Mr. Lucchese," one detective said. "Sorry to bother you, but I need to ask you – "

"Hey, fuck you, flatfoot," one of the hoods at the table interrupted. "Why don't you go outside and see if anybody's putting slugs in the parking meters?" Lucchese immediately slapped him in the face.

"*Respetto,*" Lucchese said. "Never show disrespect to police who are only doing their job. He does his job, we do ours; it isn't personal. Now apologize, and it better be sincere." The terrified mobster obsequiously apologized.

Of all the prosecutors Casso might have targeted, the threat against Rose was most certain to arouse the anger of the federal law enforcement establishment, where Rose was among its most popular and highly regarded members. A jovial man whose wit concealed a strong sense of moralism, he was renowned among federal law enforcement agencies for his handling of major narcotics and organized crime cases. He was also the subject of any number of "Rose stories," as the one in which he offered a plea bargain of ten years to the chief defendant in a counterfeiting case. "I spit on your offer," the counterfeiter said, then went to trial and beat the case. Years later, arrested in a heroin case, the counterfeiter was looking at a fifty-year sentence, at which point he was approached by Rose, who told him, "You should've taken the ten years."

Determined to smother Casso's murder plot, the FBI-police task force redoubled its surveillance of known minions of Casso, with particular emphasis on Frank Lastorino, D'Arco's candidate as the most likely callbox. A tap on Lastorino's phone detected no contact with Casso, but the connection was revealed one night when Lastorino made a traffic mistake.

Trailed by two police detectives in an unmarked car, Lastorino was driving near his home when he pulled up at a stop light. But as the light turned green, Lastorino sat there, not moving. The cops beeped twice, but Lastorino didn't move. They flashed their red dome light at him, and Lastorino suddenly took off at high speed, careening around the corner.

It was sufficient cause for the cops to pull him over. "What the fuck do you assholes want?" Lastorino said. He continued to mouth off as the two detectives laboriously examined his driver's license and registration, using the time to take a look at the interior of the car. They spotted a canvas bag with the butt of a pistol pertruding.

"You got a license for that gun?" one cop asked.

"That ain't my gun," Lastorino said. "What do you think, I'm crazy? Shit, I got like seven surveillance cars following me. I wouldn't have a gun in the car."

"But you do," the cop said. "You're under arrest for illegal possession of an unregistered firearm. We call it the Sullivan Law, in case you never heard of it. That's a year in jail, by the way." Frisked and handcuffed, Lastorino's legal situation continued to worsen as a folded dollar bill fell out of his pocket. It contained several grams of cocaine.

Although Lastorino's prospects appeared bleak, they suddenly brightened when a local criminal court judge, in one of those decisions that have made New York's judicial establishment notorious for bias in favor of criminal defendants, threw out the charges. Lastorino, he ruled, would not be stupid enough to keep a loaded gun in plain sight in his car, nor would he have cocaine in his pocket. Therefore, the police planted both items of evidence. Lastorino walked out of court smirking at the two enraged cops, unaware that the Lucchese task force wasn't finished with him yet.

Among the things the cops had noticed in his car was a cellular telephone, an item that intrigued a strategy session of the task force. Taken together, the cellular phone and the gun suggested the strong possibility that Lastorino had replaced D'Arco as the contact between Casso and the supply of money: the phone was for communication, and the gun was to protect the large amount of cash Lastorino would be carrying. To prove it, cops and FBI agents began the laborious task of checking every single number Lastorino had called on his cellular phone for the previous year. Most of them turned out to be various phone booths scattered throughout the New York metropolitan area, but there were several calls to a number in the suburban community of Mount Olive, New Jersey. Further checking revealed that Lastorino had no family or friends in that area, and certainly none who lived in a $300,000 house on a quiet street.

A surveillance net descended around the house, whose owner turned out to be a young woman from Brooklyn. For a woman with no visible means of support, it seemed odd she could afford so expensive a house. But there was something even more interesting about her: she was the high school sweetheart of a married man named Anthony Casso. One night, a tap on the home's phone heard a male voice order three dozen roses to be sent to his mother for her birthday. He dictated the accompanying card: "Happy Birthday, mom. From your son Anthony."

The next morning, on January 19, 1993, a twelve-man FBI SWAT team burst into the house and encountered Anthony Casso emerging from the shower. He was wearing only a towel.

"FBI, Gas Pipe!" one of the raiders yelled. "You're under arrest!"

"I don't like being called Gas Pipe," Casso said as he put up his hands.

Some hours later, following his arraignment, Casso decided to use his one legally mandated phone call to contact his wife. Already aware from the television news bulletins that her husband had been caught living in a girlfriend's house, she screamed, "Drop dead!" and hung up the moment she heard his voice.

"I refuse to believe this," Charles Rose said as the FBI agents began laying material on the table. "Can our friend be that stupid?"

Apparently so, judging by the haul from Casso's hideout. Agents had found $340,000 in cash concealed in various hiding places around the house (along with his 10.5-carat diamond ring), plus another $200,000 in the safe deposit box rented in the maiden name of Casso's wife at a nearby bank. More incriminating, the agents found the card file Casso maintained on members of the Lucchese Family, each one filed under a nickname to denote a criminal specialty (for example, "Patty Cars" for an auto thief, and "Tony Air" for an airport racketeer). They also found a trove of documents relating to the family's various operations, each one specifying an individual operation (filed under such easily decoded cryptonyms as "garb" for garbage and "garctr" for the Garment Center), plus the names of those involved, which union officials were corrupt, and the names of anyone receiving payoffs. (For good measure, a raid on the home of Frank Lastorino, now in renewed legal trouble, turned up an account book that Casso demanded he maintain, which detailed all the Casso regime's outlays, including lawyers and narcotics wholesalers.)

While Rose considered this astounding pile of evidence, Casso was busy in his prison cell, planning how to thwart the latest attempt to put him away. His solutions were characteristic. First, he planned to be sprung from jail during one of his trips to court by means of an ambush of the U.S. Marshal's van in which he would be transported – to be carried out by Lucchese gunmen armed with submachine guns and orders to slaughter everybody but their boss. When he concluded that the logistical requirements for this plan would be too complicated, he turned to his next plan: to assassinate federal Judge Eugene H. Nickerson, the jurist scheduled to preside at whatever RICO case Rose would present against Casso. In Casso's calculation, killing Nickerson would so terrorize the federal law enforcement establishment that it would decline to prosecute him. And, if that didn't work, Casso planned to spend whatever was necessary to learn the identities of all prospective jurors who might be assigned to his case; each would be offered $100,000 to vote not guilty.

Stupidly enough, however, the fellow inmate whom Casso was using as a go-between with his hoods on the outside was a Mafia turncoat who saw the opportunity to score further points with prosecutors. Consequently, Casso was thrown into solitary confinement, there to be confronted with a demand for exemplars of his handwriting (which the FBI hoped to match with the handwriting on the treasure trove of documents found in his hideout).

"Fuck you," Casso said. "I ain't giving you nothing."

He was taken before Nickerson, who was not in a good mood, having been informed by the FBI of Casso's plans to kill him. When Casso repeated his refusal to give handwriting samples, an angry Nickerson threatened to fine him $5,000 for each day he continued his refusal, to a maximum of $1.2 million. Casso gave in, and dutifully provided the samples – which handwriting experts had no trouble matching with the handwriting on the documents found in his New Jersey hideout.

Casso's resistance to providing handwriting samples struck Rose as odd, given the mountain of evidence he was confronting. By this point, Casso was aware that both Chiodo and D'Arco had defected to the government. Either one of them could provide devastating testimony against Casso; taken together – along with the documentary evidence – he had absolutely no hope of beating the case Rose was formulating.

"Oh, he knows very well he can't beat the case," D'Arco advised. "He's just looking for weak spots. When he can't find any, I'll tell you exactly what he's gonna do. He's gonna flip."

When Rose expressed skepticism that a man of Casso's

temperament would actually roll over to his enemies, some of whom he planned to kill, D'Arco laughed. "Don't you understand?" he asked. "Why do you think Gas has been keeping such detailed records all the time? Why to you think he used to demand from me every detail of what we were involved in, no matter how small? Because he was putting this stuff in the bank. He was preparing for the day when he might get caught, and he always planned to have some bargaining chips. He knows how many people he can put away, and he's sure you gonna want to deal."

The FBI was equally skeptical, but several agents visited Casso in prison to determine whether he was actually prepared to become the first Mafia boss in the history of American organized crime to become a government witness. Initially, it didn't seem as though he was interested, but he was actually waiting for his visitors to show their high cards. At last, the agents played one: they silently shoved a document across the table to Casso. Casso scanned the affidavit of Peter Chiodo attesting to his personal knowledge of felonies committed by the man he consistently referred to as "Gas."

- *Gangbusters is available on Amazon.com, Alibris.com & Half.com*

REVIEW & COMMENTS:

MURDER INC.

by

Burton B. Turkus & Sid Feder

There's no way to talk about the mob and not talk about the Jewish mobs of the first half of the Twentieth Century. Like the Nineteenth Century Irish immigrants before them, some immigrant Jews fought their way out of the ghetto and poverty by turning to a life of crime. It is easy to forget the powerful Jewish mobsters because, like the Irish, Jews viewed crime as a vehicle to take them from poverty to affluence...and out. Most Jewish mobsters sent their sons on to college to become doctors and lawyers, or put them in place to become successful businessmen. Ian Schrager, for example, of Studio 54 fame...or infamy...and hotel magnate with trendy establishments like the Delano in Miami and the Mondrian in Los Angeles, is the son of Meyer Lansky's gambling czar in Williamsburg, Brooklyn, the late Max "The Jew" Schrager. Max was a big numbers banker. Ian went to college and became a lawyer, before getting involved in Studio 54 and a trip to federal prison.

Lansky himself spawned a next generation of businessmen and even a military official. The only one of his children to follow a criminal path was a stepson who was murdered after he shot a mobster to death in a Miami restaurant. Gurrah Shapiro, half of Lepke and Gurrah, the duo that oversaw Murder Incorporated, spawned a son who became a forerunner in the 1960s explosion of stylish men's clothing. Henry Shapiro owned Raleigh Clothes, a men's clothing manufacturer, and Mr. Stag, a trendy men's shop in Brooklyn. "Crazy Henry," as he was called, accommodated me on junkets he ran to the Thunderbird Hotel, in Las Vegas. But it was the fathers that made the real mark on society.

Burton Turkus and Sid Feder's book, "Murder Inc.," is a wonderful look at one of the most vicious bands of primarily Jewish gangsters ever. It relates, based on the testimony of Murder Incorporated member-turned-stoolpigeon, Abe "Kid Twist" Reles, a visceral account of personalities and events within the gang. Reles was, however, a pigeon without wings, and was found smashed and broken on the ground below the hotel room where he was being protected by New York's finest (?). The book is also a colorful picture of an era long gone. Moreover, it clearly highlights the "Heyday" of organized crime by illustrating its expansiveness during the era following Prohibition, when it could use its money and muscle to control production and distribution in the garment, baking, and fur industries, to name a few. The chapter on Lepke is priceless.

One of the greatest pleasures I had growing up was to sit and talk with the "old timers," guys who had been active players during the glory days of the mob. Generally, they all regarded Albert Anastasia as the most dangerous guy they'd ever met. I was told that when Albert would squint at you through the smoke of the cigarette that dangled straight down from his lips your blood would run cold. One could imagine his huge hands beating or strangling you to death. Leaving his presence was a gift. It was also agreed that, pound for pound the toughest guy they had ever met was Lepke. Louis Buchalter: "Lepke" to his friends; "The Judge" to most of the underworld.

Lepke was the guy who ran Murder Incorporated for Albert Anastas, NOT Meyer Lansky or Bugsy Siegel, who were connected to Lucky Luciano's family, which later became known as the Genovese Family. Anastasia's family later became known as the Gambino Family. And Lepke headed up a Jewish subgroup of that family which was centered in Brownsville, Brooklyn, and whose members killed as easily as they downed kosher hot dogs and potato knishes. It was ripe with deadly but colorful characters, like "Kid Twist" Reles, "Pittsburgh Phil" Strauss, "Blue Jaw Magoon," and "Pretty" Amberg, a man so ugly that when Mayor Jimmy Walker saw him at a speakeasy it is said he swore off drinking, and a man whose signature was to leave the corpses of his victims in the streets of Brownsville in laundry bags.

And, who did they answer to? Lepke.

The book is also interesting for things it is missing; information that may not have been known by the authors at the time of the writing, but made its way through, at very least, the oral running history of the mob. This chapter, for example, relates the downfall of Waxey Gordon after a jail term for income tax evasion. More telling is how that came about, with Lucky Luciano and Meyer Lansky sending the latter's brother, Jake, to the Feds with the damning evidence against Gordon, his accounting records, in order to short circuit the escalating "War of the Jews."

Two things I find interesting. First, that this book discloses what continues to be prevalent today; how the authorities are willing to take the word of someone who "rolls over" as the gospel. For example, when Reles explains away his perjured testimony by saying two guys he knew threatened him if he testified anything but that he didn't know Lepke, Turkus accepts that as truth. Life in the streets says, "Bullshit." Everyone should keep that in mind when they read the testimony of the slew of modern turncoats like Sammy The Bull or Lewis Kasman, who billed himself as "John Gotti's adopted son."

The second is how little authorities knew about the hierarchy of the mob in those days. At one point, Turkus writes, "Anastasia was, and is, an Adonis man." Of course, that's absurd. Joey Adonis (Doto) was a member of Luciano's family, which is today the Genovese crew. Anastasia, on the other hand, was an upper level member of what is now known as the Gambino Family. Were they friends? Sure. Were they like-minded about what was going on in mob politics? Probably. But neither one was the other's man.

In spite of things like that, which are more enlightening about the time period than anything else, this is a must read for any aficionado of mob history.

MURDER INC.

Burton Turkus & Sid Feder

Farrar, Strauss & Young, 1951

CHAPTER 12: Sociology's stillbirth: the king of the rackets (Pp.331-362):

Lepke sells Lucky a bill of goods, and wins the clothing industry – more on the purge of Mafia – Longy Zwillman, and interstate crime the Senators overlooked – industrial extortion made easy – Winchell, J. Edgar Hoover and the deal that wasn't – a mob operation with Sidney Hillman?

Going all the way back to the beginning, you wonder how Louis Buchalter ever wound up that way.

His parents were decent, honest people who worked night and day for their brood. One son turned to the pulpit, and today is one of the leading clergymen in the Rocky Mountain area. Another became a pharmacist and is highly respected in his Midwestern community. A third is a successful, admired dentist. The only daughter took to teaching and, when last heard from, was the head of the English department of her school.

And then there was Louis.

He was born to these respectable, industrious people on Lincoln's Birthday, in 1897. With the heritage of the Great Emancipator's name and the environment of decent family life – what did Lepke become?

"The most dangerous criminal in the United States," said FBI chief J. Edgar Hoover in 1939; and:

"The worst industrial racketeer in America," declared District

Attorney Thomas E. Dewey.

Nor did the incongruity stop there. The family called him Lepke, an endearing diminutive of his name. Lepke grew up to be a devoted husband and family man; rarely drank or gambled. Yet, he ordered the murders of seventy or more men in his infamous career, contracting for killings with the efficiency of a management company assigning the installation work on a new building.

Where other criminals tore their plunder from the gambler, the alcoholic and the dope addict, this unimpressive-looking crime king preyed on the ordinary needs of the ordinary citizen. He cut in on the clothes people wore, the bread they ate, the motion-picture theaters they patronized. In fact, on the very work they did. The pay envelopes they earned. In the prosaic fields of labor and industry, it has been officially estimated that he extorted from $5,000,000 to $10,000,000 a year for a decade. And not only in New York, either.

Statistics show that more than sixty per cent of the clothing worn in the United States comes from the New York region. And Lepke virtually "owned" the clothing industry in the Metropolitan area. After paying off his organization, his connections, his protection – his take-home pay on this one racket alone still was a fantastic one million dollars annually.

He didn't even look like a hoodlum, and he acted like one even less. Barely five feet seven, he had an almost apologetic manner, a dimple in his left cheek, and soft collie-dog eyes that hid the piracy and homicide lurking behind them. His reputation through gangland was that he never lost his temper or became excited. The men who worked for him did not let that fool them. Sholem summed it up for all when he said:

"I don't ask questions; I just obey. It would be more healthier."

This was Lepke: Louis Buchalter, sociological enigma. Heredity, environment, upbringing...everything said Lepke should turn out law-abiding. But he became, in many ways, the most powerful crime king of all. Little publicized until 1939, few ranked him with the Lucianos, the Costellos, the Capones, the Adonises or the Zwillmans. Few, that is, except these underworld czars, themselves. They knew his talents. When the national Syndicate of crime was formed in 1934, his was one of the most respected counsels on the board of governors.

When Lepke was thirteen, his father, a small hardware merchant, died. His mother tried to keep things going, but the fight was a losing one, though. In a year or two, she was forced to seek charity with relatives in the West. Louis, she directed, was to stay with his older sister. She would care for him and see that he grew up a good boy. But, the sister related later, she never saw Louis any more after Mother Buchalter left.

In the fall of 1915, in a space of a few weeks, Lepke was picked up twice for burglary. He beat both raps, but, to permit things to cool off, he trekked to Bridgeport, Conn., to the home of an uncle. Only days after his arrival, he was caught stealing a salesman's sample case, and was put in Cheshire Reformatory. In two months, he won a parole. Instead of reporting to the parole officer at specified intervals, the nineteen-year-old delinquent went back to New York, where he knew his way around.

This was not the Lepke, by any means, of the political fix, the easy money for bondsmen, the killers under contract, the vast organized setup for extortion. He began by chiseling on pushcart peddlers and stealing packages. He had nothing "going for him" yet, as they say. In 1917, a loft burglary backfired. Lepke did a year in Sing Sing. He was out only a year when another loft job failed. That time, he served almost two years.

Now, the mob type of underworld group was just then coming into its own. Lepke was quick to appreciate that the loner had none of the protection and opportunity afforded those who ran with a pack. Even as early as that, Lepke demonstrated the cold analytical capabilities that drew special notation nearly two decades later. In the underworld, in fact, just as Frank Costello is known as "the Prime Minister" and Lucky Luciano as "the Boss," Lepke was "the Judge." In inner circle conversation, it was always "Judge Louis."

From the time he left Sing Sing in 1922 until he ran into his final series of legal headaches in 1939 and 1940, he always moved with a gang. He was arrested eleven times in that stretch, for everything from assault to homicide – and never saw the inside of a jail.

It was about that time too, that Lepke picked up with Gurrah, a youthful sneak thief then. They were a sharp contrast, the outwardly undistinguishable Lepke with the bucolic brown eyes, shunning the spotlight, and his loud, hulking, heavy-handed, slow thinking, strong-arm Russian-born partner. Early in their association they won the label of the Gorilla Boys. As felony brought fortune, this was polished up to the Gold Dust Twins. At their peak, the Gold Dust Twins were big business. There was hardly anything anyone could use, eat or wear that their claws did not try to grab.

Contrary to the general belief that Prohibition spawned the underworld gang on the American scene, the criminal mob actually sprang from the wars between labor and management, just before and subsequent to World War I.

Prohibition, of course, became a mighty contributing factor to the development. But in labor wars lay the birth of mobdom. Labor unions were not yet the powerful, rich, well-organized institutions they have become. In industrial disputes, they were on their own. Management, on the other hand, recognized – and could afford – the effective method of combating the workers. The employers simply hired one or another of the early-day hoodlum gangs to "handle" strikers, pickets or any others they regarded as fomenting unrest – especially in the billion-dollar garment industry.

Lepke and Gurrah were soon working with such an enforcement gang. Another member of the same troop was Waxey Gordon, who was to become one of the very biggest of bootlegging figures – as well as an early income-tax evasion casualty among mob moguls. In fact, Waxey's tax woes had a lot to do with generating the shuddering respect the underworld has held for this prosecution weapon ever since – when, of course, it is in the hands of a vigorous and honest prosecutor. Today, most gang bosses advise their henchmen that the mob is behind them all the way – up to and including murder – but that if they get themselves tangled up in tax troubles, they must untangle themselves alone. (Waxey sank lower and lower on the mob social ladder. In the late summer of 1951, after his name had been missing from the police blotter for several years, he was arrested while sitting in a car – with a package of heroin in his hand. Authorities announced he was the powerful leader of a huge narcotics ring. That didn't quite add up, though. No one ever heard of a ringleader being caught actually holding a batch of the "powder" in his hands. Such risks are usually for the pushers, the peddlers).

Before the twenties were very old, Lepke and Gurrah stepped up into an exclusive crew headed by Li'l Augie Orgen, whose forte was strikebreaking strategy, and Curly Holtz, who was skilled at labor-union organization. Li'l Augie Orgen is not to be confused with Li'l Augie Pisano (or Hooko, as he is more familiarly known in Brooklyn's Gowanus Canal district), who skyrocketed to power with Joey Adonis on the strength of political connections.

As time went along, hard-headed realists began to rise from the union ranks. "If the bosses hire mobsters," they reasoned, "why not the unions, too?" And the gang system of crime went into the upper brackets. By 1921 some unions already had gang gunmen on their payrolls, and were developing huge funds for the conflict. With the market thus widened, Orgen frequently rented his crew out to both sides in the same dispute, or would contract to supply both with guns, bullets and blackjacks.

With profits high, intermob competition, naturally, became fierce. The gang of Kid Dropper, a vicious, ruthless downtown torpedo, was at the throat of Li'l Augie's crew. Until, that is, Lou Cohen, one of Holtz's men, shot Dropper's head off as he sat in a taxicab with Police Captain Cornelius Willemse in front of a Manhattan courthouse. Cohen got off with a prison term. (In 1939, he was to be assassinated by his friend Lepke's triggers.)

The mobs waxed fat; so did the unions. The bitter, historic International Tailoring Company Strike and similar labor explosions brought violent civil war to the garment industry. Paul Berger, a stalwart Lepke strong-arm and collector for a dozen years or more, turned State's evidence in our investigation years later and lifted the lid on the mess.

"We had a hundred sluggers and a brigade that threw acid on merchandise of companies fighting the union," he recalled. "The union had spies working inside who tipped off who should be slugged."

A dress manufacturer was thrown from a tenth-floor window. A picket was killed. Seven men followed a worker into a trolley at 6 A.M. and slashed his face to keep him from work. It was reported the unions spent three million dollars on the struggle. The upheaval was inspired as much by Communist prodding as anything else. A reminder that perhaps some things have not changed overmuch since those days of 1926 was contained in testimony of J. Edgar Hoover before a Senate Committee in March, 1951. The Director of the Federal Bureau of Investigation alleged that Communists are infiltrated into unions generally today to incite violence and foment trouble. The end result, back in the twenties, however, was not quite what the left-wingers had in mind. The moblords glimpsed the opportunities, and when the smoke cleared, the gangsters – far more fascist than Communist-minded – were moving in.

Li'l Augie, taking sole credit for the mob's progress, considered himself an astute businessman now. While Curly Holtz continued as boss in labor matters, Augie branched out – to narcotics and other things. Neither Lepke nor Curly liked his new stock in trade. In labor and industry, the economic base of the nation, they could play it safe.

Toward the end of 1927, a labor dispute developed in the painting trade. The boss painters' association offered Augie $50,000 in cash to "prevail" on the union to end the strike. Orgen accepted without consulting his board of strategy. He issued orders to the union to cease the walkout forthwith. One union official, however, was a friend of Jack Holtz, Curly's brother. Jack asked Curly to keep the mob out of this one. Orgen was aghast when, shortly afterward, he displayed $50,00 to his boys and they demanded that he return it.

But $50,000 is a lot of money. Orgen sought out the notorious Legs Diamond and agreed to split the fee in return for help in the painter's strike. Legs was alcohol and dope and even holdups. He was a stranger to the fine points of labor racketeering. Leple and Curly regarded him as nothing more than a low-class crook. They took umbrage at Orgen.

At 8:30 P.M., on October 15, 1927, Li'l Augie and his new associate were walking along a lower Manhattan street. A black sedan picked its way through the pushcarts. Behind the wheel was Lepke. Next to him, pistol in hand, sat Gurrah. The lumbering Gurrah was about to plunge out and start shooting, in his typical muscle-headed manner.

"Only Augie," warned Lepke sharply, aware, even then, that indiscriminate, unnecessary killing led to trouble.

So, Gurrah hit the sidewalk yelling, "Move over, Diamond!" Legs fell back instinctively against the building. Li'l Augie, transfixed, was killed. Diamond got a bullet through his shoulder – for butting in. If he hadn't drawn his gun, he would not have been touched.

Lepke and Gurrah went into hiding until "lines" could be laid. Then they ambled in and blandly said to the authorities, "We understand you want to see us." All the witnesses, it developed, had suffered a sudden loss of memory. Not even Diamond himself was "able" to identify them. Li'l Augie's friends, though, had announced reprisal intentions. When the partners left court, as a result, they were accompanied by fifty detectives and policemen. To those aware of the recent strike operations of the two thugs, the photographs in the next morning's papers had but one message: the two were strolling out from a murder charge, with a protective cover that would have done justice to the President. Obviously, they could get away with murder – with a police escort! After that, their power was assured.

With Augie gone, the partners took over. Smart and ambitious, Lepke saw that their ambidextrous affiliations with unions as well as employers offered far greener fields than just hiring out as strong-arms. There was nothing to stop them from controlling whole industries. The "gimmick" was captive labor unions and captive trade associations.

"That way," figured Lepke, "you get both management and labor in your pocket." Such was Lepke's recipe for organization.

As gang wars continued to eliminate other mob leaders, he and Gurrah hand-picked the best of the suddenly detached torpedoes and built a powerhouse force of 250 triggers. They fomented or broke strikes for fancy fees. They moved and muscled and manipulated until they had their fingers – up to the armpits – in most of the rackets of metropolitan New York. In industry after industry, controlled organization was the goal; violence the means to achieve it. Lepke had a gift for both.

"Send a sixty-watter to so-and-so," he would command one or another of his enforcement agents. Soon a vial of acid, a tear-gas bomb or a stench bomb, of the general dimensions of a 60-watt electric bulb, was deposited in the business establishment of an owner who could not see paying a fancy figure to halt a strike or to belong to a protective association. How could an investigator listening in, say, on a tapped telephone, connect violence with the mere mention of a light bulb? That was the point of the jargon. The same cautious operational double talk also produced the mob-ese as "contract" for an order to kill and "hit" for a murder target, so popular with the Brooklyn branch of the cartel.

The strikes of 1925 and 1926 showed Lepke where he wanted to specialize in his chosen profession. No matter how or with whom he and Gurrah worked on other rackets as the years passed, they kept the clothing industry as their first love.

The Amalgamated Clothing Workers is a giant parent body of many labor unions, which turn out perhaps three-fourths of the country's ready-to-wear men's clothing. For many years, its leader was the respected Sidney Hillman, who sat high in the councils of the nation during World War II.

The making of men's suits requires many crafts...spongers, cutters, fitters, long and short pants workers, buttonhole makers, etc, and truckmen for transportation. As Lepke found it, each group had its own local in Amalgamated. This giant numbers some 375,000 workers now **[1951, SG]**. Even then, a quarter of a century ago, it was an army of 25,000 to 50,000. (The truckers, incidentally, have since switched affiliation to the teamsters' union.)

It was about 1927 when Lepke first cast a covetous eye in this direction – and envisioned a gold mine in a suit of clothes. Obviously, the parent group was too large to attack frontally. Lepke, however, made a remarkable discovery. The hub, the heart of this sprawling collection was the cutter, who cut out the sections of the garments from patterns, and, next to him, the trucker. They were a key that could lock the industry up tight, if they stopped work. What's more, the cutters' union numbered only 1,800 members, and the truckers' about 80. Thus, on a base of less than 1,900 workers, rested the continued operation of an entire industry of, perhaps, 50,000.

Lepke moved in on the cutters. The manner of the invasion was comparatively simple. Max Rubin, one of Lepke's staunchest organizational arms, revealed the details during our murder investigation. Lepke had early spotted Rubin as an expert on labor manipulations. He used him on many grabs.

Lepke, Rubin related, convinced certain of the cutters' leaders that it would be to their advantage if his entire crew were taken on to replace Terry Burns and Ab Slabow, who were then the local's staff musclemen. Rubin said they had been on Amalgamated's payroll since 1923.

"So, Lepke and Gurrah and Curly Holtz became connected with the union," Rubin recalled. "They took the place of Burns and Slabow."

At about the same time, Philip Orlofsky, who had been a business agent, suddenly was made manager of the cutters' local. Paul Berger, the professional strong-arm, told us that he "became a slugger for the union when Orlofsky became manager."

A year or two later, Amalgamated was rocked by what seemed to be spontaneous internal rivalry between the Hillman group, heading the parent organization, and the Orlofsky faction in the key cutters' union. Orlofsky launched a rebel parent organization, challenging Amalgamated's supremacy. Not until 1931, with battle lines drawn for the showdown, did the curtain go up and expose the "spontaneity." Lepke was quickly revealed then as the real boss — the power – of the comparatively tiny cutters' unit that could tie up the industry. He was moving in now to werest control of the whole works. In fact, Rubin already had begun operations in his behalf in the truckers' union.

The bitter run of this civil war in the clothing industry has been detailed to some extent earlier. It was here that to counter the menace of Lepke's troops, the forces of Salvatore Marrizano, or Manaranzano, leader of the remnants of Mafia, entered into the intramural war. He assured Lucky Luciano that he would "make no trouble" for Lucky's friend, Lepke. There was shooting, however, and Lepke persuaded Lucky that Marrizano actually was waging war on Lucky's newly powerful Unione. The chances are, of course, that Luciano would eventually have done something, anyway, about removing the survivors of the "Mustache Pete" oldsters in the Italian Society. Lepke's persuasiveness, nevertheless, was the convincer. Lucky fell for it, and the purge of Mafia followed. Lucky's trades were numbers and narcotics. He is never mentioned in clothing industry extortions, except in Rubin's testimony during the murder trials.

In the dispute between the Hillman and the Lepke-backed Orlofsky factions, a key man was Bruno Belea, who was Amalgamated's general organizer, and, through all disturbances, Sidney Hillman's efficient expeditere. With Marrizano removed by the purge, Lepke applied his fine conniving touch toward control of the entire industry. He suggested to his friend Lucky that Belea had been as responsible as anyone for introducing Marrizano to the dispute. And he proposed that Lucky add Belea to his other victims! He was moving in for the kill now.

One day, at the height of the interfactional battle, Lepke came to see Rubin.

"I just had a meet with Charley Lucky and Belea," he announced. "We made a deal."

"What was it, Louis?" Rubin inquired.

"The deal is for Orlofsky to give up his union. He is out; him and the others with him. We'll see they get a year's pay after the union breaks."

Some of the minute details of how he worked it will forever remain clouded in racket connivance. Certainly, the threat on Belea's life was a key move. If Lucky was on the Amalgamated organizer, Lepke would be in a good "dealing" position. A man marked for death will hardly quibble about details if a way out is offered. The treachery involved in dumping Orlofsky was just as easy for Lepke's persuasive skills. He simply sold the mob on the sound economics that "Hillman is a sucker; Orlofsky is a sucker...we'll stay with the sucker who has the most dough."

"Tell you what I want," he continued with Rubin now. "Get a hotel room where we can meet. Then get hold of Orlofsky and get him up there."

Rubin complied. At the conference, he related, Lepke came right to the point.

"I just left Charley Lucky and Belea," the ganglord informed Orlofsky. "You have to break up your organization."

That's all there was to it. In short order, Orlofsky's rebel organization, which Lepke had backed, was wiped out at Lepke's order. It had served its purpose. Orlofsky simply was thrown out. Lepke was now at the throat of the industry.

As part of the reorganization, Rubin was called to Belea's room on Eleventh Street, just off the clothing district. There, he recalled, he found Lepke with Belea. By this time nothing surprised him. Hillman's organizer told him, Rubin related, that Danny Fields, a tough torpedo, and Paul Berger were to be the "intermediaries" between the union and Lepke, because Lepke wanted to remain "out of the picture." It was not to be a permanent post for Fields. He, too, was murdered on Lepke's command in the late thirties, because he knew too much.

Berger supplied additional astonishing details of Lepke's assumption of power, and of just how high that power reached. The strong-arm said that he accompanied Mendy, Lepke's operations aide, to a certain office on one occasion to get a victim to "come across with the money." Evidently, the victim was not entirely convinced of the mobsters' position, and Mendy wanted to impress him with their influence.

"Mendy forced me to tell him everything that was going on in the union office...tell him about the bonus he [Mendy] got from Hillman for $25,000 for Lepke, after the strike," Berger testified. (The strike referred to a work stoppage in the early thirties, during which Lepke's might was confirmed to all, including management.)

It was startling. Here was a sworn charge in open court, by a man on the inside, linking the highly placed Hillman, either directly or through aides, with top-level lords of organized crime while he was head of Amalgamated! And most startling of all, at the very time this was alleged, Hillman was co-director of the Office of Production Management in the United States' World War II effort, considered in many quarters to be as close to the White House as any man in the nation!

When Lepke took over, a number of tailoring contractors were moving to small towns in Pennsylvania and New Jersey, where they could run non-union shops and escape the periodic violence in the industry. New York workers were complaining of this loss of income, particularly at that dismal stage of the business depression.

In the summer of 1932, Lepke summoned his boys and reported that there was to be a "stoppage." Although he had no formal connection with Amalgamated, here he was giving the orders. Rubin testified that, as far as he knew, Hillman called the "stoppage."

When union officials are not sure of getting people out for a strike," Rubin explained the form, "they call a stoppage. If it falls down, or there's a double cross, nothing is said. If it picks up force and people respond, then you call it a strike."

Lepke took an early hand in its direction. "The stoppage got to be called in the truckers," he pressed, "to keep the work from going out of town." To his own set, he privately added, "Whenever a manufacturer goes out of town, there is no chance for us to make a dime."

"You're the business agent for the truckers," he turned to Rubin. "No truck rolls on the street...see!"

Rubin anticipated difficulty with only three companies: the big Garfield Express of Passaic, N.J., owned by Louis Cooper, who was often called the "czar of the New Jersey clothing industry"; Branch Stores, another successful New Jersey outfit; and New York & New Jersey Truckers, which did considerable hauling to plants around Wilkes Barre,

Pa.

"They'll be tough," Rubin forecast.

"If you have any trouble, see me," Lepke directed.

Rubin had trouble. He saw Lepke, and the boss adjusted it. And in the adjustment, Lepke personally wound up owning a considerable portion of each of the three firms without paying a penny! Rubin testified to the conference on the stoppage between Lepke and Louis Cooper of Garfield Express:

"The hell with you," declared Cooper, flatly rejecting it. "I been double-crossed by Amalgamated before."

"You got nothing to worry about this time," replied Lepke. "I am Amalgamated now."

Cooper's outlook on the stoppage changed suddenly at that.

"If you'll come with me...be my partner...I'll stop," the truck executive invited, evidently quick to appreciate the situation. So, Lepke "accepted" a half-interest in Cooper's thriving firm as a gift, all legal, with official partnership papers. The he snatched for "his" company the better accounts of New York and New Jersey, which he forced out of business. And finally, he emerged from the "adjusting" with a block of stock in Branch Stores.

During the entire run of the stoppage, Berger and the other sluggers reported to Lepke nightly for instructions. "We stopped trucks and slugged drivers...things along those lines," the strong-arm said.

With labor now practically in the palm of his hand, Lepke aimed at management. Under threat of strikes or sabotage – threat and actual practice – the Gold Dust Twins extorted anywhere from $5,000 to $50,000 from individual manufacturers or boss truckers, who paid solely so that they might carry on their legitimate business. From 1934 to 1937, Rubin admitted, he "participated in shakedowns from $400 to

$700 a week...some weeks more." And he was just one of an entire company of collection men. The state charged afterward that reputable garment trucking firms alone yielded Lepke a million dollars a year for ten years!

In several cases, the twins demanded – and took – a piece of a perfectly legal firm or they usurped an entire business. Manufacturers and truck operators were frankly afraid to seek the Law's help against two racketeers who had walked out on a murder charge with a police escort. In some cases special subsidiaries were formed by large companies through which to handle the financial pay-offs.

When Lepke went "on the lam" in the late thirties, he continued to receive hundreds of dollars each week, for the entire time he was in hiding, from his interest in clothing firms into which he had muscled. In fact, as late as 1944, after he had been in prison for five years, he was still collecting sums running into many thousands annually.

(Long before the stench of Lepke was finally lifted from the industry, both management and labor came to their senses and moved to clean up. Today, the clothing industry may be cited as an example of labor and management functioning individually, as well as together.)

Even while Lepke was clinching control of the garment trade, he set his sights on his second target: the hundred-million-dollar rabbit fur industry. A needle trades industrial group, representing a considerable portion of labor, was on the way to forcing the furriers to negotiate with it exclusively – until an organizer was blown apart in Chatham, N. J., by a bomb placed under the hood of his car. Just by coincidence, of course, Lepke popped up with three small fur workers' unions precisely at that time, and gained control of everything.

His organization collected dues, fixed prices, placed a tariff on furs, supposedly to develop a union "expansion fund." Furriers were ordered to join a "protective" at a fee as high as $100,000. One recalcitrant had his place bombed and acid smeared on his face. Another had his head bashed in. There were bombings, beatings of furriers and their families – and the resistance ended.

Early in his manipulations in trade and economics, Lepke discovered what amounted to the atomic secret of labor-industry racketeering: Stop transportation and you stop an industry; control the truckers and you control the work. The methods he employed were most effective – burning merchandise, beatings, overturned trucks or trucks with machinery wrecked by sand dumped in their transmissions.

The discovery was a priceless formula when he turned to the baking industry.

Everyone ate bread. In a city of 7,000,000, reasoned Lepke, that added up to a lot of loaves – and money. Trucking is an integral part of this industry. The flour brought into New York each year is not too far from a billion barrels. Bread, when baked, must be delivered too.

Applying his special persuasions, Lepke won the bakery truckmen's local. Through it, he took charge of both management and labor. Incredible as it sounds, he exacted this "slice" from almost every loaf of bread bought by New York's millions. He even caused the price to be raised for the consumer!

Hundreds of thousands of dollars were extorted from many of the most successful baking firms. Max Rubin, Lepke's official trouble-shooter in every new venture, demanded up to $20,000 from each of the various concerns on threat of sabotage and strikes. He told us of a $15,000 extortion paid by the Gottfried Baking Company, one of the largest in New York. This pay-off, he revealed was made in the office of the Tammany District Leader for lower Harlem – and, he added, the politician got 10 per cent as a "commission." The widely advertised Mrs. Wagner's Pies, said Rubin, was a victim of a $1,500 bite on at least one occasion.

Controlling both sides of the industry, Lepke applied high-handed systems in either direction. Thus, in 1939, the drivers were notified of a wage cut. The truckers defied their "agreeable" union officers and voted to strike instead. Lepke had put William Snyder in as the union president, and Snyder, surprisingly, backed up the truckers.

"If I didn't," he pointed out, "I couldn't control them any more." To Lepke, though, failure was never explainable.

Arbitration was suggested, and one evening, fourteen delegates met around a table in a downtown restaurant. In came an inane-looking individual with receding chin and blinking eyes. He walked up behind Snyder, who had his back to the door. As the other thirteen "arbitrators" ducked – that, they said later, is what they did – the mousy man fired two bullets into the union president and killed him. The abrupt abdication advanced Vice-President Wolfie Goldis to the presidency – at least nominally. The strike never came off.

Two witnesses told detectives they heard the dying Snyder name Wolfie Goldis' brother, Morris, as his assassin. The killer's car turned out to be a rented vehicle. One Sam Tratner insisted that he had hired it for Wolfie's brother. Two waiters at the restaurant identified the brother's photograph. The "custom" of the District Attorney's office was not to take witnesses before the grand jury, to get their statements under oath, until a suspect was apprehended. It was seven weeks before this was accomplished. By then, Tratner asserted it wasn't Morris, but some stranger who had paid him to rent the car; the waiters could not identify the suspect – and the witnesses to Snyder's dying statement were never called. A man who had committed murder in front of thirteen witnesses – got away with it!

By 1932 and 1933, Lepke ruled as absolutely and autocratically as any czar over a feudal state. His power magnified in many directions, not the least of which was the protection he enjoyed. He reached into high places politically – and not necessarily on a cash pay-off basis. A force of 250 sluggers and gunmen, who could strong-arm voters at election time or vote several times each themselves – with proper prearrangement as to addresses on vacant lots or in cemeteries, for instance – was a handy item for any political machine. The commander of such an army was an asset to be fawned upon – and forgiven minor transgressions like murder and extortion.

Local 306, Motion Picture Operators Union, was wealthy and powerful. It controlled all operators' jobs in the city. It had set high minimum wages, and required every theater to maintain two operators, on salary, in each projection booth. To buck an organization as powerful as this constituted a challenge to Lepke – as well as a profit.

He started a rival union, backed by strong political tie-ups. Members were supplied on recommendation of various Tammany leaders. He offered special inducements to theaters. Before long, some movie houses were deserting Local 306. Eventually, after spending over a million dollars in the fight, Local 306 bought out its rival. And almost at once, another new union appeared – run by the same insidious "Judge Louis"! Pitched battles blazed. Then, the first rival reappeared. The struggle continued until 1936, when Local 306 was able, at last, to emerge alone – and then only because the closing-in investigations were keeping Lepke busy hanging on to more remunerative extortions.

Long before then, though, the cow-eyed plunderer had annexed vast territory to his empire. He had a "grab" in the leather workers, the milliners, the handbag makers, the shoe trade. He was providing gorillas for cabarets in a partnership with the Bug & Myer Mob. He ran the taxicab racket, was a partner in the poultry-market racket, seized the restaurant racket from Dutch Schultz, and, with Lucky Luciano, operated the cleaning and dyeing industry piracy.

After the formation of the Syndicate, in which he was a prime mover, he spread ever wider. When slot machines were hard hit in New York, he financed and organized setups in Florida, in Havana and New Orleans. Perhaps it was pure coincidence that his New Orleans' interests corresponded to Frank Costello's transfer of his establishment to the Louisiana metropolis. He was high up in the mob in Florida and Saratoga gambling. He was active in sending Buggsy Siegel out to open the California territory.

About then, too, he departed further from what he regarded as the sound industrial-labor rackets, and dipped into narcotics. Dipped? He leaped in! Government officials later said it was the most important dope-smuggling operation in the history of federal enforcement. The repeal of Prohibition had a helping hand in this.

In the early thirties, Lucky Luciano had gone into the formation of an Atlantic Seaboard bootleg monopoly group. Connected to it, in one way or another, were such characters as Joey Adonis and the abdicated Chicago ganglord, Johnny Torrio; Longy Zwillman from Jersey, Cy Nathanson of Atlantic City, the Danny Walsh outfit in Providence, R. I., King Solomon of Boston and Nig Rosen of Philadelphia. A valued workman in this outfit was Yasha Katzenburg, who was frequently called "King of the Smugglers." Police of various world capitals conceded Yasha was one of the biggest American buyers ever to appear in the international markets. When repeal broke up the liquor group, he was too good a man to be out of work. So, he was brought into a newly organized dope-importing ring.

Lepke, as the financial backer, was in for one-third of the profit. He was too shrewd to set up this operation as a continuing business; the odds were against that. The ring wanted just "one good shot," as the boys put it. By bribing a customs man, a hole was opened through which, for a short period, any amount of narcotics might be smuggled, if the mob worked fast. They went at it so fast, they were practically supersonic. They smuggled in ten million dollars worth of morphine and heroin from China in exactly six shipments!

There were simultaneous plans for a similar haul from Europe. Curly Holtz, Lepke's old co-worker in the Li'l Augie mob, went over on the buying trip. Astonishingly, federal men seized the dope he bought. Not long afterward, Curly was missing from his usual haunts. Reles told us what happened. Curly, it seems, bought only a portion of "the stuff" he was supposed to, and pocketed the balance of the cash. To keep the mob from learning of his double cross, he tipped off the Federals about the amount he had purchased. Lepke, however, had ways of finding out things. Curly has not been seen since.

Once success arrived, Lepke and Gurrah lifted themselves off the firing line and into the front office. Then the little hood who had taken to the streets at fourteen found out how the other half lives.

He had a swank apartment in Manhattan's midtown. He wintered in California, in Florida, or took the baths at Hot Springs, Ark. One of the more stylish groups patronizing the Arlington Hotel at the Spa consisted of Lepke, Lucky, Joey A., Meyer Lansky, Jimmy Hines, the New York political boss, and the local "Arkansan," Owney Madden, who had migrated from his New York alcohol addresses not long before.

Lepke summered at the shore, or, later, made annual migrations to Carlsbad, for the German baths. The businessmen of such industries as clothing, furs and baking – and, in turn, the public – footed the bill as the rackets ruler romped, de luxe style. He married Mrs. Betty Wasserman, daughter of a London (England) barber, and legally adopted her son. The killer who sucked at the veins of the honest workingman was so devoted that the stepson later said, "Louis was better to me than my own father could have been."

In November of 1933, a federal grand jury indicted 158 persons for violating anti-trust laws through "interference with interstate commerce." Actually, it was for the fur-industry racketeering, and marked the first time the anti-trust act ever was invoked on the rackets. Two of the 158 were Lepke and Gurrah. In 1935, they were convicted. Each was sentenced to two years in prison and fined $10,000.

"It is just a slap on the wrist," mourned Federal Judge John C. Knox, sentencing them. "But that's the maximum for these violations."

The judge refused to permit bail pending appeal. But two weeks later, Judge Martin T. Manton, senior member of the U.S. Circuit Court of Appeals, mysteriously and remarkably opened the doors – permitting them to post bail and walk out. And then the Circuit Court – Judge Manton presiding – reversed the conviction of Lepke!

It was, though, no more than you might have expected of Judge Manton. He was the tenth-ranking jurist in the United States – yet, as far back as 1927, he was writing decisions that made racketeers happy. In that year, Big Bill Dwyer appealed his sentence for running one of Prohibition's most gigantic bootleg rings. Judge Manton's opinion vigorously maintained the bootleg baron should get a new trial. One of those indicted with Dwyer, incidentally, was Frank Costello – the same imposing Frank C. of today's national Syndicate. Judge Manton made so many weird decisions, in fact, that eventually, a few years after the Lepke stunner, his days of playing angel to the underworld came to an end after too long. He was ignominiously removed under charges that his decisions were frequently influenced by something more than legal merits.

Lepke was free under $3,000 bail. When he was called, he did not answer. Three months later, he walked in, all tanned up. He explained that he'd been in Carlsbad taking the baths, as he was every year, and, he claimed, the call hadn't quite reached to Germany until it was too late. He asked for his bail back – and he got it, too!

At first, the soft-eyed extortionist was inclined to scoff at the rackets investigation in 1935, and the selection of Dewey as the special prosecutor. Potential witnesses who might be sought were sent out of town. Lepke continued to direct his hoodlums, even though he was under constant surveillance.

"I sneak way from the cops...I lose them...mostly in the subway," he explained to Paul Berger. Then he would meet one or another of his mob on a subway platform, in the lobby of the Flatiron Building or in Madison Square Park. His office was watched; his phones were tapped.

He himself would answer only when a caller asked for "Murphy." A dictaphone was spirited into his office. He foiled that by installing a portable radio and turning it up full strength whenever he had a conversation. And all the time, he was collecting thousands in extortion and was overseeing rackets and beatings – and murders!

Eventually, though, the boss had to follow his fugitive employees. It was no pell-mell flight. Calmly, in midsummer, 1937, he told Berger, "Things are getting too hot here; I'll have to lam. Be careful of the Amalgamated Clothing Workers."

Even from his hideaway, Lepke continued to direct the outfit. Mendy was left in charge of payrolls and finance. When there was a contract, however, consultation was ordered. Reles explained afterward that he and Pittsburgh Phil frequently sat in with Mendy and the astute Albert Anastasia on such occasions.

As the heat grew, more drastic steps became necessary. Lepke decreed his War of Extermination to silence any singing before a wrong note could be trilled. When all the canaries – real or potential – were out of the way, he was convinced he could walk into headquarters – and walk right out. What followed was a blood bath. That was when he was officially labeled "America's most dangerous criminal."

Lepke gave orders to the Brooklyn troop, through the years, for more than thirty contracts that our stoolpigeons knew about. The "hits" by his own staff and assigned gunmen, other than the Brooklyn torpedoes, doubled that figure, and then some. As the chief opponent of indiscriminate killing, he felt every one of these murders was necessary.

As the investigations crowded closer, however, Lepke really went kill-crazy. By 1939, the evil boss was desperately ordering one murder on top of another. Sometimes he had two firing squads on the road at once. At least a dozen contracts were performed by Brooklyn, Inc., in that single year alone.

The Law steamed up to a fever pitch as the terror spread. A nation-wide hunt was begun for a reported underground, harboring wanted criminals. The whisper was that doddering Al Capone, serving time for income-tax evasion and trying to look good with his keepers, had hinted of this. A special federal grand jury in Newark, N.J., subpoenaed Longy Zwillman to ask if he knew anything about where Lepke was holed up.

"I know Lepke a long time," Zwillman admitted, "but I haven't seen him in three-four years. So far as I know, he was a pleasant fellow...and clean morally."

His avowal of not having seen Lepke did not jib e with what Reles told us afterward. The Kid said that only a few months before this incident, a meeting was held at the home of Tony Romeo, alias Spring, and that among those present were both Longy and Lepke. Reles drove Lep over from his hideout, and sat in on the session. Among the leading citizens on hand, he recalled, were Albert Anastasia, Willie Moore, the New Jersey gambling man, and Jerry Rullo, better known as Jerry Catena, a Jerseyite who is chummy enough with Frank Costello to have visited with him in New Orleans and Cuba. And then there was Three-finger Brown, from Harlem. Brown claims he is a manufacturer of ladies' coats. However, the Federal Narcotics Bureau has a report in its New York office on the very active "107th Street Mob" of dope hustlers, and, as of midsummer, 1951, the report states, the head man of this crew is Tommy Luchese – who is called Three-finger Brown, because of a couple of missing digits from one of his hands.

The meeting at Tony Romeo's house that night, Reles explained, was called because Three-finger Brown had his eyes on a portion of the garment district. With the almost parental feeling Lepke had for the clothing industry, he, naturally, was opposed. Anastasia and Reles were aligned with him against the others.

"Nobody moved in on me while I was on the outside – and nobody's gonna do it just because I'm on the lam," Lepke laid down the law. "There's no argument…The clothing thing is mine."

Reles said that when Lepke showed them he felt that way about it, that's all there was, and the meeting adjourned.

Zwillman's grand-jury testimony of an apparently somewhat casual friendship with Lepke did not quite fit another of Reles' sworn revelations. This one concerned the only time in his life Kid Twist was in real terror. He had been subpoenaed by the New York federal grand jury investigating Lepke's disappearance. He was about to grasp the knob of the door to enter the jury-room, when two men sidled up. They advised him, he said, to testify that he didn't know where Lepke was; better still, that he didn't even know Lepke. And, he said, they further cautioned that if he so much as whispered anything different, he knew what would happen to him. In read dread – for he knew these men – the Kid went in and perjured himself to the eyes.

"Who were those two men who threatened you at the door to that grand jury room?" I asked him.

"They were Longy Zwillman and Willie Moore," he swore.

Now, for two New Jersey bosses to have come to New York to protect a director of the national Syndicate, who had his fingers in rackets and murder from California to New York to Florida, smacks mightily of interstate crime – and here a remarkable peculiarity appears. Interstate crime is what the Kefauver Senate Crime Committee was set up to investigate. Yet, when Longy and Willie appeared before the Committee in 1951, neither was asked a single question concerning this incident involving interstate crime. This disclosure, sworn to in open court, might, under proper interrogation, have uncovered some highly interesting information as to the scope of a national organization whose members are so devoted to each other. The Committee's questioning of Moore centered, rather, on how he bets the horses when he goes to the race track. Much of Longy's appearance was taken up with his vending machines, plus an interrogation by Senator Charles Tobey, an avowedly pious New Hampshire politician, as to whether Zwillman is known as "the Al Capone of New Jersey." Longy's answer was "no," – enlightening, indeed, to a study of interstate crime.

Lepke on the lam was the white-hot center of one of the most intense, concentrated manhunts that crime-fighting has ever undertaken.

For the first time in history, New York police set up a special squad to track down a single fugitive. Twenty detectives were assigned to the picked detail. FBI agents ranged halfway across the world on the hunt. The City raised its reward offer to $25,000. The federal government announced it would match that. One million "wanted" circulars were distributed all over the nation. By contrast, only 20,000 were sent out for the Lindbergh baby kidnapping.

There were rumors that Lepke was in Havana, in South America, off the coast of Mexico on a yacht, in Poland setting up a kidnap enterprise. All were checked. And all the time – for the entire two years he was hunted with the $50,000 price on his head – Lepke never left Brooklyn! Part of the time, he was within a mile of police headquarters. On dozens of nice afternoons, Kid Twist took him for a drive on the public highways, or he went walking alone on the streets.

In his walks, he happened one day upon a public garage, in front of which was a long wooden bench, where hangers-on gathered on pleasant afternoons. Lepke felt secure behind his brand-new mustache and dark glasses. Anyway, who would expect a man, sought the world over, to be sitting on the bank of the Gowanus Canal? So, on several sunny days afterward, Lepke dropped by and lolled among the neighbors. Occasionally, he even invested two dollars on a horse with the gentleman who obliged the bench-warmers.

He was sitting there one afternoon when a sedan slammed to a stop in front of the bench. Before anyone could move, four menacing men got out and flashed shields. Lepke cast a glance this way and that, but there was no way out.

"Line up," commanded the plainclothesman. Their tone indicated this was a mission of utmost importance. They pushed the idlers into an uneven rank – including Lepke. There were seventeen of them, and the detectives set about methodically searching every one, not omitting the sweatbands of their hats and the inside of their shoes. Lepke got the same. They never batted an eye at him; he never batted an eye at them. Finally, the officers said "ah." They yanked one fellow out of line, and bustled him triumphantly into the car, as if he must have tried to blow up Brooklyn Bridge, at least.

"The rest of you bums – beat it, or you'll all go in," the detectives threatened. The rest of the bums beat it – including Lepke, the man who was being sought all over the world with a $50,000 price on his head. The one they kept, alas, had a few horse-bet slips in his pocket.

His friends, Albert Anastasia and Kid Twist Reles, were careful administrators of Lepke's hideout spots. Right from the start, they demonstrated they were scientists at this sort of thing. For, while the hunt went on across the earth, they hid Lepke in a dance hall! This was the Oriental Palace, a trap in Coney Island once owned by Louis Capone. Later, Reles listed the visitors who came while "the Judge" stayed there. There were Mendy Weiss and Albert A, and Moey Dimples, Lepke's agent in the Florida-New York gambling mob, and a character who went under the weighty tag of "Fat Sidney." He had two claims to fame: he weighed 350 pounds and he was married to a movie star.

The Oriental, however, was too prominent. People were always coming in and out. After a while, Mendy had the alternative. A modern six-story apartment had only recently been completed in the Flatbush section. Mendy had personally laid out the plan for one of the suites, as part of a contemplated narcotics enterprise to be operated from a fashionable apartment in a respectable section. The flat was designed so no one could notice a thing. Mendy's interior decorating featured secret panels and storage nooks and special bolts and one thing and another. Pending the cooling off of the current investigations, however, the operation was held in abeyance. Mrs. Dorothy Walker had been ensconced in the place. She was the widow of Fatty Walker, who had wound up second best in a gun fight in New York's notorious Hotsy Totsy Club. Lepke was spirited out of the Oriental and moved in with the mobster's widow.

Lest there be scandalous implication attributed to this idyllic arrangement, be assured that the relationship of the widow and the moblord remained pure and platonic. On this subject, the Law stipulates there must be three coincident factors: opportunity, capacity and, most important, inclination. Passing lightly over the first two, it can be said that the inclination of even a myopic gentleman would be reluctant to discern, in the Widow Walker, charms to arouse the baser emotions. And Lepke's eyesight was perfect; his tastes discriminating.

Lepke's sojourn there, however, did include virtually every other diversion. His contemporaries paid their respects, and they came laden with gifts. The expected penitentiary existence of the hunted fugitive was entirely absent. Instead, it was one continuing round of lavish living, sparkling with vintage wines, finest cigars and viands to titillate the appetite of a maharajah. And Lepke presided over the entire gay company. From this bizarre spot in the next several months, a number of contracts were dictated. It seemed, from every angle, the perfect hideout.

But a man with a $50,000 price on his head is very hot. Such a cash prize might give anyone ideas. Eventually, too, Mendy was forced to flee from narcotics charges. Available triggers and aides were dwindling. The hideout arrangers, Anastasia and Reles, decided a new place was necessary – one that could be kept top secret from all but the closest of Lepke's co-workers.

Then Anastasia remembered. About two years before, one Eugene

Salvese had come around and said he hailed from Albert's home town in Calabria, in Italy, and Albert had given him some odd-job work. One day, Salvese needed a certain paintbrush which was back in his living quarters. Anastasia offered to pick it up for him, and there had met Maria Nostro, who was also Calabrese. She had the basement-first-floor quarters in this shabby house, and Salvese lived with her. Albert and Maria got to talking about the old country. Pretty soon Albert asked if a friend of his might use Maria's first floor once in a while. Maria readily acceded. So, occasionally, Lepke had gone there to meet his wife, who was brought to the rendezvous by Louis Capone.

That first-floor of Maria's quarters was just the thing, Albert recalled now, in midsummer of 1939. The entrance was through the basement, an excellent security arrangement. Maria willingly let them take the first floor for three dollars a week. (The mob would have paid probably a hundred times that, if necessary.) in the dead of that same night, Lepke slipped from the Widow Walker's modern rooms into Reles' car, and was transferred to Maria's threadbare "duplex." Lepke had grown his thick black moustache – the Groucho Marx variety – and he had put on fifteen or twenty pounds. To Maria, he was never anyone but "Charley."

Lepke was now, after two years, more secure than ever. Law enforcement was, if anything, farther from finding him on August 1, 1939, than on August 1, 1937. All he had to do was stay put, and he probably could hide out until the ink on the warrants faded into illegibility.

And then Lepke surrendered!

A most interesting story has been handed down as to just why the fugitive moblord, apparently safe for as long as he wanted, voluntarily gave up. The story goes like this:

The FBI felt it had to beat state authorities to Lepke in order to "save face," after two years of futility. So, J. Edgar Hoover sent a flat fiat to Joey Adonis and Frank Costello, the ranking "brass" of Unione Siciliano: Unless Lepke came out of his hole and gave up *to the* FBI, every Italian mobster in the country would be picked up. Mr. A. and Frank C. could not afford to let this happen. They sent an ultimatum to their old pal, "Sorry, chum – surrender to the Feds or we'll have to deliver you personally."

Lepke recognized an edict when he heard one. He set out to do the best he could for himself. The federal government had a narcotics rap against him, good for a maximum of ten to fifteen years in prison. Dewey already had announced that he had sufficient evidence for the State to put him away for five hundred years.

Lepke made a deal with the Federals. He would give up and take his narcotics sentence – provided he remained in federal custody. And on that basis, he surrendered – with the avowed assurance of the federal government that it would protect him from the state.

That is the accepted story – but the evidence says that is not what happened. Beyond the evidence, moreover, is the contention in this accepted version that J. Edgar Hoover was making deals for guarantees he knew were impossible to keep. And in the name of the federal government, at that. Besides, as a director of the Syndicate, Lepke would hardly have acceded to any edict that did not come from the full board of governors. In research for this book, the authors have come upon just about conclusive information that something altogether different lay behind Lepke's capitulation.

A manhunt, remember, was going full blast. The heat was on the underworld as it has been applied but rarely, blistering the ranking racketeers from coast to coast. Much of the country-wide extortion enterprises were singed. What's more, the "industry" would remain locked up until this Lepke thing was settled – not only in New York, but any place the mob did business, which was all over the United States. The pocketbook of the cartel was affected.

Naturally, a tremendous amount of advice began to pour in on Lepke from his close associates among the Syndicate's top magnates. As the rackets were hurt more and more, sentiment veered in one direction – Lepke should surrender before operations were ruined across the country. After all, they pointed out, the temptation of that fat reward, plus the pressure the Law was increasing day by day, created a greater and greater risk that he not only would be uncovered, but would stop a bullet in the process. The smart thing to do, then, was to turn himself in.

Lepke was suspicious of their motives. "Those bastards are more interested in their own take than they are in my hide," he growled to Reles on several occasions.

Nevertheless, even as imperturbable a man as Lepke could not fail to feel the tense urgency. And Lepke was an imperturbable as a square yard of hard concrete. Months of being cooped up alone produced in him none of the mental depressant – the "stir-crazy" effect – that it did in most lammisters.

"He's the toughest kind," insisted Major Garland Williams of the Federal Narcotics staff, after a study of Lepke's known characteristics for a possible clue to where he might be. "Give him some books and magazines, and he's content to hole up in one room for six months."

But now Lepke's own friends and business associates were putting the heat on. The unshakable moblord became fretful. Then the thought of a new danger crept in. "Judge Louis" knew the credo of the cartel – that no one man matters against the well-being of the organization as a whole. The suspicion seeped into his mind that the ever-increasing counsel to give up was really only a lightly disguised decree; that if he did not move voluntarily, the board of governors was going to call a kangaroo court on him, much as they all respected and admired him. Lepke had handed out dozens of death assignments; had sat in on scores of murder meetings. As a result, the more he pondered these suspicions, the more uncertain he became. He was in so strange a

---

state, for the unexcitable Lepke, that for three nights the only sleep he would risk was on a couch in a room with one small window – and then only while Reles stood guard, pistol in hand.

Now, aside from the Kid, about the only others Lepke felt he could still rely on – about the only others, in fact, who came to see him any more – were Albert A. and Moey Dimples, Lepke's long-time lieutenant. As the Florida-New York-Saratoga gambling delegate, Moey was feeling the pinch more than most. He only had the gambling going for him – and even Saratoga was hot from the Law that August.

Dimples, naturally, thought often of the situation. To him, it seemed that all the Federals were after was to get their hands on Lep, to give him a "reasonable" jail term. The recognizable danger lay in the possibility that the boss would be turned over to the state, where Dewey had five hundred years waiting for him.

One day, Dimples walked into the hideout fairly bubbling, and he dropped a blockbuster into the indecision and uncertainty.

"A deal is in with the Feds," he announced. "The guys told me to tip you off."

Lepke listened avidly as his henchman explained. He had been delegated to bring the word, said Dimples, because not many visitors were permitted at the hideout any more. The deal had been approved by J. Edgar Hoover and the Department of Justice, Dimples went on. Lepke was to surrender to the FBI and answer only for the narcotics violations. It was guaranteed that he would not be turned over to the state for prosecution. Later, Reles corroborated it for us.

"The understanding was that he would get ten to twelve years, and would not be turned over to Dewey," the Kid recalled when he sang.

To Lepke, hammered at from all sides, the word that the government would guarantee him against the risk of a life sentence was a rope to a drowning man. One lone voice, however, dissented. As a matter of fact, through all the controversy, all the urgency, one man consistently counseled against surrender. That was Albert Anastasia. To each new proposal to give up, the curly-haired boss of the troop had one invariable word in rebuttal: "Why?" Now he was still opposed.

For two years, Albert had kept Lepke hidden, and Lepke was as secure now as the day he'd gone into hiding. More, in fact. Few, even, of the mob, were aware of the hideaway in Maria's mean quarters. Reward or no reward, Albert insisted he could harbor Lepke for years in more spots he knew. Moreover, the underworld is fully cognizant that nothing hurts a prosecution's case more than delay. Witnesses – particularly stoolpigeons – are not easy to keep overlong in a co-operative frame of mind. Public clamor cools off in time. Determined, aggressive prosecutors move on to other offices.

"So, what's the hurry?" Anastasia countered Dimples' report of the deal. "You can always walk in. But while they ain't got you, they can't hurt you."

Here again is convincing proof against any ultimatum from Adonis and Costello, dictated on command of the FBI or otherwise. Anastasia was, and is, an Adonis man. Had an edict been issued by Joey A., Albert never would have been against it – and vociferously against, at that. In fact, Albert stayed with Lepke to the very end, assumedly ready to protect him from gunmen or law enforcement.

Lepke respected Albert. Through these months, the commander of the killers had proved that Lepke could trust him with his life; even with his clothing industry racket. On the other hand, this deal Dimples detailed removed all risk of falling into the hands of the state. That changed the picture; the odds were now going for him. Besides, highly as he regarded Anastasia's opinion, Albert was but one against every voice in the Syndicate. In the end, Dimples' report swung the balance.

On the night of August 24, 1939, a car pulled away from No. 101 Third Street, Brooklyn. A swarthy, hard-faced man was at the wheel. In the rear, sat a meek-looking little fellow in dark glasses, with a red-headed woman and a baby. Just looking at them, you'd guess that a generous car owner was agreeably taking a neighbor's small family for a ride on a hot evening.

The automobile drove across the bridge and proceeded among the dark and towering offices and warehouses of Manhattan's east Twenties. It continued until the driver sighted a parked car, for which he evidently was searching. He stopped. The quiet little man got out and joined a man in the parked car. From some yards away, where he had been waiting, a sturdy heavy-set man walked over and entered the car. That is how Walter Winchell, who was the man in the automobile, and J. Edgar Hoover, waiting close by, "captured" the most wanted man alive, shortly after 10 P.M. on a hot August night.

The hard-faced driver from Brooklyn was Albert Anastasia. The mild individual in the back seat had been Lepke. Louis Capone's sister-in-law, pressed into service, was the redhead, and the baby she carried had been borrowed from a friend. The masquerade was deemed necessary to prevent recognition while the party was navigating the streets of the metropolis. Albert A. had lined up all the details. Through himself and agents to whom he delegated some of the arrangements, he made the necessary contacts, including the one with Walter Winchell, the syndicated columnist of the *New York Daily Mirror*. And he did it while wishing, all the time, that Lepke would change his mind about giving up.

Hoover spoke to Lepke when he entered the car – and almost with the first sentence, a ton of rock landed on the extortion executive. Anyway, he told a friend long afterward, that is what it felt like. For, from the FBI chief's very first words, Lepke realized there was no deal; there had been no deal; not Hoover nor Winchell nor the Department of Justice nor anyone else had been a party to any deal! And then it hit him: Dimples had double-crossed him. Dimples, who used to say, "I'm with you a million per cent, Louis"...Dimples had sold him a bill of goods!

There was one brief final touch to the story of the hired hand who double-crossed the boss so he could never get out of it. In 1943, one evening, a shooting match shattered the decorum of a midtown restaurant in Manhattan. When the smoke cleared, a man lay there dead. He was identified as one Wolinsky, alias Moey Dimples.

Lepke was in prison by then, with little chance of ever getting out. A friend brought him the news – a friend who shall remain nameless here, and who incidentally was not aware of the "deal" that wasn't.

"You know," reported the friend on his return, "when Louis heard that Dimples got it…I never saw him look happier. I always thought Dimples was his pal."

Considerable feeling developed between state and federal law enforcement after the surrender. Justice Department officials refused to permit Dewey even to question Lepke. New York police were no end riled. They revealed that during the manhunt, the FBI had made an agreement: anything the police learned about Lepke anywhere in the country outside of New York, they would turn over to the G-men; anything the FBI found out about him, involving New York City, they promised to give to the police. Police authorities charged now that the Federals had broken their word – had not let them know that Lepke had established contact, or was even in New York.

This conjured up a shuddering picture. Suppose a New York policeman, unaware of what was in the wind, had seen that tiny group and that suspiciouis business of switching cars. And suppose the officer had recognized Lepke and started shooting. Whose responsibility would it have been had the Director of the Federal Bureau of Investigation and one of the most widely known columnists been killed in the gunplay?

The federal government convicted Lepke for his narcotics smuggling at the end of 1939 and sentenced him to fourteen years. Only then was Dewey permitted a crack at him – and promptly convicted him for his nefarious bakery operations. For this, "Judge

Louis" drew thirty years to life.

The government took him back then, put him in Leavenworth and said the rackets czar would have to serve out his narcotics "rap" before anything else. Thus, he would do fourteen years for the Federals and then start thirty-to-life for the State. The irony of it was that, for years to come – as many as he lived, probably – the public would still be paying the freight for Lepke. He would be fed and housed and live off the same taxpayers on whom he'd been living by extortion all his adult life.

His hands ran with blood – all law enforcement in America was positive of that. But all were just as positive that the Law had done as much as it could to him. Lep had covered up too well to be caught in murder.

Then, two months later, we stepped up and announced we had the murder to pin on him; and we had an indictment to show we meant business. We had opened up on the national Syndicate some time before, but what with the Brownsville and Ocean Hill torpedoes to be nabbed in our own front yard, Lepke's name had not previously been mentioned.

That was in the spring of 1940. For the next year, I was deep in convicting Pittsburgh Phil and Buggsy, in the trial and retrial of Happy and the Dasher, in running out to California to supply data in the murder case against Buggsy Siegel and Frankie Carbo, and in furnishing information to New Jersey to put Bug Workman away for the Dutch Schultz slaughter. In all that time, I was almost unaware of the Lepke case. Varioius others in the District Attorney's office handled it, and apparently, in that year, it was not put together for trial. What happened, I don't know. The first I really knew about it was, one day, after the second conviction had put Happy and the Dasher away for keeps, the file on the Lepke case was dropped on my desk.

To get Lepke from federal authorities for trial, I went to

Washington and saw James V. Bennett, the Federal Director of Prisons.

"If you have a murder case, and can prove it, he's yours," agreed Bennett. He made one stipulation: unless we could convict Lepke of murder in the first degree and make it stick, we would have to give him back to serve out his narcotics sentence. So, Lepke came to Brooklyn on lend-lease for murder.

- *Murder Inc. is available on Amazon.com, Alibris.com & Half.com*

REVIEW & COMMENTS:

REVOLT IN THE MAFIA

by

Raymond V. Martin

Besides being a great read, this book is part of American mob lore in such a way no one not directly associated with the Brooklyn mob of that time realizes…till now…and it is especially close to my heart. First, what makes this book head and shoulders above other accounts of the Gallo-Profaci mob war, like "The Mad Ones," is that Inspector Ray Martin was there, living it. He didn't just do a literary exercise in research decades after the fact, and believe any faulty remembrances or outright bullshit from those he interviewed. Of course, he was on the other side; the law's side, and only knows what reached his eyes and ears at the time. However, that time was one when men…mobsters…still took secrets to the grave with them, and there was much going on in the background that the inspector was never aware of.

If you've seen Godfathers I & II, which I assume you have if you're interested in mob material, you'll remember scenes from those movies that were directly taken from the real events in Martin's book. Puzo either read them or knew of them indirectly and incorporated them into his fiction. One was the killing of Luca Brasi, and the delivery of his jacket wrapped around a fish. Suddenly, all of America was saying, "Luca Brasi sleeps with the fish." That parallels exactly the tossing of "Joe Jelly" Gioielli's jacket wrapped around a fish from a moving car on Avenue U. Who was Joe Jelly? He was probably the toughest of the tough in the entire Gallo crew. Jelly had a vicious German shepherd that used to chew up any living thing that came close enough to it. When the dog would be ordered destroyed by a judge after some attack, Joe would get another dog, put it down, and bring his original dog back as the one he'd bought.

The second major theft of a real Gallo incident by Puzo is the one covered in Chapter 10. Larry really was strangled like Michael V. Gazzo playing Frankie Pantangeli was in Godfather II, but in the Sahara Lounge, on Utica Avenue, Brooklyn, instead of where it was staged for the film. Larry bore the rope burn around his neck till the day he died, at age 41, of cancer. He also bore the memory of the beating he took at the precinct, as detectives tried to find out who had done the shooting. Larry never told them, but got his own revenge with bullets, leaving the one who betrayed him crippled in one arm for life.

If I could have named this review as an original piece, I would have called it, "Ode to Larry." I've been acquainted with a lot of mob guys in the course of my life. Couldn't stand some of them; liked some of them; even became close friends with a few. However, with no disrespect to any of them, Larry Gallo was the best guy I've ever come across. Amazingly, I have never come across anyone, even enemies, that didn't have the same opinion of him. I was fortunate enough to know Larry well when I was a very young man looking for a father figure and to prove my manhood. He taught me not just what it was to be a successful mobster, but what it meant to be a man. When my other wannabe pals got plucked by different wiseguys, one of whom was the Sally D. mentioned in the following chapter, who gave them carte blanche to step on toes as they flexed their mob muscles to prove they were worthy, Larry ripped me a new ass every time I stepped out of line. I'd get frustrated and wonder out loud if he was an angel when he was young, but he'd calmly answer that he'd seen and done everything and I didn't have to behave recklessly to prove myself; just listen to him. Later, when two of the guys who'd encouraged my friends to do what they wanted then report back to have it taken care of were killed, my pals' enemies began purging them one by one; young, tough, stand up guys found dead every other day. Then I understood.

When I had an argument with a drunken bar owner at 4 a.m. in the Foursome Diner, I was called downtown later that day. Larry told me he'd heard about the incident. I told him word for word what had happened. His next question floored me.

"Were you drinking?" he asked.

"Nicky was drunk," I replied.

Larry went on to tell me that he didn't care about Nicky because he had no responsibility for him then asked again if I had been drinking. When I said I had, he immediately told me I was wrong. He said that he would consider me wrong in any beef I had in the future if I had been boozing it up. As a result, I stopped drinking; had an occasional party if I was with people I was absolutely sure of, but never drank regularly. I never wanted to be "wrong." Even today, I'll have one glass of a dry Italian red wine (Nero d'Avola's my current choice) if I'm dining with others who are also drinking it, or a once in a blue moon after dinner aperitif, like Frangelico. Larry saved my liver as well as my life.

I learned from Larry Gallo that one became a big man by the number of friends he had, not by the enemies he'd made. I learned the difference between someone who couldn't pay money owed and someone who didn't want to pay; and how to treat each. Following those lessons, I brought food to guys who owed me and had lost their jobs, and even laid out money to put one man with a family into a hot dog wagon business of his own when he was down on his luck. When the last guy was approached by organized crime detectives asking about shylock money he owed me, he refused to confirm it. In fact, not one of my customers at the time did.

It's impossible to know about the man in my ramblings or in Inspector Martin's book. What it is possible to do is understand what a day to day mob struggle that takes lives is like, and how much of what we think of as fiction was lifted from real life. This is an important book. Read it.

© 2011 R.I.C.O. Entertainment, Inc. All rights reserved.

Sonny Girard

REVOLT IN THE MAFIA

Raymond V. Martin

Duell, Sloan & Pearce, 1963

Library of Congress Catalogue #63-16821

CHAPTER 10: A Strangling at the Sahara (Pp.145-157):

My telephone rang at headquarters. Larry Gallo had been strangled at the Sahara Lounge. Patrolman Blei had been shot in the face. John Scimone had been picked up dazed in a gutter where he had fallen from a white Cadillac speeding from the scene.

It was Sunday afternoon, August 20, 1961, five days after the Canarsie swamp case. As my command car, driven by Jim Goggin, screamed toward the Sahara Lounge, I wondered how Larry Gallo happened to be there. I knew the Sahara. We had kept an eye on it from time to time. It was a mob hangout in the Flatbush section of Brooklyn operated by Charles Clemenza, a friend of Joseph Profaci. Gallo must have known it was enemy territory. Was he over-confident? Did he feel that his efforts to lift the crown from Profaci's aged and ailing head were finally on the verge of success? For several days we had been getting vague reports about conferences between the Gallos, Carmine (Sonny) Persico, and Salvatore (Sally D.) D'Ambrosia, the Don's former Button Men, and John Scimone, the Profaci chauffeur. We learned later that Scimone had phoned Larry Gallo earlier that afternoon. Though he sounded excited, Scimone said only that he had good news. The rendezvous was set for 5 P.M. at the Sahara. Both were on time. A light gray rain was falling as Scimone greeted Larry Gallo with a handshake on the sidewalk. To indicate how good the news would be, Scimone gave Larry Gallo a crisp $100 bill folded sharply in two. Scimone took Larry by the arm and walked him through the open side door of the lounge.

It was dark in there except for the dim bar light by which Charley Clemenza was polishing glasses. He greeted the two men, asked how things were, said how glad he was to see them, and why didn't they have a drink. He poured two shots for them. They drained the drinks at the bar. They talked and made little jokes. A careful dresser himself, Larry Gallo admired Clemenza's handsome tie and diamond stickpin. Clemenza poured two more drinks. Scimone excused himself to go to the men's room hidden in the rear shadows of the lounge. Larry, his foot on the rail, continued talking across the bar to Clemenza.

He saw the rope through the glass darkly as it flipped over his head, around his throat. It was swift, tight, and twisted before he could get his hands up. While his hands clawed at the noose, the knee in his back pinned his belly to the bar and his fingers lost strength. The open palms of death cupped his eyes. He fell to the floor. The rope loosened briefly and the blackness receded into blues and reds. His eyes reached out of his head. He looked through the darkness at a man he knew. The rope yanked tight. The blackness returned. His heart stopped beating. He excreted into his pants – a sign that clinical death was seconds away.

The sunlight knifed into the Sahara darkness as the side door opened wider.

"Is everything all right in there, Charley? The door was open."

"Everything is fine, Sergeant," said the proprietor, keeping his voice steady. "Just cleaning up a little. You okay?"

Sergeant Meagher saw the legs of Larry Gallo extending toward the dim light behind the bar. "Is that something on the floor?"

Behind the darkness a voice said: "Take him!" A second voice responded: "Okay!"

"Not here!" shouted Clemenza. "I don't want trouble here!"

The police sergeant's gaze returned to Clemenza. Two figures broke from the shadows and raced through the door. Sergeant Meagher yelled: "Blei! Watch out, Blei!" Patrolman Melvin Blei was stepping from the patrol car. As he straightened up on the sidewalk, a man with a drawn pistol hurtling toward him extended his arm and fired a bullet sideways into Blei's face. Blei staggered back against the hood of the police car, trying to stop the flow of blood from his cheek with his hand. Three men ran, jumped into a parked white Cadillac, and gunned the car crazily down the street and around the corner.

Meagher ducked into the patrol car, picked up the radio microphone, and called headquarters. "Larry Gallo murder attempt, Patrolman Blei shot. Sahara Lounge—Utica Avenue and Clarendon Road. White Cadillac three or four men in it took off from the scene. Get an ambulance. Blei is bad."

Precinct Radio Control Broadcast Signal No. 41: Emergency. All patrol cars proceed to Sahara Lounge. Utica and Clarendon. Forty-one. All cars to Utica and Clarendon.

The white Cadillac, its doors open and the keys still in the ignition lock, was found abandoned on East Thirty-fourth Street, near Snyder Avenue, four blocks from the Sahara. John Scimone, who had been sprawling face down in the gutter, staggered to his feet as a patrol car pulled up. There was a large bruise on his left cheek and his face was swelling around the left eye. The patrol-car cops held Scimone to keep him from falling. They were brushing the dirt from his clothes when they heard the 41 signal blasting from their car radio. They noticed a pistol under the Cadillac. They took it and the ignition keys and Scimone to the Sahara Lounge. Within eight minutes fifteen police cars from several different precincts gathered there.

"It was a routine check," Meagher explained to two detectives standing with him on the sidewalk. "The Sahara doesn't open until six. I thought I'd better stick my head in. Something was wrong. When I got to the door, the dog didn't set up a racket. He keeps a wild Doberman in there. Tear your arm off. The dog wasn't there. Three of them inside the place. They brushed me back as they went for the door. The way the light came in I saw their faces. I could pick them out, I think."

Inside, the dead Larry Gallo was coming back to life. The blue face slowly received color from the now pumping heart. Larry's eyes blinked up at the dark ceiling. Fresh blood delicately pin-pointed the skin breaks in the bright red rope burn around his neck and throat. His lips moved. "The bastard," he said. "The dirty bastard. He gave me a C-note. He gave me a C-note!" Then he saw the cops squatting beside him and standing above him. He became conscious of the fact that he had dirtied himself and he groaned with disgust. With the help of a cop, he moved shakily to the lavatory to get rid of his underpants and to clean up as well as he could.

The bullet that entered Patrolman Blei's cheek had lodged under his nose. Despite heavy bleeding and shock, he was not in a critical condition, the doctor said, before rushing him by ambulance to the nearest hospital.

Scimone sat in a chair in the Sahara Lounge whose lights were now blazing. "I didn't see anything," he said. "Larry's my friend. I was buying him a drink. I went to take a leak. I didn't see anything."

He kept pressing a handkerchief to his face but his eyes were alert and his voice was strong. "Yeah, they stuck a gun in my back and made me go with them. Them guys threw me out the car. They tried to kill me. I never seen them before."

"What were you doing here?"

"I came in for a drink."

"With Larry?"

"Yeah, I came in with Larry."

"How did you know the place would be open?"

"It was open."

Clemenza next. "What can I tell you?" he moaned. "I'm busy cleaning and I see cops and there's noise. My God, it's an awful thing!"

"How come the place was open? The Lounge never opens before six."

"I was cleaning up a little. I wasn't open for business."

Larry Gallo returned from the lavatory. His glare swung from Clemenza to Scimone. I prompted him: "Tell us what happened."

"I don't know," he said.

"Who strangled you?"

"It was too dark to see."

"What were you doing when they got the rope around you?"

"I was having a drink."

"Where?"

"Over there by the bar."

Clemenza again. He shook his head violently when asked if he had served Larry Gallo a drink. "How could I serve him a drink? The place is closed till six o'clock. I didn't give him no drink. I didn't even see him."

I took Meagher aside. "How did you spot it?"

"Routine, I guess," he said. "The place is not supposed to open until six. The side door was open. I walked in to check."

I said: "Take them downtown." Clemenza put on his jacket,

buttoned his collar and slid his tie up. He asked if he should lock the door. We told him it wasn't necessary. We left six men to secure the premises. At the precinct we booked Scimone and Clemenza as material witnesses. We also held Larry Gallo as a material witness, partly for his own safety.

Scimone kept protesting his innocence. He and Larry were great friends, he asserted. Larry stared at him with his lips unconsciously cocked to spit. Clemenza kept chirping about nobody being there. He hadn't served Larry Gallo a drink, he hadn't seen Gallo—it was too dark to see anybody. Not Scimone either, he hadn't seen Scimone. His nonsense annoyed Scimone. "Sure, I was there, Charley," said the Profaci triggerman with authority. "You give me a drink and you give Larry a drink, and then I went to take a leak. You musta seen us—you getting old or something?"

"Oh, that's right. You're right. I remember now. All that excitement. I got mixed up. Oh, yeah. I seen Johnny and Larry. It was them others hiding in the dark I didn't see."

I asked whether he didn't see the rope go over Larry Gallo's head. "No, I didn't see nothing like that," he said. "I was busy working around. I didn't pay no attention."

Larry Gallo put his hand to his throat. "Son of a bitch," he said, with a half-smile. "I was coming around when the cop came in, you know. He leaned down and give the rope another twist."

"Who did?"

"I don't know."

I persisted. "Who wanted to strangle you, Larry?"

"Nobody would want to do a thing like that to me, Mr. Martin," the mobster said, looking steadily at Scimone. With an obvious effort, Scimone disentangled his eyes from that gaze and stared at the floor.

Sergeant Meagher thumbed through the mob books at headquarters. He picked out photos of Sonny Persico and Sally D. D'Ambrosio. He never had any contact with them before, or with the mob generally, but he thought they were probably the men who brushed him back as they bolted through the open door of the Sahara. "I'd be sure if I saw them again," he said. In writing up his report Sergeant Meagher did not mention the rogues' gallery photos because he believed, as I did, that it would be better to wait until he could see Persico and Sally D. in person. He did, however, describe the assassins. One was slim and young, about five feet six, with round, bulging eyes, receding forehead, small hooked nose, small chin. That fit Persico. The other was well built, taller, in his late thirties or early forties, balding (the assailant had worn no hat) with a round, full face. That fit Sally D.

I was not surprised. It was characteristic of the Mafia to use as executioners men who were so close to the intended victim that they would not be suspected. Yet Carmine Persico had trained as a hoodlum under the Gallos; he was one of their products. Sally D. had been a friend of Larry Gallo for years. And John Scimone? He had never been a friend of the Gallos. Fork-tongued Johnny must have been playing a double game right along. What about Tony Bender? What about Ruby and Jiggs? Did they also belong to Joseph Profaci? Had they also played a role in waltzing the Gallos toward death, the Gallos who thought they could take three giant steps to power but who never got beyond the first step? I pulled myself up short. This was no time for speculation. There would be time later. I said nothing about Sergeant Meagher's identifications to Gallo, Scimone, or Clemenza. We assigned them cells and locked them up.

Events tumbled over each other. We tried not to run in ten different directions, but there were at least ten different directions in which to run. The white Cadillac was checked out. It was registered in the name of Alphonse Cirillo. I sent two detectives to Alphonse's home in Brooklyn to tell him of the dramatic events.

Cirillo looked innocent. "I left the car in front of the house," he said. "Somebody must have taken it. I forgot to take the keys out."

Alphonse's brother Aurelius was a well-known Profaci associate. Alphonse had no idea where Aurelius might be. Aurelius was not at his apartment and his wife had no knowledge of his whereabouts. When he continued to be missing, we concluded that he had driven the Cadillac.

This was the point at which we lost control. An assistant in the district attorney's office checked the mug shots independently after reading Meagher's descriptions. He selected Tony Abbatemarco as one of the assassins. Tony Abbatemarco did look a little like Sally D. The district attorney's office had Tony Abbatemarco picked up and brought to Patrolman Blei's hospital bed. Blei was in a state of shock though the doctor said he would be all right when the bullet was removed from his head. His face was swollen, his eyes puffed and closed. When the district attorney's representative entered his room with a police representative, as required by law, and confronted him with Abbatemarco, Blei looked out from under his bandages and thought Abbatemarco might be the man who shot him. Though he would normally push for an identification, since a fellow cop had been shot, the police representative expressed doubts. They ought to wait, he suggested, until Blei was in better shape. The D.A.'s man emphasized the fact that possibly an immediate arrest might break the case wide open and cripple the mob. Resolving uncertainty in favor of time, the D.A.'s man instructed the police officer to place Abbatemarco under arrest. He would seek an indictment against him of attempted homicide, he declared.

Tony Abbatemarco protested vehemently. Larry Gallo was his close friend, he said. The arrest made it appear that he had double-crossed his friend. It occurred to me when I heard what had happened that Blei's identification might lead to Abbatemarco's death at the hand of the Gallos, who had saved him previously from Profaci's vengeance.

By the time Abbatemarco was brought to the precinct, he was a bundle of fury and fear. He asked to see me. I told him I believed his story and that I thought the facts would stand up for him. I had to add that at the moment things were out of my hands. I did not order the arrest and I could not cancel it. I thought Blei was wrong, yet in view of the underworld custom of using a friend to set up a hit, even Abbatemarco must realize that he might conceivably have been the one. To myself, as I thought about it, it seemed more and more unlikely that Abbatemarco was involved. He didn't fit the role.

In custody, Larry Gallo usually retreats into aloofness. The news about Abbatemarco's arrest, however, shook him up. "Are you nuts!" he said. "Abby is my guy! He's my friend."

"So is Scimone," I said.

"Sure, sure," he said impatiently. "They're all my friends. C'mon, Inspector. Abby had nothing to do with that."

I made up my mind to level with him. "I know it," I said. "It was Persico and Sally D. The Cirillo kid was driving. Maybe there was another guy out front with him. Scimone set it up."

Larry Gallo sucked his cheeks in, his round eyes popping a stare at me. He released three long, slow whistles from his puckered lips. "When does my uncle, the lawyer, get here?" he asked.

"Iovone? Soon, I suppose. Why?"

"Why? He's my lawyer. I wanna confer."

"Be smart," I said. "Sign a complaint against Charley, Persico, Sally D., and Scimone."

"You think I'm smart?"

"No, I don't. Maybe your uncle's smart?"

His uncle, the lawyer, arrived at the precinct and talked with Larry

Gallo. Larry would sign a complaint, they told me.

The complaint would not say that Larry had seen Persico or Sally D. at the Sahara or that he knew that they had tried to kill him. He would sign a complaint that stated that the police told him Persico and Sally D. assaulted him. He would claim no personal knowledge. If he were asked to testify against either of these men at a trial, he would refuse. It was not much of a complaint in legal terms but it had some tactical value as far as Gallo was concerned. He wanted the Profaci gang to know that he might not sit still and wait for his death, that he might not choose to play *omerta* all the way. We had the complaint drawn in the manner suggested by Larry and his attorney and Larry signed it.

Based on Meagher's impressions and on Larry's unusual complaint, I sent a wanted-for-questioning alarm for Persico and Sally D. As anybody might have expected, they had disappeared. The next day was another busy one. County Judge Samuel S. Leibowitz, a tough and highly competent judge, held Larry Gallo, John Scimone, and Charles Clemenza in $100,000 bail each as matrial witnesses. He fixed bail at $7,500 for Alphonse Cirillo, the innocent automobile owner. This was on the morning of August 21. Around two thirty the next morning a highway police patrol picked up a blue Cadillac along the Belt Parkway in Queens. Two bullets had gone through the windshield. The keys were still in the ignition lock. Our President Street detectives took one look at the blue Cadillac and confirmed that this was the car in which Joey Gallo had been driving around daily for the past two weeks. They had the license number in their books. We concluded tentatively that Joey Gallo was dead. Why else would his car be left deserted on the highway? Presumably, he had been shot, pulled from the car, and taken away to be finished. Larry yesterday, Joey today. Where would it end?

The blue Cadillac had been registered in the name of Lila Luftschein. I knew about Lila though we had never met. She was part of my file system. She was listed under Gallo associates as the girl friend of a hoodlum known as Sonny Pepitone. She and Sonny had met when she was managing the office of a smart Manhattan supper club.

They had been going steady for some time.

We picked up Lila Luftschein, who proved to be a good-looking woman in her early twenties. She seemed quite unconcerned. She gave her name. She was the owner of the car, she said, but she often loaned it to friends. Somebody had borrowed the Caddy. She could not remember who it was. She had heard of Joey Gallo, of course—she read the newspapers—but she had never, she said, met him.

When word reached Sonny Pepitone that Lila Luftschein had been brought to headquarters for questioning, he rushed to her rescue. There was no mystery, he said. He had been driving the car along the highway when another car pulled alongside on the right. The bullets were fired through his open right-hand window and went out through the windshield. He was not hit, but he lost control of the car momentarily and skidded to a stop. He opened the door on the driver's side and ran across a couple of fields until he found himself in Idlewild Airport. He rested there while his nerves quieted down, then he went home. It was a miracle he wasn't shot, he said. He had no idea who fired at him. Asked what he was doing on the Belt Parkway at that hour, he said he had gone out for some fresh air. He made no bones over the fact that he had borrowed the car from Lila Luftschein. At this point Lila recalled that she had loaned the car to Sonny. We released them with a request that they keep themselves available for further questioning.

Later that same day Joey Gallo, alive and well, was seen by my men on President Street. We concluded that the Profaci mob knew he had been driving the blue Cadillac regularly for some time. They probably followed it. What they did not know was that Joey turned the car over to Sonny the previous evening. Then, when the Belt Parkway seemed to offer a suitable opportunity, the Profaci pistols shot at the wrong man in the right car. Once again they had botched a Gallo killing.

We were not finished with Lila Luftschein. One of our paid informers reported that she was scheduled for assassination because she knew too much. She expressed skepticism about this.

Nevertheless, we urged her to seek protection. Reluctantly, as a hedge against the possibility that the tip was true, she went before Judge Leibowitz and said: "I fear for my life." the judge ordered an around-the-clock guard at her home. Later we learned that Lila was right. The informer had invented the whole story to get money for a main-line narcotics fix. Quietly, without the newspapers picking it up, the guard was withdrawn.

Where was Joe Jelly? I began to wonder about him as soon as I could catch my breath after the attack on Larry Gallo. It seemed to me that nobody would try a hit on Larry without first disposing of his bodyguard, Joe Jelly. I sent Lieutenant Tom Madden around to see Mrs. Gioielli. She appeared to be calm and unworried. Her husband had left on a trip two or three evenings before, she said. She did not know where he had gone, she added, but she was sure everything was all right. I asked Lieutenant Madden to repeat his visit at ten o'clock every morning. For two mornings Tom received the same reception. On the third morning Mrs. Gioielli was crying. Something had upset her, but she would not say what it was. Finally she broke down and said she wanted to report Joe Jelly as missing.

I checked with my President Street squad. Nobody had seen Joe Jelly for two or three days before the attack at the Sahara Lounge. The last person reported to have been inquiring for him was Sonny Persico. The night before the garroting Persico came up to Sid Slater, a roving Gallo associate with restaurant experience, and Hyman Powell, secretary of the Jewelry Workers Union, to ask if they had seen Joe Jelly. Neither one had. He was probably home, Slater suggested. Persico wanted Slater to phone Joe Jelly and ask him to meet them at a certain Bensonhurst bar. Slater did not suspect a rubout or anything like that, but he knew Joe Jelly disliked being disturbed and he was very much afraid of Joe Jelly. He refused to make the call. Persico shrugged and said he would make the call himself. Neither Slater nor Powell had any idea whether Persico did make the call. Certainly Joe Jelly was now missing.

The United States is a civilization on wheels. We looked for Joe Jelly's car as well as for him. We couldn't find either one. Months later we learned that the car, a 1959 air-conditioned Cadillac, had been delivered to a junk yard and cut up into scrap. The junk-yard owner had only a hazy recollection about the car. It was a wreck without plates, he said, and he had purchased it for cash from two men whom he did not particularly notice.

I put most of my detectives on the search for Joe Jelly. The next evening an unfamiliar car rolled through the streets of the Bath Beach section. As it slowed down near a candy store on Avenue U which served as Joe Jelly's hangout, the rear door of the car opened and a dark bundle flew through the air. It landed on the sidewalk at the feet of a cluster of young men. The bundle consisted of Joe Jelly's coat wrapped around a dead fish. It was an underworld obituary notice.

Elimination of the bodyguard of Larry and Joey Gallo had terroristic value, so the Profaci mob was advertising. In Mafia shorthand, the symbolic fish meant that Joe Jelly had been killed and dumped into the ocean. In this case we concluded that he had been taken on his final voyage out of Sheepshead Bay. In addition to the party boats that operate out there for deep-sea fishing, many yachts and small boats berth at Sheepshead Bay. Sally D., who was a gambler as well as a gunman, had a thirty-two-foot cabin cruiser tied up there. Joe Jelly's body was never recovered. We assumed that it had been properly weighted, cemented, and dropped from a boat far from shore.

- ***Revolt in the Mafia is available on Amazon.com, Alibris.com & Half.com***

REVIEW & COMMENTS:

THE LAST GODFATHER

by

Anthony M. DeStefano

If Joe Valachi was the first to sound the eventual deathknell of traditional organized crime in America, Joe Massino has virtually nailed the coffin shut. Massino was the biggest in a growing number of mob executives to scream when his shoelaces got tight. Sammy the Bull was not a boss but a second in command; Little Al D'Arco was the least likely to be put in any position of power (when I was told he had been made acting boss of the Lucchese Family, I really thought my leg was being pulled); Ralph Natale, of Philadelphia, was a disappointment, but never carried himself with the demeanor of a boss. Joe Massino, on the other hand, was a bona fide boss. He was extremely close to John Gotti, who volunteered to act as guardian for the Bonannos till Joe got out of prison and could handle things himself; not the kind of company that suggests weak knees. Massino's own actions over the years gave no indication that he would ever fold; "work" he did and time in prison he did.

Why is the rodentarization of Massino so important? Because of the fact that he was a boss and a well respected boss, it was the final straw in a growing mistrust of authority in the mob. There is a system of "going on record" with any business, legal or illegal, or other acts that can either yield money or a backlash from other mobsters or the authorities. That means reporting those things to the guy above you, who in turn reports to the guy above him until it goes to the boss. It is said that it is for the protection of the one reporting so that he can be backed up if something goes awry and there's some kind of beef as a result. While true to a small extent, it's really to protect the higher ups from indictment as a result of associating with the underling and to know how much money is being made to insure a proper amount makes its way upstairs. Unlike the laws of physics, in the world of organized crime, what goes up never comes down; gravity does not apply to money, which only flows upward. In the distant past there was no worry about the upper echelon ever ratting out those who put stuff on record. They might have one killed for a misstep, but would keep his secrets from the law. The only reasons NOT to go on record were fear that a misstep might be punishable or, most often, to avoid sending a piece of the profit upstairs.

That system is now destroyed.

No longer do street guys have to worry about the day to day people they interact with ratting them out, but those above. Few with any sense will go on record anymore. What that means is that the "organized" in organized crime will become less of a factor each day. Does that mean crime will go away? Of course not. What will remain in organized crime's wake will be disorganized or chaotic crime. The old adages about mob neighborhoods being safe any time of day or night will be old stories, like westerns. Chaos will rule and no one is safe in that environment. Joe Massino is not the only one responsible for the new normal, but he's the one that finalized it for all time.

Since Joe in some ways closed the book on the traditional organized crime structure in America, I only thought it fitting to reprint the last chapter of DeStefano's book. It is a proper close to a fine book that should be on every mob aficionado's reading list, and is available on Amazon, Alibris, and Half.com, among others.

Enjoy the government cheese, Joe.

THE LAST GODFATHER

Anthony M. DeStefano

Citadel Press 2006

ISBN 0-8065-2735-8

CHAPTER 27: ENDGAME (Pp.284-294):

When they want to hide things from prying eyes on the sixth floor of the courthouse in Brooklyn, the metal fire doors get closed. When the black doors are shut, there is simply no way to see who enters and leaves the courtroom where Judge Nicholas Garaufis presided.

It was sometime late in the afternoon of July 30, after the jury had come down with its second verdict giving the federal government over $10 million of Joseph Massino's assets, that court officials closed their fire doors. The hallway was sealed for privacy.

Just before the doors were shut, a federal marshal had walked into Garaufis's chambers and had a word with one of the judge's staff. Federal judges have a number of support staff working for them. Schedules need to be arranged, problems solved, and paper work handled and for that the jurists have a bevy of clerks, assistants, and other aides. Practically speaking, judges are helpless without them, particularly when the unexpected happens.

On the afternoon of July 30, the unexpected happened. One of Garaufis's staffers came into his chambers to say that Joseph Massino wanted a word with him.

The judge's private office faced Adams Street, the main venue for the Brooklyn Bridge and in the late afternoon of July 30, Joseph Massino

383

stood before Garaufis as the traffic went by and the sun was reflecting off the apartment buildings across the boulevard. A court stenographer was the only other person in the room.

Massino had a straightforward but monumental request of Garaufis: the convicted mobster wanted a new lawyer appointed for him so that he could explore possible cooperation with the government. The meeting was short and after Massino was taken back to the holding cell, Garaufis told Greg Andres about what had happened. The judge needed a list of lawyers the government was comfortable with in the role of "shadow counsel" for Massino. Of course, David Breitbart and Flora Edwards were not to be told of this backroom maneuver.

So it was that one of the most seismic events in law enforcement's long struggle against organized crime got underway. Massino was a beaten man. He faced not only the certainty of life in prison and the loss of every tainted penny he had ever made but also the prospect that he could be executed if convicted—a strong likelihood—in the next year's trial for the murder of Gerlando Sciascia. It seemed clear to Massino that he had one card left to play and that was go to with Team America. In all likelihood, this was not a spur of the moment panicked decision by Massino. He had seen the progress of the trial and that the various witnesses were unshakeable in their testimony. The verdict shouldn't have surprised him.

Everybody else had become a rat, so with his own life at stake Massino must have figured an endgame strategy for himself long before the verdict. As a mobster, Massino had a tendency to figure ways of running from trouble. He went on the lam in 1982. When FBI agents paid him a visit in 1984, Massino seemed so spooked that he ran out the back door of his social club. He was a man who had always tried to have an escape plan. He had played the mob game like the good old man he was. But reality now was not in some emotional notion of blood loyalty spawned in Sicilian culture. No, reality was now the fact that in a coffin was the only way Massimo would get out of prison. There had to be another way.

From the government's list of lawyers Garaufis appointed Edward C. McDonald as Massimo's shadow counsel. The use of attorneys as "cooperating" lawyers has been criticized by some in the legal community as an anathem to the traditional role and function of a defense attorney. For some it left a bad taste in that an attorney became involved in a legally approved subterfuge on the trial attorney who had zealously defended someone like Massino but yet didn't know the client had changed sides. However, the use of shadow counsel is legal and used regularly.

McDonald had been head of the old Brooklyn Organized Crime Strike Force in the 1980s, ironically the unit that had prosecuted Massino in the 1985 Teamsters case. Leaving government service, McDonald became a partner in a Manhattan law firm, specializing in criminal defense work.

Massino didn't start cooperating with the government right away. There were initial proffer sessions to go through before any agreement could be signed. The government was in the driver's seat and had to be convinced he could help law enforcement. Massino's initial approaches to the FBI were met with skepticism and he was rebuffed, said one law enforcement official.

The first glimmer the FBI had a new mob mole came in early October 2004. At an overgrown lot in the Lindenwood section of Queens, abutting the border with Brooklyn, federal agents and city police began digging. The place had seen excavation nearly twenty-three years earlier after Alphonse Indelicato's body began rising through the soil. Immediately, word leaked out that the FBI Bonanno squad was involved in the dig in a search for the remains of the still missing three captains murder victims. Agents Jeffrey Saller and Kimberly McCaffrey, dressed in their FBI raid jackets and accompanied by agency evidence collection agents, watched as the excavators brought in heavy equipment to tear up the ground and concrete at the site.

It wasn't a total surprise that the FBI would start digging again at the Ruby Street lot. One body had already been found there and immediate speculation centered on a new confidential informant having identified the location as a burial ground where other victims could be found. Some thought Salvatore Vitale, who had already told the FBI that Massino had said the three captains had been disposed of together, might have been the source. But according to one law enforcement official, Massino, in an informal effort at cooperation that didn't cost him much, had told the FBI that police had not looked hard enough when they first found Indelicato's body.

The digging went on for about three weeks and after some false alarms the forensic team recovered human bones. It took over two months for the medical examiner to make DNA comparisons, but it seemed like the dig had been productive. A credit card belonging to Dominick Trinchera and a watch traced to Philip Giaccone had been unearthed. On December 20, 2004, the FBI announced that the human remains found at Ruby Street were those of Trinchera and Giaccone.

Massino's secret dealings with the government, though still tentative and with no cooperation agreement signed, continued through the fall. He had not told his family what he was doing but there were hints Massino dropped that he was feeling abandoned by his crime family brethren. When it was announced in court that prosecutors would not be seeking the death penalty against his two codefendants in the Sciascia murder case, John Spirito and Patrick DeFilippo, Massino became depressed over the exultation shown, said a source familiar with the events Massino was still on the hook for death and after the way his top lieutenants had turned on him he had become very bitter and felt abandoned, the source said.

With McDonald as his advisor, Massino continued his secret talks with the government. This was all done with his regular lawyer, Flora Edwards, kept in the dark while she gamely went on representing Massino in the upcoming death penalty case. In fact, Massino had asked Edwards to stay on the case after it became clear that David Breitbart would not be able to continue.

Just before Thanksgiving word leaked out that U.S. Attorney General John Ashcroft intended to seek the death penalty against Massino for the Sciascia murder. The ruling was formally announced in court by prosecutors Greg Andres and Nicholas Bourtin on November 12. The Ashcroft decision was another part of the government squeeze play on Massino.

Another move by the feds came on November 23, when Massino appeared in court to answer charges to a superseding indictment in the Sciascia murder case. This time the government added two more defendants, acting street boss Vincent Basciano and reputed Bonanno soldier Anthony Donato, accusing them of racketeering acts unrelated to Sciascia. Both in court and in the holding cells, Massino had a chance to chat with Basciano as they all entered not guilty pleas. Massino's machinations with the government remained a closely guarded secret.

On November 29, things took a curious turn. According to a letter filed in court by attorney Flora Edwards, Massino received a copy in the mail of a *Newsday* story about the fact that Garaufis had required closer monitoring of his health status. The article was confiscated and Massino was moved into a segregated housing unit (SHU) and no longer in the general population of the Brooklyn federal jail, said Edwards. Massino told his family of the move into solitary and the fact that the newspaper article had been confiscated.

Edwards said Massino's movement into the SHU made it difficult for him to prepare for trial, all because of a critical newspaper story. On December 22, said Edwards, prosecutor Andres told her that he had recommended that Massino be prohibited from attending the codefendant meetings but wouldn't explain why, saying Garaufis was "fully aware of the facts and circumstances." Edwards said she pressed Andres for an explanation but that he stated the movement of Massino into solitary confinement had to do with Bureau of Prison policy regarding inmates on "death penalty" cases. Edwards continued to ask Garaufis to intervene. Little did she know the real story and the fact that the system was playing with her.

With hindsight, the movement of Massino into the SHU and the government recommendation that he be kept from meeting with codefendants Basciano, Donato, DeFillipo, and Spirito should have been a red flag. But a red flag about what? Never before had a crime family boss become a cooperating witness. Government explanations, which can now be viewed as cover stories, seemed plausible. Perhaps Massino had been plotting more crimes or was using codefendant meetings to pass messages to his underlings?

Massino's wife and daughters were also getting strange vibes. Before his move into solitary, he seemed more embittered to them, family sources said. He had lost about twenty-five pounds and in visits after he was placed in solitary he seemed distracted. Massino had said he was angry with the fact that there had been talk about a plot to kill Andres and said it all indicated that the Mafia had degenerated into a pack of animals, said one family source. From his rhetoric, Massino seemed to signal to his wife and daughters that he was considering becoming a cooperating witness. If you do, his family told him, you are on your own.

It was on the night of January 26 that Massino's immediate family learned that they shouldn't try to see him at the Brooklyn federal jail. He had been moved to the Manhattan federal jail, a sign that he was cooperating they were told.

The next day in the Brooklyn federal court another indictment was filed against acting street boss Vincent Basciano for the December 2004 murder of Bonanno associate Randolph Pizzolo. The court papers indicated that a cooperating witness relayed comments Basciano had made in a courthouse holding cell in November about the homicide. The indictment alleged that the cooperating witness also stated that Basciano had proposed the murder of prosecutor Andres, something Massino had alluded to in talking to his immediate family. Astonishingly, the incriminating comments had actually been tape recorded by the witness. Who was this "cooperating witness"? the indictment didn't say, but in a matter of minutes after the court papers were filed word leaked out: the new witness was none other than Joseph Massino. At the jail Massino met one final time with Edwards. He avoided eye contact with her. She left in a few minutes.

On Eighty-fourth Street in Howard Beach, the news that Massino had become a government informant and had taped his loyal surrogate Vincent Basciano was first disseminated over the all-news radio stations and was another in a long series of enormous emotional jolts. Josephine Massino stayed in seclusion, attended to by a close female friend who had sat with her throughout most of the trial. Quick-tempered daughter Joanne railed against her father and in a blast of anger said, "I am done with him, I am ashamed that he's my father."

In an e-mail interview with *Newsday*, Massino's daughter, Adeline, portrayed her father as embittered and having lost the support of his family with his decision to become an informant.

"My mother, my sister and I [have] no reason why he is doing this and probably never will," Adeline said. "Maybe he himself doesn't know that answer."

At least to his daughters, Massino's decision was a betrayal of the code of loyalty to friends he had always preached to them. They also felt betrayed because they supported him throughout his trial, even in the face of embarrassing disclosures about his infidelity. They also feared that their father's actions could endanger themselves and their own families, a not unreasonable sentiment in the dog-eat-dog life that now characterized the Mafia. Adeline said that her mother in particular had been hurt by Massino's actions during his married life and that she could no longer support him. There were hints that a divorce might even be in the cards.

Massino's turning was not officially acknowledged for some months. But the indications he had become a star government witness were plentiful. The clearest signal was the disclosure in May 2005 that the Department of Justice, led by Ashcroft's successor Alberto Gonzales, had decided to reverse itself and not seek the death penalty against Massino. It was an indication that Massino had done some significant cooperating and was catching a break.

Speculation abounded about what damage Massino could do to his Mafia brethren. By any measure, it was believed that he could hurt a lot of people. Basciano aside, Massino could also be expected to testify against other Bonanno defendants, including reputed Canadian crime boss Vito Rizzuto, who also faced charges stemming from the murder of the three captains and other allegations of racketeering. Rizzuto was fighting extradition from Canada after U.S. officials had disclosed in a letter filed with the Canadian courts the evidence against him in the three captains case.

Massino also had information about the Gambino crime family and he could prove troublesome for some of its members, including John "Junior" Gotti, the son of the late boss. Massino's information about the killing of the three captains could also be used to bring additional charges, if the prosecutors wanted to go that route, against the late John Gotti's brother, Eugene, who was already in prison.

Massino's cooperating with the government delayed his sentencing in his racketeering case until June 23, 2005. Garaufis's courtroom again filled and in the crowd of spectators were Donna Trinchera, the wife of slain capo Dominick Trinchera, her daughter, Laura, as well as Donna Sciascia, the daughter of murdered Canadian mobster Gerlando Sciascia. The appearance of Sciascia's family members was a clear sign that Massino would also be wrapping up that murder case with a guilty plea.

At 12:48 P.M., a grim-looking Massino entered the courtroom from the holding cell. He was wearing a gray suit and had an open-necked white shirt. He sat at the defense table next to attorney Edward McDonald. Unlike his demeanor during trial, Massino appeared nervous. He kept scratching his face and putting his hand up to his mouth. In the back of the courtroom were FBI agents Jeffrey Sallet and

Kimberly McCaffrey. Sallet had been transferred to Washington, D.C., with a promotion while McCaffrey continued the delicate task of handling Massino.

Neither Josephine Massino nor her daughters were in court. Minutes earlier, Josephine had entered Garaufis's chambers with her attorney and acknowledged to the judge that she had signed a forfeiture agreement. She was the owner of record for some of the properties listed and Garaufis had to be satisfied that Massino's wife had signed off on what was to be a massive surrender of most—but not all—of the property she and her husband had acquired. Her spouse was not present in the room. After the formality with the judge was over, Josephine Massino left the courthouse, although she was unable to avoid being spotted by *Daily News* reporter John Marzulli.

At 12:51 P.M. in the hushed courtroom, Garaufis asked Massimo to stand up. The judge had a few preliminary questions, asking the mob boss how far he had gone in school. Massino answering the eighth grade at PS 73. Prosecutor Greg Andres, who had entered the courtroom with a large cup of coffee from a local gourmet shop, handed up to Garaufis the cooperation agreement Massino had signed earlier that day. So it was official, Joseph Massino the mob boss had signed on as a government witness.

It was well known that upon his conviction for racketeering in July 2004 Massino was going to get life in prison without parole, as well as a stiff fine. Massino acknowledged to Garaufis that he was indeed guilty of the crimes for which he had been convicted by a jury. By doing that, he squelched any chance of appeal and dropped the pretense that he was innocent. The Sciascia murder case was still open—but not much longer.

At 1:06 P.M., Massino said "yes your honor, guilty" when asked if he had orchestrated the Sciascia murder. Garaufis asked Massino to explain.

"As boss of the Bonanno family, I gave the order to kill George from Canada," said Massimo.

That simple sentence in itself was amazing not just because Massino admitted his guilt but also because he had dropped the pretension that the crime family was his patrimony. He didn't say "Massino" crime family as he wanted the enterprise to be known. No, Massino instead acknowledged the supremacy of Joseph Bonanno's legacy. It was the "Bonanno family." Massino had just been renting t he hall.

Pressed by Garaufis, Massino said that the killing was carried out by "Johnny Joe," who he said was a "goodfella," Patty DeFilippo, and "Mikey Nose." By his words, Massino implicated John Spirito, whose full name he didn't know, DeFilippo, and reputed Bonanno member Michael Mancuso in the Sciascia murder.

Part of Massino's bargain with the prosecutors was that he had to turn over a great deal of his wealth to the government. He didn't write a check for the $10 million, but he could have come darn close. Massino agreed to give the federal government $10,393,350 in assets. An astonishing $9 million of that was in cash ($7.3 million) and other assets like gold bars. He also turned over the property housing the CasaBlanca Restaurant in Queens as well as two other buildings on Fresh Pond Road. Those properties had been held in Josephine's name. The staggering amount of cash showed that Massino had done very well for a neighborhood touch who never made it out of grade school.

Although the forfeiture agreement didn't spell it out, Massino was able to work out a deal that allowed his wife to keep title to the marital home in Howard Beach, his family's home in Maspeth where his elderly mother lived with her other son, John, and the old house off Grand Avenue where Josephine Massino had been raised. Josephine was also able to keep title to some real estate in Queens and Florida, the agreement indicated, something that allowed her to garner rental income.

Donna Sciascia had filed a letter with the court but asked that it not be disclosed. However, Laura Trinchera, the daughter of one of the slain three captains, allowed her letter to be read in open court and Garaufis did so for the benefit of the public and the news media. Trinchera's letter was the heartfelt statement of a daughter who never got to grow up with her father and lived for years not knowing where he had gone.

"I am grateful that our family now has closure and now my father is resting in his proper place," said Trinchera. "We now have a place to go and say our prayers.

"As far as Mister Massino, he took the opportunity to live out his life, to see his family grow. He took that away from us," she said. "I am here today to support Mister Massino's facing mandatory life in prison. I feel that better late than never."

Garaufis had been presiding over the Bonanno crime family cases for over two years and wanted to have his own say. There had been sixty-seven members and associates of the crime family named in various indictments and fifty-one, including Massino, had been convicted. The overwhelming majority had pled guilty.

"The evidence produced at Joseph Massino's trial last year told a sobering story of an organization devoted to the pursuit of crime and corruption. That evidence detailed the system utilized by organized criminals—and in particular, the Bonanno/Massino crime family—to conduct business, extract revenue from both legitimate and illegal activities, and enforce its rules against members and non-members alike," said Garaufis.

The judge said that the rituals and personalities of the mob "have been deeply romanticized in the popular media of the past thirty years, seemingly with ever-increasing frequency." But the true nature of that life made it prey on human frailty, greed, weakness, and fear, he said.

For the Sciascia murder, Massino was given a life sentence that was to run consecutive to the life term he received for his conviction in July 2004. He was saddled with a $250,000 fine as well.

Since he was cooperating, Massino would be able to seek a reduction in his sentence, assuming the government was happy with his cooperation and filed on his behalf a letter with the court saying so. These so-called 5K letters, named after a section of the federal sentencing guidelines, had become like gold to Mafia cooperators because they could lead to freedom from a long prison sentence.

The sentencing of Joseph Massino took about forty minutes. When it was over, a dour Massino quickly shuffled his way out of the courtroom in the company of federal marshals. He didn't look at any of the spectators. But those who did see his eyes peered into his soul and found nothing. His gaze was as cold, gray, and dead as gunmetal.

- ***The Last Godfather is available on Amazon.com, Alibris.com & Half.com***

MOB CALENDAR

Sonny Girard

Sonny Girard's

MOB CALENDAR:

*Months have a variety of mob events that occurred in them.

This calendar presents the most memorable.

JANUARY: 18th Amendment to the Constitution (Prohibition) ratified.

There is probably no more important event in the history of organized crime in America than the ratification of the 18th Amendment to the Constitution, or, Prohibition, on January 16,1919. Petty local gangs that preyed on their own neighbors, using mugging, extortion, muscling voters to support politicians willing to pay back with favors, and kidnapping as means of supporting themselves, suddenly found themselves the only ones who could and would deliver to the American People what they wanted even more than before Prohibition: alcohol.

A case of booze that cost $25 to bring into the country brought back about $1,000, at a time when a men's wool suit with two pair of pants cost about $15 and a pair of leather wing tip shoes cost only $3. More important than just money for personal wealth and *bribery, Prohibition turned the mob from local thugs into national figures. Movies and magazine stories glorified them. As an ancillary benefit, they were forced to buy trucks to transport their goods and warehouses to store them. Add that to their experience in running speakeasies, and it's easy to see how they became restaurateurs, nightclub owners, real estate moguls, liquor distributors, truckers, and union bosses once the Great Experiment had ended.*

If the 1931 meeting in Atlantic City that included Lucky Luciano, Al Capone, Meyer Lansky and many of the mob leaders from around the country was the birth of organized crime as we know it today, then the ratification of the 18th Amendment was American's impregnation with its seed.

Amendment 18 of the U. S. Constitution – Liquor Abolished.   Ratified: 1/16/1919

1. After one year from the ratification of this article the manufacture, sale, or transportation of intoxicating liquors within, the importation thereof into, or the exportation thereof from the United States

and all territory subject to the <u>jurisdiction</u> thereof for beverage purposes is hereby prohibited.

2. The Congress and the several States shall have concurrent power to enforce this article by appropriate legislation.

3. This article shall be inoperative unless it shall have been ratified as an amendment to the Constitution by the legislatures of the several States, as provided in the Constitution, within seven years from the date of the submission hereof to the States by the Congress.

FEBRUARY: St. Valentine's Day Massacre:

If any city epitomized the struggle for control of its Prohibition liquor distribution, it was Chicago. The Italian Outfit, led by Johnny Torrio and Al Capone, had been battling a mixed ethnic crew of Irish, Germans, Jews, and, yes, Italians, led by Irishman Bugs Moran. Besides the money involved in the alcohol business, it was a time of war in the streets. In New York, Sicilians led by Salvatore Maranzano were at war with Sicilians from another region of the Island; their leader Giuseppe "Joe The Boss" Masseria. The idea of competing with a bastardized group led by a non-Italian was as insulting as the amount it cut into their business.

Al Capone decided to end the war quickly.

On St Valentine's Day, 1929, seven men occupied a carting garage under Bugs Moran's control. Five were, in fact, Moran's men. The garage's mechanic and an optician who liked hanging out with Moran's hoods comprised the balance. Capone sent a group of shooters dressed as policemen to the garage where he knew the Moran Gang was waiting for a shipment of bootleg whiskey. The pseudo-cops lined everyone in the garage up against a wall, facing it, hands on it above their heads...then opened fire with both a machine gun and a sawed off shotgun, killing everyone. The one person they unwittingly missed: Bugs Moran. When a police sergeant arrived and witnessed the carnage, he exclaimed, "What a massacre!" giving a name to one of the most memorable mob murders in history and a number of films.

MARCH: Joseph Petrosino murdered in Sicily

When a criminal case came to light in the Little Italy area of New York, at the turn of the 20th Century, there was usually only one call from police brass: "Get me the Dago!"   The Dago was 5'3" Giuseppe Petrosino, a hardworking Italian immigrant from Italy, who had worked his way up from shoeshine boy outside the Little Italy police station, to street cleaner, to the first Italian Lieutenant Detective in the city.

Petrosino's impact on crime fighting was enormous. He was a pioneer in forensic studies, picking apart piles of dirt or pockets and linings of the clothes of men he arrested.   He was a master of disguise before "undercover" was a common law enforcement practice. At times he would pose as a Hasidic Jew, a rag picker, or a common laborer.   It was in the last undercover capacity focusing on a group of Italian anarchists that he discovered they wanted to assassinate President McKinley.   His close relationship with former Police Commissioner Theodore Roosevelt, now Vice President of the United States, got him a face to face with McKinley, who refused to believe anyone would want to harm him, and refused to increase his protective team.   As Petrosino had warned, President McKinley was assassinated by an anarchist, Leon Czolgosz, while he spoke at a Pan American Exposition in Buffalo, New York.

As time went on, Petrosino's no holds barred style of dogged investigation followed by arrests and/or beatings built a reputation that drove many Italian criminals, popularly known as Black Handers, to other cities or back to Italy. One of the latter was Don Vito Cascio Ferro, who went on to become one of the most famous dons in Sicilian history. Petrosino was murdered while on a supposedly secret (it had been leaked by a superior in the Police Department) mission to Sicily to gather warrants against those who had fled to New York and deport them. Legend has it that Cascio Ferro had Petrosino set up to meet a phony informant on the night of March 12, 1909, left a dinner with Palermo's society, murdered Petrosino at the meeting spot, then returned to the gathering to finish his meal.

Petrosino's funeral procession was followed through the streets of Manhattan by more than 250,000 mourners. He remains the only American detective ever to be killed overseas in the line of duty. A small park in Lower Manhattan bears his name.

The don met his match later, when Il Duce, Benito Mussolini, declared war on the Mafia. Cascio Ferro was imprisoned in Ucciardoni Prison until he died. His cell became a kind of shrine, with only top Mafiosi allowed to occupy it thereafter.

APRIL: "Crazy Joe" Gallo gunned down in Umberto's Clam House

Joey Gallo was indeed crazy. A typical story about him as a young man is that he left a crap game for a few minutes, then returned with a handkerchief over his face to stick up the game, then returned immediately after that to gamble with the money he stole. Everyone was afraid to confront him. The police were afraid to arrest him when they had a warrant, and had to plead with his brother, Larry, to have him surrender.

He went to prison because one of his men had set up a scheme whereby Joey would threaten a very wealthy nightclub owner, named Teddy Moss, that he was his new partner. The plan was that Moss would call Joey's man, who would arrange a phony meeting where it would be settled that the owner was "around" him, that Joey would leave him alone, and the bar owner would put Joey's man on payroll; the money would later be split with Joey. All went well at the meeting until Joey's man made his rehearsed speech about the owner being under his wing, and that Gallo should leave him alone. Joey reacted by slapping the owner and informing him that no one could protect him from Joey Gallo. Next stop for the Teddy Moss, the NYPD. Detectives attended a subsequent meeting between Gallo and Moss at Luna's Restaurant, on Mulberry Street, in Little Italy, where they heard the bar owner plead for more time to come up with the extortion money and Joey respond that he should take all the time he needed, on Joey...in the hospital. Next stop for "Crazy Joe," prison.

When Joey came out of prison, Joe Colombo, his official boss (their old partriarch, Joe Profaci, had died and Colombo had been elevated to the top position) was in trouble over the heat brought by the Italian American Civil Rights League (see June). Joey, who had little respect for Colombo, stepped into the conflict. His brother, Larry, having died of cancer was not around to control him. When Colombo was shot, Joey Gallo was blamed by many Colombo followers for having instigated it.

Had Joey not been "Crazy Joe," he would have avoided the mob stronghold of Little Italy like the plague. Instead, he chose to rub noses in the dirt by celebrating his birthday with a late night snack at Umberto's Clam Bar on April 7, 1972. When one of the Colombo men reported to his friends that Joey was just down the street, eating at Umberto's, they immediately grabbed some stashed weapons and turned the evening into Joey's last. His supposed bodyguard, Pete the Greek, took a bullet in the ass as he defended (?) his boss by diving for cover. Same old Pete.

MAY: Frank Costello shot; steps down as boss of Luciano Family

The birth of organized crime as we know it was a messy one. It began with mass immigration from Southern Italy at the turn of the Twentieth Century that spawned Italian ghettos controlled by "Black Handers." As gangs formed based on Old Country regions or even cities and towns, wars for control regularly left bodies in Little Italy streets. When young Turks like Lucky Luciano, Vito Genovese, and Frank Costello overthrew the old Mustachios in a bloody coup and formed their own of the five crime families, all that violence was supposed to stop; and, while Luciano ruled, it did. The internal order maintained itself even after Thomas Dewey sent Luciano to prison for thirty-five years on trumped up prostitution charges. Genovese was on the lam in Italy for a murder in the U.S. and Costello was named acting boss.

The family's peace ended after WWII when the witness who could get Vito electrocuted was gone and he returned home. Unlike Costello, who was a smooth, classy diplomatic-type who kept himself aloof from the day to day street operations, Genovese was a pitbull who reveled in mob crime. Costello fancied himself a businessman who rubbed elbows with New York's hoi poloi. Genovese, on the other hand, was known to have thrown the husband of a girl he wanted to marry to his death from a tenement rooftop. Getting rid of Costello so he could take over was child's play to Vito. He sent one of his underlings, a former prizefighter named Vincent "The Chin" Gigante to dispose of Costello. On May 2, 1957, Chin caught Costello by surprise as he entered his expensive uptown apartment building. "This is for you, Frank," Chin yelled as he fired. Maybe it was the fact that his words startled Costello and made him turn toward the sound, which resulted in the bullet grazing his head instead of going through it that later turned Gigante into one of the least heard bosses in history.

If Costello had had the temperament of Genovese or Luciano, Gigante would have been the first victim in an internecine bloodbath. Ever the diplomat, he dogged it and stepped down, happy to spend the following days at his favorite restaurant, Monsignore, than Campbell Funeral Home. He testified that Gigante had not shot him, letting Chin off the hook, and retired to the life of a Manhattan society gentleman. Vito's mark on the family was so profound that he displaced its founder, Lucky Luciano, as its namesake, forever changing it to the Genovese Family.

JUNE: Joe Colombo Sr. shot at 2nd Annual Unity Day rally

There has been no boss since Lucky Luciano to have the impact on society as Joe Colombo. Borne out of an arrest of his son, Joe, for melting down U.S. coins for the silver content, Joe began a movement that transcended mere picketing of the FBI Building with hand-lettered signs protesting discrimination against Italians. He formed the Italian American Civil Rights League and straddled its legitimate world and the world he ran as boss of the Colombo mob family.

Colombo's public accomplishments were many: pulling TV commercials off the air that he felt were insulting to Italians; forcing the words Mafia and Cosa Nostra to be removed from the shooting script of "Godfather" before he would allow cameras to roll; pressuring the U.S. Justice Department to ban those same references from all their correspondence and inter-office memos; starting a feeding program for hungry youths of all ethnic backgrounds; staging a "rat pack" concert at Madison Square Garden to raise funds for IACRL projects; etc. He interviewed on TV and was "Man of the Year," and staged a Unity Day rally at Manhattan's Columbus Circle that drew 50,000 people, press, politician & celebrity speakers—and FBI retaliation.

The next year saw unbearable heat on the mob as the Feds struck back. Other bosses, including Carlo Gambino, told Colombo he had to step down as head of the League. He refused, arguing that the whole movement would collapse without him as its public leader. Friction worsened that year as "Crazy Joe" Gallo left prison and went head to head with Colombo for money and power sharing. At a diminished second Unity Day affair, on June 28, 1971, with merely 20,000 on hand, Colombo stepped up to the podium—and was shot in the head by a black ex-con with press credentials who was widely assumed to have been sent by Gallo with a tacit okay from Gambino. Colombo lingered for nearly seven years in a diminished mental state as a result of the head wound before expiring. As he had predicted, the Italian American Civil Rights League collapsed without his leadership.

JULY: Carmine Galante gunned down in Joe & Mary's backyard.

Having designs on being boss can be dangerous. Wanting to do that while there is a sitting boss or defying him can be deadly. Lillo learned that the hard way.

The Bonanno Family had been at war with itself for decades, from the time Joe Bonanno got run out of town for hatching a plot to dethrone other bosses to become the first one since Salvatore Maranzano to declare himself "Capo di Tutti Capi." It was finally settled, with Philly "Rusty" Rastelli with a firm hold on the family, and Lillo as his underboss. When Rusty went to prison, Lillo named himself boss, which split the rank and file into sides. After a lot of pressure, he was able to get himself confirmed as Acting Boss. But, after a lot of years in prison, Galante let power go to his head and was also like a dry financial sponge, soaking up money that wasn't meant for him, but as a slush fund to help others coming home and more. The combination added to the bad feelings he'd already made with the boss and his loyalists. On the afternoon of July 12, 1979, while enjoying a meal at Joe & Mary's backyard garden, he was riddled with bullets as those who were supposed to be his bodyguards happened to be in the bathroom, just like Luciano was when his boss, "Joe the Boss" Masseria, got the same treatment over a dish of pasta in a Coney Island restaurant nearly half a century later.

AUGUST: Lepke Buchalter surrenders to Walter Winchell and J. Edgar Hoover

Louis "Lepke" Buchalter was the most wanted man in America. He, along with Albert "The High Executioner" Anastasia, was a top executive of a Brownsville, Brooklyn street crew known as "Murder Incorporated." When Lepke's underlings started rolling over for the authorities, some unwilling to do prison time when arrested but more fearful that they would themselves be murdered because of his paranoia about being implicated in killings he'd ordered by "rats," Lepke was indicted for various State and Federal charges. Rather than turn himself in, Lepke went "on the lam," hiding out in Brooklyn while his loyalists tried to work out a deal in which the Feds would take him into custody and supercede any State murder charges that carried a death sentence.

As the authorities turned up the heat on other mobsters for information on Lepke's whereabouts, so did mob grumbling about their suffering to protect one man. Finally, Lepke was told by other top mobsters that a deal had been struck, whereby Lepke would turn himself into FBI Director J. Edgar Hoover directly, with newspaper columnist Walter Winchell as the go-between. Lepke went along with the deal that promised he would never face State murder charges, but only do federal prison time, and rendezvoused with Winchell and Hoover. Unfortunately for Lepke, the deal he had been promised had never been struck. He was eventually turned over to the New York State Criminal Justice System, was tried, found guilty, sentenced to death, and given the electric chair.

SEPTEMBER: Night of the Vespers; more than 60 moustachioes murdered in two days

Modern organized crime in America was born between September 10th and 11th 1931.

The history of the mob goes back to the 13th Century, in Sicily, when Sicilians rose up to drive the Bourbon invaders out at the ringing of the church Vesper bells. Sicilians, who had always had a foreign force dominating their country, became inflamed when a drunken Bourbon Sergeant, Pierre Drouet, assaulted a bride-to-be who was waiting outside the church for her groom and the priest to join her. Drouet tried to have his way with the attractive female, struggled with her and her clothes, and accidentally banged her head against a rock, killing her. Their alleged cry, "Morte Alla Francia, Italia Anella," or, "Death to the French is Italy's cry," is the legendary birth of the word "Mafia."

A similar uprising occurred in 1931 against the old line Mafiosi who had come from Sicily during the great migration of the early 20th Century and ruled their gangs as if it were still the 18th or 19th Centuries. They were clannish and needlessly violent, which, to the younger Americanized mobsters, like Lucky Luciano and Al Capone, hurt their chances to make money. It was about business when they eliminated more than sixty of the old guard across the country over a forty-eight hour period.

Law enforcement and writers cast doubt on whether the incident was more myth than reality since they can't account for that number of murders during that period of time. What they don't understand is that all of those killed were immigrants, many having arrived here illegally with their families because of criminal records in the old country. When one of them disappeared, as many of their bodies were disposed of, their spouses would have been too fearful to report it. One of the disposal methods of the day was to incinerate the cadavers in pizza ovens overnight then brush the ash remains out in order to bake pizzas for their hungry customers later on. I am also certain of the events having happened because of one old moustachio I knew who had been shot, but allowed to retire instead of taking a second round of bullets, and Lucky Luciano's co-defendant, Little Davey Petillo aka Betillo, who recounted his sanguinary contribution on that day.

In any event, the period following the "Night of the Vespers" saw the eradication of the old ways and the ushering in of organized crime as we know it today.

OCTOBER: Albert Anastasia gunned down in barber shop

Albert Anastasia, known as the "Lord High Executioner of Murder Incorporated," because that group of murderers answered directly to him, was one of the most intimidating figures in organized crime at that time. Mobsters with a number of notches on their own belts reported chills going through their bodies when they sat across a table from him for some dispute or other. A cigarette usually dangled almost vertically downward from his lips, making him squint icily; his huge hands appearing as though they could rip a man apart in seconds.

Anastasia was also one of the founding members of the modern day organization that was born at the 1931 gathering in Atlantic City. That meeting was hosted by Lucky Luciano, and included mob figures from around the country, including Meyer Lansky, Frank Costello, and Al Capone. He fell under the Family headed by the Brothers Mangano. Both disappeared some time afterward, making room for Anastasia to step into the top spot. He was loyal to Luciano, who headed up what is now called the Genovese Family, and to Frank Costello, who substituted for Luciano when the latter went to prison. He respected them for their brains and sophistication. He hated Vito Genovese. When

Genovese had Costello shot, Anastasia wanted to exact revenge for his pal, but Frank quickly threw in the towel and retired. Genovese wasn't very secure. Neither was Carlo Gambino, who wanted the same kind of opening at the top that Anastasia had created when the Mangano Brothers were killed. Besides, as rumor had it, Anastasia had created a side income for himself by selling "buttons" to unworthy mob wannabes for fifty thousand dollars each.

On November 25, 1957, while "The Mad Hatter,"as Anastasia was also known as, enjoyed a hot towel wrapped around his face during a shave at the barber shop in the New York's swanky Park Sheraton Hotel, two gunmen entered and blasted him out of his chair, making room for Gambino to become boss.

NOVEMBER: Appalachian meeting busted up by State Troopers

Okay, we've got a meeting at a house in the woods upstate New York, and we don't want to attract attention. What should we wear? Hmmm, polished wing-tip shoes? Silk or mohair suits with white on white shirts and expensive ties? Fedora hats, gold and diamond jewelry? That should make us blend. Oh, and we'll all go in black Cadillacs.

Sound ridiculous? Well, not to the leaders of the major organized crime families when they called an emergency Commission meeting on November 14, 1957. There were issues that had to be dealt with; some issues generally known, some not. One major issue was Albert "The Mad Hatter" Anastasia, who had purportedly been selling memberships in his Family, or "buttons" for fifty grand a pop. That practice, and "The Mad Hatter" along with it, had been stopped weeks earlier when two gunmen had murdered him as he was being shaved in a barber's chair. The Commission's task that day was to confirm Carlo Gambino as the new leader of that Family, which they did before being raided by a local trooper who had noticed the unusual amount of Cadillacs at Joe Barbera's estate and had called for backup to investigate. As the raid ensued, many of the nation's top mobsters took off into the surrounding woods in a futile effort to escape, making the incident not only a nationwide news event, but fodder for comedians across the country.

DECEMBER: Paul Castellano killed in front of Spark's Steak House

A lamb cannot rule over a pack of lions...even if the lamb roars. That was the fatal mistake for Paul Castellano, a man who should never have been boss. While Big Paul became boss of the Gambino Family by virtue of his cousin, Carlo Gambino, having anointed him before his death, Paul could not gain the respect of the street troops that made that Family one of the strongest in New York. He was at odds with followers of Family Underboss Aniello "Neil" Dellacroce, who felt they needed someone who had already walked in their shoes; had come up through the ranks the hard way; had stolen, been arrested, gone through battles, done "work" for the Family. Castellano was a businessman, who had reached the top by earnings and nepotism. Because of his background, Castellano conducted the Family in a manner that could have earned him the nickname "Dr. No." Everything that was brought to him for an "okay," which might have brought some heat his way, got turned down. "Don't do this; don't do that," kept Big Paul safe, but didn't help underlings earn a living...which he didn't either.

Paul's downfall began when he demanded information about the drug arrests of John Gotti's brother, Gene, and close pal, Angelo "Quack Quack" Ruggiero. Drug involvement had been banned for the Gambino Family by the old man himself, going back decades; penalty, death (though Sicilian-born relatives of Gambino's were heavily involved). Gotti resisted turning over tapes. Paul made it obvious that he would use that as an excuse to come down on hard John Gotti.

Neil Dellacroce had been the only stumbling block for Big Paul bringing down Gotti, using his position as underboss and support from street soldiers to protect his protégé. On Government tapes played at least one during a mob trial, Colombo Family executives are heard advising that if Gotti doesn't strike first, Paul will. John took the advice. On December 16, 1985, as Paul Castellano and his right hand man, Tommy Bilotti, stepped out of their car to dine with "loyal" pals at Spark's Steak House in Manhattan, Gotti gunmen blew them away. The lion had eaten the lamb.

Also by Sonny Girard:

BLOOD OF OUR FATHERS

"An authentic thriller from a mob guy who's obviously been there."

-- **Nicholas Pileggi, Author of** *Wiseguy (Film name: Goodfellas)*

With razor-sharp honesty, Sonny Girard, an ex-mobster himself, tells the story of "Mickey Boy" Messina, just paroled from prison for a crime he didn't commit, and in love with his brother's ex-girlfriend, Laurel, a complication on his road to becoming a "made man" in the Calabra Crime Family. Mickey Boy's mother, Connie, carries a secret of an affair that could cost her son his life. Chrissy Augusta, a top mobster's teenage daughter, walks a dangerous tightrope with a secret lover from another *Cosa Nostra* family. All three affairs collide with tragic results in the midst of a bloody mob war.

From Little Italy social clubs to mob bedrooms, BLOOD OF OUR FATHERS is a tale of intimacy, loyalty and betrayal in the underworld – an underworld caught up in a war that threatens the life of everyone associated with it. Three love stories in a mob setting rather than a mob story, BLOOD OF OUR FATHER portrays family secrets, authentic organized crime politics, and bloodshed that crackles with vivid detail.

"Girard shines as a storyteller...(he has an) authoritative grasp of the Mafia's inner workings."

-- Publishers Weekly

"This story is not just for guys. It's like Jackie Collins meets Mario Puzo. I loved it."

--Katherine Narducci, Actor (Sopranos, Bronx Tale, etc.)

"Sonny Girard captures the heart of the mob life without glorifying it or attacking it; just tells it like it is."

- Jennifer Graziano, Creator and Executive Producer of "Mob Wives" franchise, VH-1

Also by Sonny Girard:

SINS OF OUR SONS

Not since Mario Puzo's Godfather *has a novel so passionately captured the soul of organized crime as did mob insider Sonny Girard's astounding debut,* Blood of Our Fathers. *Now Girard brings us the extraordinary successor, an explosive drama of the changes rocking the American Mafia...*

In one swift stroke, an assassin's bullet elevated Mickey Boy Messina from foot soldier to boss of the Calabra Crime Family – and left him with a legacy of pain and confusion. Now Mickey Boy is walking a delicate line, caught between the thrill of a power he never dreamed would be his, and Frank Halloran, a rock-hard parole officer determined to bring him down; between Don Peppino Palermo, a treacherous old Sicilian boss scheming to change the face of New York's organized crime, and Laurel, Mickey Boy's smart, sexy, no-nonsense wife. For her sake – and for the sake of Hope, the baby daughter he prayed for to end his line of mob inheritance – Mickey Boy is filled with a new ambition: to lead his people away from their criminal tradition and into the legitimate world. But in a dark society laced with misplaced trusts, and peppered with sudden and violent revenge, the road into daylight has always been paved with blood and sorrow...

"Sonny Girard...takes you on a journey into the real mob: how they killed, intriguing, suspenseful, with an insider's view of life in the mob"

- Tony "Nap" Napoli, author of "My Father, My Don"

"Nobody knows the inside outs of mob life better than Sonny. No bullshit; no lies."

- Frank DiMatteo, Publisher, Mob Candy Magazine

[Sonny Girard is] "...A man who knows the world of crime."

-- Bill O'Reilly, *The O'Reilly Factor, Fox News Channel*

Also by Sonny Girard:

SNAKE EYES

Small-time mobster Neil DiChristo is a happy-go-lucky bookmaker who prefers wine, women, and good food, not necessarily in that order, to any serious work or crime. One morning he is dragged out of his house by a team of FBI agents who have put together enough false information to throw him in prison for life and mark him as an informant to get him killed. All they want, they say, is for him to get close enough to a Russian operative to bring him down. It seems the only chink is the Russian's gambling habit, and DiChristo's credentials in that area give him the greatest chance of gaining the supposed spy's confidence. With no good option available, he reluctantly agrees.

From the opening page, Neil DiChristo is catapulted into a bizarre world of intrigue, murder, and more sex and romance than is healthy for anyone—where nothing is as it seems and his fate is beyond his control. All Neil wants is to be left alone.

Fat chance.

"Girard shines as a storyteller."

—Publisher's Weekly

"Sex and romance, mobsters and spies. What more could a girl ask for?"

—Kim Delaney, Actor (*NYPD Blue* – ABC TV).

"Sonny certainly knows all the players, and when it comes to this kind of book he's as good as anyone."

—James Caan, Actor (*Godfather, Vegas/NBC-TV, etc.*)

"Girard captivates the reader. He is an accomplished storyteller."

—Literary Journal

Autographed hard copies of all Sonny Girard's novels, Snake Eyes, Blood of Our Fathers, and Sins of Our Sons are available at www.SonnysMobCafe.com

ABOUT THE AUTHOR

Sonny Girard was born on the Lower East Side of Manhattan but raised but raised in the Red Hook and Navy Yard sections of Brooklyn: Mob Country. He has spent the greater part of his adult life on the inside of organized crime, not as a hanger-on or sycophant, but as a full time participant.

The target of a three-and-a-half year undercover investigation by New York's Organized Crime Control Bureau. Sonny was characterized by the New York Post as a "...middle echelon member"of one of New York's five mob families. His arrest resulted in a three year sentence in State Prison, where he maxed out in facilities like Sing Sing, Dannemora, Downstate, and Arthurkill.

Convicted later of racketeering under the R.I.C.O. Organized Crime Statute by Rudy Giuliani's office, and sentenced to seven years in Federal Prison, Sonny Girard again served the maximum time allowed under the law. It was during that time that he wrote the first of his three novels, "Blood of Our Fathers," which was published by Pocket/Simon & Schuster.

Due to his unique mob experience and ability to communicate about the inside workings of organized crime, Sonny has been in demand for various media interviews in the U.S., Canada, and Italy. He has appeared on Fox News Channel's "The O'Reilly Factor," HBO's "Politically Incorrect" during "Mob Week," ABC-TV's "Nightline," and RAI-TV, in Italy, where he has also been featured in that country's nationally distributed newspapers, "Corriere della Sera" and "Il Tempo."

www.ingramcontent.com/pod-product-compliance
Lightning Source LLC
Chambersburg PA
CBHW051936090426
42741CB00008B/1173